Queen Kinni

written by Beverly A. Burchett
and
Fatou K. Goumbala

QUEEN KINNI
by Beverly A. Burchett and Fatou K. Goumbala

ISBN # 978-0-9817111-1-9

PUBLISHED BY BLACKCURRANT PRESS COMPANY.
ALL RIGHTS RESERVED.
COPYRIGHT (C) 2006 BY BEVERLY A. BURCHETT
AND FATOU K. GOUMBALA. ALL RIGHTS RESERVED.
EDITED BY DENISE M. JOHNSON
ALL RIGHTS RESERVED. NO PART OF THIS PUBLICATION MAY
BE REPRODUCED, STORED IN A RETRIEVAL SYSTEM, OR
TRANSMITTED, IN ANY FORM
OR BY ANY MEANS, ELECTRONIC,
MECHANICAL, PHOTOCOPYING,
RECORDING, OR OTHERWISE, WITHOUT THE PRIOR
WRITTEN PERMISSION OF BLACKCURRANT PRESS COMPANY.

PRINTED IN U.S.A.

CHAPTER ONE

He shoved her into her own room with such force that she missed the bed entirely and went sailing head first onto the stiff wooden floor planks scratching and scrapping her body against the edges of the bureau drawer and the metal frame as she fell. The house was eerily quiet except for his heavy footsteps against the hallway tiles as he raced back into his room, opened a single drawer then slammed it shut. The radio couldn't drown out the loud thumping of his size eighteen hard leather soles thundering back or her arduous, heavy breathing, wheezing for air as she tried desperately to regain balance and consciousness. She was literally hunched over for the pain emanating out from her twisted elbow and her now swollen skull when he returned. He threw the door open and the knob smacked into the sheetrock cracking its surface. There he stood for a brief moment with a glint in his eyes that gave way to her understanding as to what might come next. She wondered if he would use the belt or if he had some other weapon in mind. Evil hadn't a shape or texture for her anymore but instead a smell and an intensity of which he reeked. Between the dirty, salty sweat on his forehead and the redness circling his pupils she became paralyzed. With her feet feeling as if they were cemented to the floor, she couldn't move. It didn't matter though because he lifted her up with one hand and hurled her down hard onto the bed. She felt the coils jarring into her back and neck as she landed with a slamming jolt. She never ever liked it when they were alone in the house. He looked meaner than hell, eyes glistening scarlet.

"Leave me alone! Leave me alone," she yelled but it came

out in a raspy whisper because her lungs felt collapsed.

This latest commotion was a continuation of the argument they'd been having earlier. The thought of him hitting on her because she disagreed with him upset her beyond reason. Yet she was, as usual, prepared to fight. Her nerve was way up. Her fists curled and ready but he didn't reach for his belt this time. Rather he grabbed hold of her leg and with great effort began yanking at her pants, snatching them at the foot along the fold of the double stitching. He yanked and yanked until he pulled them clean off and they lay in a tangled heap at the foot of her bed.

"What are you doing?" she yelled kicking at his knees and screaming at the top of her lungs for him to stop.

At first she figured that he wanted her to feel the welts on her bare flesh but there was something else in his eyes that wasn't quite adding up to his usual whippings. He looked more licentious and ravenous like a wild dog.

"Leave me alone! Leave me alone! Stop! Stop! What do you think you're doing?" and this time audibly with a tinge of disbelief at what she perceived might be happening.

He reached behind him and turned the radio volume up to drown her out. 'Who can hear me now?' she thought. Then he reached down her body touching every inch along the way, toward her underwear. That's when her entire world stopped and spun on its head. She completely ceased movement altogether and just looked at him in shock as he began pulling her panties down at the waist. She instinctively reached for them as well all the while holding tightly to the thin bands trying desperately to keep them resolutely up and securely on. She kicked and hollered with all the strength she had in her but his hands were large and strong and before she knew it, her underwear were off too, flung and disappeared somewhere in the room. At this point she was so horrified that she became deathly afraid. Yet in anguish, she kicked and screamed some more.

"Stop! Stop! Gotdamit! Stop!" she shouted, "What are you doing?" she sobbed.

Then he pinned her down with his knee pressing down fiercely against her legs so that she couldn't move. She kept saying over and over again in her mind, 'Oh, my God! Oh, my God!' Oh, my God!' She just couldn't reasonably comprehend what was on his mind. It was unreal. It was revolting. She actually felt physically ill. Again his stare pierced her, all of her, examining every hidden, private place. She tried to shield herself from his hideous face as his bulging eyes began ogling her and then of all hellish things, he began fondling her with his huge grotesque, dirty fingers. They roamed so indecently that all she could think to do was cry for the shame of it. With her arms flailing about she screamed some more though it was of no use. Then she tried to ball up into a rigid posture in order to fend off his improper ravaging but his strength was overpowering.

"Stopppppp! Leavvvvvvve mmmmmeeeee alone! Leave me alone! What are you doing? You have no right," she yelled, she begged, she pleaded but again to no avail.

It was as if he couldn't hear her at all. He was so single-minded in his evil, immoral quest. Then he grabbed at her legs again, one with one hand and one with the other and pried them apart. It was then that she realized that she had had them knitted together at the knees for dear life. He wrenched them so determinedly that she was split farther than the muscles could bear. It was an agonizing hurting that tore throughout her entire body as he stretched her wide open.

"No! Stooooop! Stop!" she shrieked.

She cried for salvation from this terror, this fiend who then focused all his energy on what laid between her legs. He glared at her tiny womanhood disrespectfully and seemingly forever. She prayed for that to be the sum total of his intention. If Allah was with her that day, that was what she believed in him for but no relief came. He pressed down on her thighs with one hand while unzipping his pants with the other.

"You can't do this to me! You're not supposed to do this to me," she yelled at him shaking fiercely with anger now from behind a pillow.

She had covered her eyes with it hoping that if she couldn't see him, he couldn't see her but that was the reasoning of a little child.

"Shut the f- up. I do whatever the f- I feel like," he barked back at her as if she was nothing, as if she was filth.

"I'm not ready for this! You can't do this to me!" she screeched.

"Yes, you are," he smiled so repulsively that she didn't even recognize him anymore.

Grabbing hold of her favorite Pepé shirt, he ripped it right down the middle of the cute little draw string. Then he whacked the pillow she was holding so harshly that he chipped her front tooth and caused her to bite down on her tongue.

"L'eeeeeave mmmme'lone. Leave me alone," she mumbled with a sore lip bleeding, "Stop! Stop!" she cried, "You're not supposed to be doing this to me."

He just bore his eyes down at her bare breast, which hadn't fully grown in yet.

"But you're my father," she simply said to him very much as an appeal.

Surely there was something wrong in all this. That he would presume to take his own daughter.

"Shut the f- up! Shut – the - f- up! I do whatever the f- I feel like. You are my child so if I want to have you, I can. Now, shut the f- up I tell you! Shut the f- up," he said repeatedly.

"No, you can't! No, you can't," she kept on screaming at the top of her lungs trying to raise her thin small voice above the loud music and the hectic sounds of the city's own harsh den.

"You want to hang out all night with your friends. You think you're grown now, don't you? You don't think you're old enough to marry? I'll show you how old you are," he said drooling spit from the corner of his mouth.

"I'm telling mom. As soon as she gets home I'm going to tell her! I'm going to tell her, I swear! You can't do this to me. You just can't do this to me. You just can't," she continued through uncontrollable sobs.

He slowly reached around down by his ankles. She thought he was at long last searching for his belt of which she believed she'd be grateful if he had. However, before she knew it he had once again snatched the pillow from in front of her face and thrust a nine-millimeter into her forehead. The compression left a dent and she could feel the coldness of the barrel all the way down her spine. She didn't look closely at the gun. Rather, she kept both eyes on him. She just knew from his unswervingly quiet tone that he was deadly serious.

"You tell. You go right ahead and tell…," speaking ever so softly, "…that will be the last breath you take," he said with a chilling calmness in his voice.

At that, she had stopped breathing momentarily. She believed he'd do it. He'd kill her. Actually she was preparing herself for the worst and there was a remarkable tinge of tranquility that came with that thought. She was going to die. He was going to pull the trigger and her brains would be splattered all around her room. Though she did not think she was ready to die, there was nothing she could do about it now. If she fought him, he'd shoot.

If she tried to run, he'd shoot. Time seemed to have stopped entirely because she had it to formulate her opinion on this matter. Oddly, she realized that she still had some control even in this horrific time of trouble. She could die fighting or she could simply give up. She began to realize then that she would rather die than have him do this incestuous deed to her. So she yelled all the more.

"Kill me! Kill me!" she begged, "Please, kill me," she screamed for it, "Please!"

She truly wished that he had because right after that she thought he had rammed the barrel of that giant weapon inside of her in a most unnatural and awful way. She had no idea that she could be in so much pain. A sharp avalanche of throbbing riddled through every inch of her. The wind was knocked right out of her and her head recoiled back from the shock wave that struck as she scrambled to breathe. That thing penetrated so deep that she could feel it all the way up to her neck and at the back of her throat. It nauseated her and she started choking from it and from the blood that had settled in the bottom of her mouth. It tore a pathway into her that was not where anything should ever lawfully go let alone a trespass. It ripped through flesh and bone boring a hole in the skin and destroying anything that lay in its wake. It severed something entrenched within her very soul.

"You're my pro-per-ty and I can do what-ev-er the f- I want to you. You're li-ving un-der my roof and as long as I say so you will do what I like," he pitched and shook on top of her as if his mighty fists were pummeling her broken body.

His massive weight crushed her ribs which battered her windpipe. She was being devastatingly suffocated and she began to feel light-headed. Then the odorous smell of his breath assaulted her as much as he and she could barely stay conscious for the torture and the putrid nature of it all. She felt as if she had this tender open wound that someone was recklessly pounding with the prying side of a hammer. With each insertion of this thing her guts gave way as if they might spill out. It was as if she were being sawed in half.

She didn't want to die this way.

She didn't want to die this way.

She didn't want to die this way, but if it were going to be this way, if there was ever such a time in her life, she was ready. At this point, she even longed for it. Then she began to sink into the persuasion of it, of death and with that keeled over.

Unfortunately for her, moments later, shaken and disoriented, she awoke discovering that she had only passed out. She couldn't believe it; she saw the only man she had ever called father, now no more than a stranger, exiting out of her room and casually going into the living room. With tremendous effort, she slowly, painstakingly, managed to close her sore, aching legs. They were bruised along the sides of her inner thighs where he had been pressing down on her. They were tight and inflamed and had stiffened in that ungodly position. She could even see the indent of his handprint still there reminding her that she had not been dreaming. She curled herself up into a fetal position and sobbed until her whole room shook and seemed soaked and sticky. Everything hurt on her and in her. She knew that she would never be clean again. For her there wasn't enough soap in the universe to wash away his uninvited touch. Each time she recalled his hands in her and about her, his private members along side hers, she vomited onto her bed and floor.

"G'et 'op," she heard him say from down the hall.

She was in a fog. His voice sounded hollow and distant and formless. She couldn't bring herself to obey anything. Even her own inner voice told her to stand and run but nothing about her body could lift up anymore. Her very core and will had been diminished to mere fractions of what they once were.

"Get up I said," he demanded storming back into her room.

She gestured to him that she couldn't; somehow though, she didn't say a word nor move a muscle.

"You're disgusting. Look at you, Kinni. You're disgusting," he told her and rolled her into a seated position.

She remembered thinking that he could not refer to her in that manner without recognizing that he had something to do with it. She looked down to her side visually searching for her pants. That's when she saw the blood that had soaked through the sheets, mattresses, and was plastered on the walls and floor. It covered her and some of it got on him too. It seemed to be coming out of the furniture. She thought she was peeing on herself only to realize that there was also blood flowing out of her vagina. She must have fainted because the next thing she knew she was sitting in the back seat of a taxi and she heard her, now lower than earth-scum father tell the driver, "Mount Sinai Hospital."

She heard a male's voice but she couldn't see where it was coming from.

"She's coming to. Just one more," a man said.

She was completely at a loss as she saw an intravenous drip taped to her hand. It was the first thing she saw when she finally opened her eyes. She was flat on her back staring into a square box of bright lights. She didn't know where she was but that she was groggy and disoriented. Then she noticed that her legs were flung wide open again. She panicked thinking that her father was coming in for another round. She just couldn't bear that. So she quickly tried to swing her thighs round to close them but they were fastened into these oval metal hoops, so she sobbed.

"Hold her arms," the male voice said and a woman came out of nowhere and gently reached out to hold her hand. Kinni had no idea who either of them were but the woman had a real calming effect, her touch was warm and comforting. Before Kinni knew it, her cheeks were smeared with tears. She looked over and saw the woman's nurse uniform then everything that had just transpired flooded back to her memory. It was such an emotional pit of despair. She believed that the nurse must have suspected something horrible had taken place in her home because she was so kind and began to wipe Kinni's eyes with her sleeves. Kinni was so uncomfortable lying there with her feet in the air and everything that her father had just done to her in plain sight for the whole world to see. The shame of it was insufferable and cut deeper than the depth of an ocean. Meanwhile, these stranger's hands were doing something to her womb and backside.

"There. She's good," the man said.

He peaked out from around her legs while slowly lowering them onto the mat. Kinni could do nothing but curl into a ball and weep some more. The nurse continued her kindness by rubbing her back never letting go of her hand. Kinni found out later that she had needed six stitches and wouldn't be able to sit properly for several days. Apparently the wall of her uterus was ruptured on all sides and she had lost several pints of blood. That was just the physical damage. The emotional ripping and tearing had placed a gapping hole in her soul for which her father would someday dearly repay, possibly with his life.

Kinni was home in bed when her mom returned with her brothers, Deebal and Jumu, and little sister, Sara. They were all still bursting with the joy they had experienced going to the park that day. Kinni still couldn't move. She couldn't greet them and match the excitement that they had for living. She couldn't talk for all the tears she'd shed. Her throat was dry, lips were chapped and she was exhausted. For her the nightmare never seemed to end. After she and her father came back home from the hospital, he had to help her tidy up her room. She watched him with such disgust and anger that her eyes were bruised and puffy from squinting. He tore the sheets from her bed and threw them into the trash out back in an effort to hide his crime. He mopped up the blood too which seemed to have covered every surface in the whole three-story house. Then he had to help her climb onto bed because she couldn't do it all by herself. Her hatred of him grew with each brief encounter, each bumping of shoulders threatened to tear her heart apart. Yet, the extent of his remorse was that he couldn't look directly at her. Otherwise he was his typical arrogant, boorish self. She couldn't believe how he explained everything to her mom.

"What in the world. Matar, what happened to Kinni?" her mother asked him in a panic when she discovered that they had just gotten back from the hospital.

"She tried to kill herself," Matar yelled back at her defensively.

"Tried to kill herself? What?" she asked.

"Yes, Binta. That's what I said..." Matar explained, "...with a broomstick."

'How is it...' Kinni thought, '...that she believes anything that comes from his lying mouth.' She just couldn't understand. Yet believe it, Binta did. For it was common knowledge around Kinni's home that she was the bad seed. This description was mostly promulgated by her father and as the man of the house, the sole breadwinner he had a certain persuasiveness with his women and children. Since Kinni already had this reputation of being rebellious he just sold Binta that same bill of goods.

"Well, I told her that I want her to marry! She is old enough, but she doesn't want to obey me, me, her father. Well, if she doesn't want to live here anymore. To hell with her," Matar said.

He went on to say that Kinni didn't want to mind his rules and his authority and that this was his house. So, apparently Kinni's reaction to Matar's regulations was to push a wooden broom handle up her behind until she broke something and practically bled to death. That would have never been her choice of poison notwithstanding. 'Who could believe such a ridiculous tale,' Kinni thought while lying there listening through her closed door. Yet, unbeknownst to her, her father was manipulating her family's image of her and murdering her character with each lie. They were all a little terrified of her after that incident and began to think that she was indeed going crazy.

Chapter Two

Kinni Bragia died that day and not a quick painful death either, as with a simple firm twenty-two caliber pistol tap to the back of the head at close range. That would have been the decent thing to do. Of course, dying of old age where the body slowly eats itself away from acid poisoning, where friends and family have time to tire of you would have been a real nice elegant choice too. However, she wasn't afforded that luxury either. Her death happened before she had even grasped that her very fate was at hand. It was snatched from her just as she was about to discover its value and purpose. There was a wealth of understanding on the subject of life preceding it that she was still chewing the fat of, when abruptly, she was thrust into the void of unformulated, unrealized dreams, the illusion of the eternal restful sleep, the broken promise of reincarnation, the black hole of existence which prophets and soothsayers so poetically call the hereafter. Yet, no one really knows what, if anything, comes after. Each human being is so limited in their thinking and can only speculate, theorize and imagine to the point where it makes them feel less uncomfortable, like they have control over life itself. Yet, without any legitimate authority, everyone is utterly helpless and their so-called theories are as frail and as flimsy as cheap toilet paper. Kinni could now say with some accuracy what comes after because she lived the anguish, torture and torment of the living dead.

That night she waited until everyone was asleep. Then she crept into her parents' room stealth-like with the large Ginsu chopping knife that her father loved so much in her hot little hand tucked beneath her pajama top. His favorite thing to do in life was to sharpen that thing over and over again. It annoyed her mom to no end that he would slide it across that large block of steel acting like a Kung Fu master. On television they claimed that these blades could cut through anything. Kinni so desired to put their theory to the test as she tip-toed down the long hall. She made sure that her breathing was deep and low. She didn't want to wake anyone and have them disturb her plans, spoil her fun. As she walked in darkened shadows, she couldn't help but think back to the first time she began to suspect that her father was an absolute monster. It all started one typical evening. Her mom had just finished feeding the kids then prepared a plate for her father who never really ate with them except on special occasions. He took one mouth full then pushed the plate across the table, scrunched up his lips and pouted like a child. The saucer hit the floor and broke to pieces leaving her mom with a big mess to clean of food and broken glass.

"I don't like it. It tastes like she-it!" he coughed trying to spit it out of his mouth.

"Oh, you don't like it, huh? Well, you have other women. Why don't you ask one of them to make you something else," she told him sternly.

He slowly turned toward her feeling insulted because he thought that she was being disrespectful. So, he reached across the table and punched her hard in the jaw. Kinni ran in when the commotion spilled out into the living room. There she found her father brutally beating up her mom with his bare fists. His hands swung indiscriminately. They punched her about the face, the arms and the stomach. Kinni instinctively rushed over and grabbed hold of his leg trying to pull him off of her. She was kneeling down covering her face in her hands, sobbing. She was only five years old. She had never seen anything like that before.

"Leave my mother alone," she screamed at him in disbelief at what he was doing.

He swatted her away like a bug and she stumbled to the floor backwards. Unharmed, she got back up and went at him again.

"Leave her alone," she yelled, "Stop it!"

He kicked her hard this time and she went flying into a table where this African incense was burning sweetly ironically in order to refreshen the room. Her left arm landed right onto the flame. As it burned her she continued to scream both for her mother and for her aching arm which immediately welded itself to the fire. All the while she screamed at her father, "Leave my mom alone! Leave my mom alone!"

Binta was Matar's first wife of three.

"Shut up, bea-itch!" he snarled at Kinni with so much hatred it was hard for her to take.

He never swore at her before and the harshness of his words wounded her deeply. She had never felt fatherly love from him but he had always been decent toward her and her mom.

"Kinni! Kinni, look at your hand," Deebal and Jumu cried.

She couldn't feel the burning any more. Instead she felt every blow that Matar heaped upon her mother and it seemed as if he were battering her too. Kinni had this overwhelming sensation to protect Binta. After all, she was three months pregnant with Kinni's first little sister, Sara. Even at that young age Kinni knew that this type of stress wasn't good for the baby. The fight ended when Kinni started bleeding out from her mouth and nose. Matar simply stopped hitting on her and walked out of the front door. Matar never used alcohol or drugs and Kinni thought that maybe if he had then she could understand it. She could rationalize his brutal behavior maybe even cut him some slack but he didn't do it for that reason. She could even understand it if he had a horrible childhood or if his parents were total nightmares. Yet that wasn't it either. He, in fact, was treated like a little prince in Gambia. After all, he was a male child and that carried a sense of grand entitlements. It was understood that he would one day receive his father's modest inheritance and therefore live in a comfortable lap of luxury. Within reason he got everything he desired growing up. No, her father did these things because he wanted to. They gave him pleasure. He did these wicked things because he said, "This is mine for life so I'm going to treat it however I want to forever."

Kinni's little brother, Jumu, who was no more than two years old ran into the bathroom and brought back some tissue for Binta's face. Meanwhile, frightened Deebal pulled Kinni's arm out of the fire. She had a huge bubble of skin oozing pus and blood all over her clothes.

"Oh, my God, girl, look at your arm!" Binta shrieked.

Nothing hurt Kinni more than what her father had just done. She sat on the floor stunned, numb and staring blankly into space. She couldn't believe that her mother was able to turn her attention to anything other than that horrifying display. Why wasn't she still reverberating like the door Matar slammed still shaking on its hinges?

"Go," Binta said to her scared son, "Go and get mommy some ice and some perfume for your sister's arm."

He scurried off leaving Kinni shattered and Binta tearful. Little Jumu knelt beside them both and simply cried. Jumu was a mere toddler and didn't really know what else to do. As Kinni looked across into his sweet little face she could tell that he was just as terrified as she was. She hadn't known that she could be so brave until that moment. She was the eldest and at that tender age she began to realize that that carried certain responsibilities. Kinni's little brother, Deebal returned handing Binta a single cube of ice. Then he walked over to Kinni and started spraying the perfume onto her arm. She shrieked in pain as the alcohol fused the flesh to the bone. Although the family was miles away from Gambia the tradition of cheap perfume being used as a medical remedy, never left them.

Kinni thought long and hard about that day as she opened the door to her parents' room. There was nothing to it. It gave way without even squeaking. She knew that fate was on her side. She stepped one, two, three, quietly up to her parent's bed and she looked down on her, soon to be deceased, father. He looked dead already to her, pale and gray. It was ironic and maybe what she was about to do was even a little redundant but she was going to do it nonetheless. She was going to do whatever the f- she felt like. After what he did, she figured that this was the least of what he deserved. She gingerly leaned in real close to his head. He smelled like the butt of an elephant. It must have been the cigars he smoked and his rotten teeth. He was roaring out a snore that filled the air with stale breath and a loud racket. She pulled the blade out easily as not to accidentally cut herself. It was exciting for her to see her own reflection in it. She looked so resolute and determined and ready. She held it length-wise across approximately two inches above the intended target. She waited maybe two seconds and then ever so quickly, she swiped it right across his thick neck. It made one long thin red line that was barely visible. She thought that she hadn't done it correctly but then blood began to spittle out and that's when his eyes popped wide open bulging beyond their sockets. He looked scared to death. 'Good,' she thought and almost laughed out loud. 'Serves him right. She was scared too,' she reasoned. What he had done to her before didn't mean anything to him and his sudden panic now didn't mean anything to her. He was terrified. He awoke reaching for anything he could grab hold of, gasping for precious air but there was precious little for him to swallow with his severed windpipe. She reached over and pretended to help him but instead she was holding one hand over the opening of his fat nose and with the other covered his deceitful lying lips. Blood was gushing everywhere same as when he decided to stick his swelled penis inside of her delicate body forever severing the last bit of innocence she possessed. She held the knife up again this time in order to lop his head clear off. He was steadily dying a nice slow and very painful death but she wanted to hurry it up a bit and she especially wanted to make sure he knew who was doing it. So, she shifted her weight and stood by the bed in such a way so he had no other choice but to see her standing there with the bloody dagger. She thrust the blade in again and again and again speedily, manically and aggressively. She couldn't stop stabbing him. That's when her mom awoke, wondering why Kinni was standing beside her bed, and then seeing a knife in her hands, what she was doing. Binta was startled and perplexed when she noticed Kinni grinning mischievously from ear to ear. Then she followed her eyes down to the gaping hole that used to be Matar's neck exposed and raw emptying his bodily fluids onto the woolen blankets.

"Hush now," Kinni told her, "Hush. Be patient. Just a little bit longer. Just wait. I'll finally be able to buy you that mansion you always wanted on outskirts of the holy city, Mecca. We'll go on pilgrimages and bow down to Allah, our God. We'll picnic there under the sun, the moon and stars, loving our freedom to worship in peace as we choose, without Matar's prying eyes. We'll be free, you and I, finally free."

Then they both quietly waited for Matar to expire until there was nothing left of him but an empty sack of blue colored, wrinkled skin.

Just the thought of what she had done filled her to overflowing emotions of extreme satisfaction. Kinni wasn't worrying about the consequences of her actions. She wasn't thinking about her brothers or her soon to be born sister having to grow up without their father. It didn't even occur to her. And she flat out refused to entertain the notion that her mom might have loved the bastard despite every malicious thing he had ever done to her. The way she figured it, she wouldn't be made responsible for her actions. After all she'd tell the authorities that her very own father viciously raped her and that would be justification enough for her taking revenge. Like the Bible says, "…an eye for an eye…" People had gotten away with murder for all kinds of idiotic reasons here in America, why not her?

CHAPTER THREE

"Hello, can I speak to Kinni?" the boy asked.

"Who the hell is this?" barked Matar in a huff.

"I'm Kinni's friend, Joe….from Miss Lopes' class. Is she at home, sir?" Joe asked politely.

"Why the f- are you calling my daughter?" snarled Matar.

"Excuse me…excuse me sir, but I spoke to you nicely. I was just calling about Poor Richard's Almanac, you know, Franklin. She's my homework partner. We're just gonna' study. I have a question. Can I talk to her or not?" Joe asked in bewilderment trying his hardest to be respectful.

"No, you can't. She doesn't want to talk to you. You are no one to her. Don't call here again. She says that she doesn't want to speak to you ever again," Kinni's lying father told him.

"Huh?" said Joe to the sound of the receiver being slammed down in his ear.

That conversation took place just four months after the rape. She was not at home to defend herself. Kinni's friend Joe told her in some detail exactly what was said a week later. When Kinni did arrive home that evening before she could even get all the way through the front door, she was smacked into a wall. She hit it in such a way that her head starting ringing and her eye was scratched and bled.

"What are you doing giving boys your number? I told you not to give nobody this number," he growled at her intimidating her.

"What are you talking about?" she asked steadily trying to support herself on the doorframe.

"Who the hell is Joe?" he asked as if he already knew the answer.

"Joe? Joe?" Kinni asked trying to figure out who had called too.

Her head was now throbbing and she just wanted to go and lie down on her bed. So she began walking in that direction.

"He says you go to school with him," Matar said as if he thought that that was a lie.

"Oh, Joe…he's my study partner…" she tried to explain.

"Study partner my ass! You're lying! You're lying! Didn't I tell you you're mine? Didn't I tell you that?" Matar screamed.

"I'm not yours or nobody's," she told him, "He's just a friend."

"You're a dirty liar," he replied.

Then he took off his belt and beat her with it, not with the leather strap part but with the hard metal buckle. He whipped her all on the back of her legs and on her butt.

"Stop! Stop! Stop hitting me!" she howled.

As Kinni screamed he just got more vicious and struck her even harder. It hurt so badly that she collapsed under the pressure of it. Once she was on the floor, he tightened his grip so he could get a better swing at her. She rolled over and over trying to dodge the blows. Some landed on her arms and others on her stomach. Then one cracked against her knee with such force that he stopped for a moment to assess his own damage.

"Stay still!" he yelled, "…or the next one is going to your head."

She froze. What else could she do? He would have killed her. Then he hit her three or four more times on her butt again and then he mercifully stopped. He backed away from her grinning. Tearful and blooded, she knew that she had to stand up to him. She had to take courage.

"I'm tired of this shit," she mumbled, "I'm leaving," she sobbed.

"You leave and that will be the last breath you take," he replied.

"Then just kill me. And if you do kill me one day they're going to find out that you did it," she stood up to him trying to match him strength for strength.

She had had enough. She knew that he was just a big bully. What grown man goes around beating on women and children?

"Do what you got to do with me! I don't give a f- . I just don't care anymore. I'm going to live my life the way I want to from now on. So go on and do whatever you think you got to do!" Kinni screamed, "...but you're not going to do any ole nasty thing to me no more, nothing. The next time you do, I'm going to call the cops," she threatened.

She went walking towards her room to get away from him. She couldn't believe that he was acting like a madman on account of Joe. Had he met Joe he would have realized that there was no cause for concern. Joe was a little scrawny kid with thick glasses, pimples and crocked teeth. Sure, he was a friend of Kinni's and she liked him but he was not a boyfriend or anything like that. In her mind she figured that her seriously demented father wouldn't be overreacting about something that didn't even merit a glance let alone a beat down and an argument.

"Leave me the hell alone!" she shouted at him from a fare and safe enough distance.

"Oh yeah! Oh yeah," he said.

Then he whipped out his nine as if out of nowhere and slammed the bottom of it right at the base of her neck where the spine starts and her neck ends.

The Declaration of the United States was signed on July 4, 1776. Kinni's teacher, Miss Lopes, informed the class that

Benjamin Franklin was one of the signatures at the bottom of this important document. The whole class took turns with her magnifying glass in order to see it. He, Ben Franklin, was also known as one of the Founders of this great country, writer, scientist, and entrepreneur. He had written and published a yearly almanac entitled, "Poor Richard's Almanack". It appeared continuously from 1732 to 1757. The almanac was a bestseller for a pamphlet published in the American colonies; print runs typically ran to 10,000 per year, so Kinni and her fellow students were told. In it he wrote once, "Doing an injury puts you below your enemy; revenging one makes you but even with him; forgiving it sets you above him." Kinni woke up three days later groggy and lying face down in her pillow. She had been unconscious all that time. She had on the same clothes she was wearing the day her father and she fought. It was pitch dark outside, she noticed when she was finally able to pry her eyes apart. She couldn't move her neck at all. It was completely stiff. She tried to crane it up so that she could at least see what time it was but couldn't without severe shooting pains throughout her entire body from head to toe. She could hear her mom's voice calling for her from the living room. She was trying to remember what had happened to her but couldn't hear her own thoughts with her mom talking so loudly to her through the closed and evidently locked door.

"What are you still doing in bed?" Binta yelled.

Her voice seemed to trail off as she walked away from the door to ask Matar about it.

"What is she still doing in bed, Matar? Do you know?" Binta asked him.

"She argued with me so I had to do it," he replied defensively.

He had actually locked Kinni in her room, she confirmed by that statement. Then Kinni heard Matar come over and unlock the door. She had a splitting headache when she finally was able to throw her legs out to the side of the bed. She tried to get up when it occurred to her that the back of her head was too heavy to hold up. Then she thought about the harsh words her father had spoken to her. She recalled that he walked back into his room and slowly came back into the living room with his nine millimeter. She remembered thinking that this was it for her. She just knew that he was about to shoot her and that this time he was really going to do it but instead he came up behind her and struck her with it. She didn't know that anything in life could hurt so absolutely. Revenge was all she could think of. She seethed with it. It threatened to burn a hole through her soul.

"Why is she sleeping? She has things to do around here," Binta kept asking Matar.

Kinni had a lot of chores to do - the bathroom and kitchen. Nothing got done though whilst she was knocked out. And she was knocked out cold. Her brothers Deebal and Jumu did nothing around the house. Housework was women's work. She managed to see the clock out of the corner of her eye. It said nine thirty.

"I don't know," her father said, "Why don't you go ask her."

Binta went over and tapped on Kinni's door.

"Y….es," she answered wearily.

"Kinni, what's wrong with you?" her mom asked.

Kinni quickly stood up and sat atop her bed. Binta walked in and saw Kinni holding the back of her neck.

"Kinni, you know you have things to do, what's wrong?" she asked her calmly.

"I'm not feeling well," she said trying not to move her head too much because it felt that if she did it would have fallen off her body.

Binta lovingly held onto her hand.

"Okay, baby. I'll do the dishes. You hungry?" she asked.

Kinni nodded no and nearly cried from the pain. Her mom left her room and as she did, Matar passed by and sneered at Kinni.

"Did you know that your daughter has boys calling here?" Matar asked Binta in a very accusatory tone.

Kinni could tell that he wanted to get her into trouble with Binta.

Then her mom asked her, "Is that true, Kinni?"

"That's Joe…Joe, my homework partner," Kinni told her.

"Matar, that's just Joe, her homework partner," Binta said to Matar while walking back into the kitchen.

"I don't care! I don't care!" he ranted just like an over sized spoiled child.

Binta simply turned and stared at him as if he needed a nap.

"I don't want boys calling here okay?" he shouted and with that slammed the kitchen door on Binta's face.

"Mind your business. That's my daughter," Matar told her.

Kinni crept into the bathroom, washed her face and then placed a bandage on her neck because she noticed that it had been bleeding there too. It left a bump about the size of a quarter. It looked as if something was growing out of the back of her head.

Binta asked her, "Why are you wearing the bandage? What happened to you?"

When Kinni finally made her way into the kitchen, she wasn't ready for the third degree. She just brushed the whole thing off.

"It's nothing. I fell," she never liked lying and especially not to her mom.

She deserved better than that but she never told her what had happened to her that day. Actually, she was scared to go to her with any of the horrible things her father did to her because then her mom would have to deal with it; she'd have to deal with her father. *"Did you do something to her? Touch her? That's what Kinni said."* She didn't want things to go down that way. Plus, her father and she were home alone a lot. She didn't want it to be harder on her. So, Kinni never told her mother these things.

Chapter Four

Just before summer break, Kinni was informed that her grandmother had taken ill, and because she was getting on in years someone would be needed to take care of her. Matar and Binta asked Kinni if she wanted to go to Gambia, Africa and be her grandmother's aid.

"Kinni, you're old enough now to take a trip overseas by yourself," Matar told her, "Besides, I'll have someone there to meet you at the airport."

This was not an unusual request for a Gambian girl, though she was born and raised in the United States. She knew that being the oldest she was the most likely candidate for such a task. She would go there for the summer and return just before school started again in September. She had never been to Gambia and heard that it was beautiful from the stories Binta told her. As she mulled over the idea for the weeks prior, she began to look forward to it, anything to get away from her confining reality. She was not allowed out of the house except for going to school after the alleged broomstick episode. During those nights locked up at home, Kinni spent most of the time dreaming up different ways of killing her father. She had not carried out any of her plans yet but the varying methods to dispose of him were becoming more and more vivid and seemingly obtainable. Leaving the country was probably the best thing for her to do.

Kinni remembered packing all of the things that she held dear, that Binta had bought especially for her trip, her Sergio Valenté Kalahari jeans with the V's stitched across the back pockets, her

Roc-a-wears, which she could not part with and all of the *wife-beater* tees that she could fit inside her suitcase. Binta even bought the suitcase with all of its many compartments and retractable wheels. Binta had washed and ironed all of it including her underwear. She brought her a new toothbrush and toothpaste, every kind of hair product Kinni desired. Then she made her put her passport in a secret zipped compartment. Kinni felt as if Binta thought she was still a five year old.

"Mom, it's okay," Kinni told her, "I'm not a little girl."

Binta wouldn't hear of it and fussed even more so including wetting her fingers in her own saliva and finger combing Kinni's lovely hair back in place. Binta and Matar rode with Kinni in the cab to the John F. Kennedy airport. Then they sat with her and waited for her flight to arrive. They seemed rigid with nerves but Kinni kept reassuring them that they had nothing to fear because she was a big girl capable of taking care of herself. She'd say that to Binta and Matar would glance over at his wife and smile. Binta hugged Kinni in such a tearful way that Kinni grew worried of what awaited Binta back home in her absence. She was her protector after all. Kinni thought that as long as she was around Matar wouldn't hit on Binta. Binta guaranteed Kinni that everything would be fine. So, after more tears and a few more long embraces, Kinni finally boarded the plane. She had never been on a plane before in her life and that proved to be a most marvelous experience even though she had already grown homesick for her mom and little sister, Sara and her two brothers.

The flight was uneventful. 'Praise Allah,' Kinni thought. There was mostly a view of the vast Atlantic Ocean and not much else. Kinni mainly stared out of the small airplane window at the horizon line until there was nothing to see except darkness. Looking down on the world in that way was exhilarating for a girl who had never been outside of Harlem. She couldn't sleep as did everyone else on her flight. She was too anxious at what lay ahead for her. Her grandmother had always been kind to her and she felt honored to return the favor. The whole trip took approximately seven hours and it arrived at Banjul International Airport early the next morning.

There was a sudden burst of energy when Kinni deplaned. It was as if the entire country had come to greet her. Then before she could take a good look around, she was shuffled over to Immigration, same as everyone else. She stood on a line for what seemed like hours as officials combed through everyone's personal documentation, Yellow Fever certification and malaria shot verification letters from everyone's doctors, passports and endless questions about one's intention for their particular visit. Once that was all done Gambian people just started approaching Kinni at all sides wanting to offer her a ride or to carry her belongings to wherever she was going, for a small fee of course. She recalled her father saying that someone would meet her there and not to worry, and a man did approach her straight away. Kinni thought, 'He looks vaguely familiar.' He was tall and thin wearing the typical Gambian suit with sandals upon his feet, same as she'd seen on her no good father, but she wouldn't hold that fact against him. The stranger greeted her warmly.

"Kinni, I am pleased to meet with you. I'm Jibril Nadau," he said politely in Wolof.

"I'm pleased to meet you also. Are you my uncle?" Kinni asked him.

He peculiarly didn't respond in a way that made her feel a little nervous. At first she just assumed that he had not heard her. They walked down the road in silence. She thought that they must be related. She had not met everyone in her extended family and had never been to Africa so she felt sure that that was who this man was, seeing as he knew her name. People continued to accost her trying to grab her bags, asking for money in return for their services. Jibril, the unknown man allowed one young boy to take one of her bags. Kinni, unsure of the boy's intentions, immediately snatched it back away from him. The young boy didn't quarrel with her he just started saying something to Jibril in French and pointing in Kinni's direction. Kinni couldn't understand the language but she knew well enough what the boy was saying.

"Give him your bag back," Jibril rudely demanded of Kinni.

She turned her head towards Jibril and just stared at him indignantly.

"Who the f- do you think you are? Family or not, I don't have to take this s-," Kinni told him.

Again, no response, Jibril just grinned at her with the biggest set of teeth she'd ever seen. The young boy gingerly took her bag and carried it to a nearby taxi line. One rolled up to Jibril's feet, ahead of the others waiting patiently. The driver jumped out and reached for the back door while Jibril stood stiffly and impatiently for him to do so.

"Get in," Jibril ordered Kinni.

Again, she stared at him irately. He was beginning to get on her nerves.

"Who the f- are you anyway? I'm not going anywhere with you," she told Jibril point blank with her arms firmly wrapped around her waist and her feet in a *hit me and you die* stance.

"I'm from New York City, son, not from some backyard you call a country in the middle of no-where," Kinni glared at him waiting for him to step towards her so she could get a good swing in.

Without much warning he simply shoved her against the car

doorframe and tried to force her into the back seat of the cab.

"Take your hands off of me or I'm going to call the police," she yelled loud enough to draw attention to this stranger trying to hoist her into a car against her will.

She didn't come all the way over to Africa to be abducted. Thank Allah, the police finally heard her screams and three of them came charging over to the car. She felt safe as they rushed in her direction and let down her Harlem bad-ass pose for a moment. She wanted to show Jibril what a flat out fool he was and just who the heck he was dealing with. However, the officers didn't even look in Jibril's direction; instead they grabbed hold of her. They lifted her clean off her feet and tossed her into the back seat no questions asked. In shock she sat frozen watching the officers approvingly pat Jibril on the back. Then she steadily howled until her throat throbbed. She kicked everything she could reach with both her feet and hands. She was hysterical with rage. Yet that did not stop the taxi driver, the police or Jibril with the nasty grin from whisking her off to a place she knew not of. Again she asked, "Who the f- are you?" as they drove pass the airport hustlers, the markets, the city buildings, and especially pass her last glimpse at freedom. She glanced out of the rear window at a sign that read Welcome to the Republic of The Gambia and realized that she was a long, long way from home.

Kinni didn't know what was coming next but from the harassment at the airport she knew that it was not to *grandma's house we go*. Instead, they arrived to her brand new prison, this unknown man's palatial palace. It was huge, gorgeous even. She was shocked when she saw it. She didn't know what to think. She figured it would be some dark alley someplace where women never escape after he's had his fill. She knew something about men like him and wasn't unfamiliar with their appetites. Obviously, he was a rich man who had bought off the police and possibly the whole damn country. She didn't like feeling this vulnerable. 'Where is my grandmother? Where is my family? Why did this stranger greet me at the airport? How did he know I was arriving? Had he just guessed that some young girl would be getting off the plane, alone and in a strange land?' She was utterly stupefied. Yet there she was at his place, his lair without a friend in the world.

"Get out," he shouted as an order and not a request.

"Who the hell are you?" she ordered right back at him.

Then she ran right up to his face and pointedly waged her finger at him. Scared or not, she wasn't going to be treated like dirt.

"I'm your husband," he spat back at her and pushed her to the ground.

"What? What? What?..." she asked not of him but of the universe.

'It's not possible,' she thought. She must have misheard him. 'Did he say husband?' The earth seemed to have spun around leaving her disoriented with its rotation. She was dizzy now with a mix of fear and trepidation. She was nauseous and overwhelmed with disbelieve. What type of world did she live in where a person can be sold by her own family? She was sick with grief and remained lying there on the ground wallowing and whaling for hours. She was inconsolable. Later that day Jibril came out of the house and snatched her up to her feet. Then he jabbed at her back with his fist pushing her into the house. She didn't have enough energy to resist. She was too tired to fight, too tired to cry anymore, too angry and utterly deserted to be anything save frightened. She needed some time to think. Then as soon as they got to the threshold of the door, he reached into her suitcase and began searching for something.

"Give me your passport," he demanded throwing her bag on the floor.

"No," she replied, as if to say 'make me'.

Kinni dared him to continue this little discussion and that was the first time he slapped her. The palm of his hand came across her face open and hard. Then a moment later before she had time to process the pain or brace herself, the back of his hand came crashing down, the one with the diamond ring on it. She tried to maintain her footing but the force was too great. As she fell he continued three or four more front and back hand slaps with her kneeling steadily trying to shield herself from his advances.

"I am your husband, dam-it," he taunted, "You do as I say. Now give me your passport."

"No," again she told him while wiping blood from her mouth and trying to stand up to him once more.

"You will give me your passport," he demanded leaning into her and raising his hand for another round of blows.

"I'm not some little girl that you can just smack around whenever you feel like it. I'm from America. I have rights. I will call the cops," she warned him in futility.

At that he laughed while walking away carrying her suitcase with him and throwing it into a room at the far end of a long hallway. Then he went about his business as if she wasn't even there for three whole days.

Chapter Five

Around the fourth day or so her official role as Jibril Nadau's wife began rather abruptly and unofficially. During the days that he had not spoken to her the maid was showing her around. Kinni didn't think much of it at the time. She figured that she would always be there helping out and serving her as well as him. Kinni had no intentions on staying at all, and she just assumed that the maid was giving her a lay of the land, showing her the ropes, that sort of thing. That morning when Kinni awoke, however, the maid was packed up and gone and Kinni was left to do all the chores including the cleaning up after Jibril's three unruly children. She stubbornly refused to lift a finger to do anything that Jibril required of her and she was belligerent with all of his kids. By twelve noon that same day, Kinni had been whipped within an inch of her life with a thin tree branch. She decided to give in a little at least in an effort to save her life. Apart from the chores, he, her new husband, had given his children her suitcases and the content within. They loved her brand new sneakers because they were from America and wore them around the house as if they were slippers crushing the backs and sliding around on the marble floors. After a short while the shoes looked as if dogs had chewed them to bits. She hated him, this Mandinka man but she really loathed his children. They were spoiled rotten. Each morning they'd wake her up by drinking water and then spitting it in her face for a laugh. Jibril laughed right along with them without the slightest concern for her feelings. Before leaving the maid had kindly given Kinni one of her dresses to wear because of the children's destruction of her clothes. So for the remainder of her stay in Gambia she wore the same old housedress day in and day out. She only took it off to clean it, but even that didn't happen very often.

So with no money and no way home, Kinni's new job was to clean the entire house, an enormous house by anyone's standards. The floors were to be mopped every single day. In a hot climate such as Gambia it was easy to track things into the house and therefore her mission was to make it seem as if no one had been there. There were four bathrooms and no one seemed to know the importance of flushing the toilets or picking up after themselves. The showers were filthy every day from the children playing in as much dirt as they could find then endlessly washing it off. They had a distinct aversion to the dirty clothes hamper which bordered on the pathological. Kinni spent most of her day picking up filthy articles of clothing thrown throughout the house. God forbid they picked up a rag, a broom or mop or bothered to hang their clothes back up in their closets. Then there was the endless shopping for food. Kinni went to the market three or four times a week. They didn't eat much but since a great many things were imported, freshness was a factor. She'd take a few clothes sacks and walk three miles to the nearest market escorted by one of Jibril's many guards. It was understood that she couldn't take a taxi going only coming back. Jibril lavished his children with every whimsical treat but the equivalent of a two-dollar taxi for her would have broken his coffers.

Then, on yet another hot sticky day, his children went off to stay with some relatives for a short visit. Jibril and Kinni were alone for the first time since she arrived in the Gambia. It didn't take her long to notice that there was something different about him. He started looking at her for one, paying attention to her movements, where as before he just treated her like the maid. She could tell that he wanted something from her that was not going to be given easily. It was then that she recognized the similarities about him and her father. Then without much warning he was all over her. He reminded Kinni of a wild animal. Everything about this man was repugnant. He didn't even bother to take her into the bedroom or the couch. They were right there on the marble floor that she had just scrubbed. He pushed her down onto it and simply fell on top of her. She felt this pole pushing against her thigh. It hurt as did his skinny bony knees digging into her legs. He was making disgusting noises and slobbering all over her face. She kept turning her cheek away from his lips every time he tried to kiss her. His fish smelling breath was repulsive and hot.

Then he rolled onto his feet and pulled her up with one smooth tug and dragged her into the bedroom. She hadn't slept with him in his bed yet. She had been sleeping in the maid's quarters up until that day. He yanked her over to the bed and threw himself on top of her again. His bones felt like needles digging into her flesh. She began to cry though she didn't want him to see it. He slapped her because she just refused to open her legs for him. She was so tired from the cleaning that eventually she did out of shear exhaustion. He didn't even bother to take off her underwear. He stuck his penis inside of her by pushing the fabric to the side. Kinni didn't know what she hated more, this Mandinka husband enjoying himself or the speed at which he did it. She had never seen anyone move that fast. He flopped around on top of her and shoved that thing with such force that she thought she was going to pass out. She felt as if someone was jabbing the inside of her vagina with a hot, skinny twig. It was torturous. She couldn't imagine that anyone found this to be pleasurable. She prayed that it would be over quickly.

It was, praise Allah, but then Jibril grew quiet and then suddenly violent. That was the second time that he smacked her. It hurt more this time because she was lying in such a defenseless position. His hand came down brutally across her face. The back of his hand crashed on the other side with the force of a baseball bat to her jaw. She was bleeding out of the nose. Then came the front of his hand and the back at least ten more times.

"You dirty filthy thing," he yelled.

She had no idea what he was talking about. She imagined that he was going to kill her.

"How dare you," he screamed.

All the while he was loosening her teeth and putting holes in her cheek. Then he took her by the hair and dragged her off the bed. She held onto his arm all the while trying to get him off of her.

"Get out of my house you horrible thing," he said.

He pulled her down the hallway and over to the one and only telephone in the house. She was bleeding about the mouth and now her head smarted and jarred from the sting of someone pulling her hair out from the root. She had a lovely head of hair that fell beautifully upon her shoulders. Though he wasn't concerned about that, how she felt or how she looked. He was interested in throwing out the trash, which apparently was her. She had no value to him what so ever. He released her with a push and dialed the phone. She was on her knees now awaiting her fate. She thought he was dialing the crocked police. She'd be thrown into a foreign prison for more of the same of what she was experiencing here with him.

"Matar, it's me, Jibril," Jibril said.

Jibril had Kinni's father on the phone. She could hear his deceitful voice on the other end.

"Hello, how are things?" Matar asked him.

"You lied to me! You lied about all of this," Kinni's so-called husband screamed.

"What are you talking about?" Matar yelled back defensively.

"She's been spoiled! She's been spoiled! She's not a virgin!" Jibril screamed again and again.

Binta must have gotten on the phone because Jibril suddenly became calmer.

"Binta, I'm sorry but there was no blood. How do I tell everyone that my wife is no good? I will be the disgrace of the community. I will not be able to show myself if there is dishonor in my house. You know that?" Jibril calmly explained to Binta.

Kinni jumped up and snatched the phone out of his hands. He started to smack her but decided to just let her have it. He did that because Kinni's parents were on the other end and he didn't want them to hear him hitting her.

"Mom…mom…mom…" Kinni cried.

She wanted to say so much more but suddenly she didn't know where to begin.

"Yes…Kinni. How are you, my daughter?" Binta asked Kinni in a most loving way.

Kinni could tell that she felt guilty, that there were tears in her eyes also. She was an accomplice to this unholy union. She and her father devised this devastating scheme. Kinni was a slave in Gambia and it was partly her doing. Kinni realized that someday she would have to come to terms with that fact.

"Why?" she cried, "Why have you done this to me?"

She was distraught and missed the sound of her mother's

voice terribly. She felt betrayed though she longed to see her, to be near her. She wanted Binta to wrap her arms around her and tell her that everything was going to be all right.

"I want to come home," she begged her, "Please, please send money so I can come…."

Her so-called husband, Mandinka coward snatched the phone from her hand at that moment. Though she wasn't all that he hoped for, he would not hear of her leaving. He told Binta to put Matar back on the phone.

"You owe me something for my trouble," Jibril advised Matar.

Kinni listened closely. She was beginning to put all of this whole situation together.

"I deserve some kind of compensation for this treachery," Jibril said in a most devious manner.

This was extortion. This had nothing to do with her.

"I know I didn't have to pay a dowry but this is not a pure virgin. You said no dowry and I thought for a pure virgin but she has been tasted before. This is not fair and you know it," he told Matar.

So, she was sent without any money changing hands. Her father sold her to this horrible excuse for a man for free. Kinni sank into the floor. She dared her father to tell him why she wasn't a virgin.

"I believe that I should have some compensation to be fair," Jibril said.

Her father must have told him what he wanted to hear because he nodded and smiled and then said his good-byes. The sound of the receiver clicking made Kinni feel as if a jail cell was closing her in. Now she had no hope of returning to America, to her family. She was definitely his slave. All of her fears had been finally confirmed. Jibril turned and spat on her.

"You filthy, filthy girl. Your father said that you were a whore with some boy named Joe and that's why he sent you to me. He told me that I can do whatever I like to you. He does not want you back," he spat again and it landed square in Kinni's eye.

'Joe,' Kinni thought, 'My lying father had the nerve to mention Joe's name for his crime.' As for, Jibril, he didn't care anything what so ever for her except for what she could do for him. Kinni had never felt so alone in her entire life. There was nothing she could do. Her family had abandoned her and now she was on her own to survive however she might. It was a lot to take in all at once. Jibril took her by the hair again and once again dragged her into the bedroom. All of this must have aroused him because that metal pipe of his was standing erect looking for a warm place to land.

There was nothing tender about this man, this Mandinka. There was nothing romantic about his, for lack of a better word, lovemaking. He treated her coldly almost as if she wasn't even in the room. There was a distance that he created between them whereby he could have been with anybody else including being all by himself. And his lips were the worst part about it. They swallowed her entire face when he, for lack of a better word, kissed her. The wetness and sloppiness of it was so gross that she wanted to vomit in his mouth. The lip flesh was always chapped and cracked and he pressed against her so hard that it left scratch marks all over her face. His tongue inside her mouth was rammed all the way back to her tonsils and it moved and explored in such a way that threatened to choke her. She was so uncomfortable that she couldn't think of anything except trying to get him off of her. The more she wrestled the more excited he became so she became as stiff as a two by four. He did to her the way she saw him doing everything, without any finesse or style. He was just a pig jerking and rolling all over her touching without permission, concern or regard. He was like a giant drill trying to nail her into the bed. As he came this time he grabbed a fist full of her hair and pulled her closer into him with it. She screeched in bitter torment. To her dismay, this reaction seemed to please him also. He stayed inside of her until she cried like a baby then he let go and pushed her over. She had never imagined that life could be like this, that people could be so mean to one another. She kept wondering what she did to deserve it. Could being born female have such severe consequences? Was that her only crime?

Chapter Six

Life as Kinni had once known it was over. She went from relative obscurity to the great unknown. Things weren't great at home but she did have some creature comforts. She went from having her own room, her own clothes that actually fit her, a closet filled with shoes and sneakers to a hole in the wall room within the confines of a mansion or jail. She went from being solidly young and single to being the wife of someone she barely knew. She was thousands of miles away from anything that she could relate to or recognize. She was severely abused daily and she didn't know how she could escape from any of it except by dying. She wouldn't have married this Mandinka fool if forced at gunpoint. Yet, there she was servicing everyone in the house including the bratty children's little guests. When Jibril's little ones, Jasseh, Jebel and Janxa, also known as his princes and the princess, had their friends over, Kinni didn't think she could survive the night. Between them hitting on her and pulling at her whenever they needed a glass of water or something eat, and them assuming that she was entertainment to be kicked around for their pleasure, she didn't know which was worst - Jibril or his kids. They weren't sweet at all like her brothers and her sister back home who'd run around laughing and playing as children do. They were instead small replicas of their father and separate mothers.

Like Kinni's family, the Nadaus were an assortment of different mothers but one dreadful constant father. She discovered that her Mandinka husband had four wives before her and each had run away from home as fast as their little feet could carry them as soon as he agreed to their divorces. Each of them was the same as her a product of a verbal marriage. No papers were signed, no blood tests drawn, no ceremony and no real bone-fide legal action of any kind was given for their nuptials. These previous wives wanted to marry rich and Jibril was that but when they actually discovered that that also meant they'd have to live with him, that's when they began to plot their escape. One of them didn't give him the son he so eagerly wanted so naturally she had to go. She left everything behind, the maid told Kinni, except her newly born baby girl. Another gave him a son but refused to let him touch her for the remainder of their marriage. Of course he forced his way as best he could but the rumor was that she had strong enough thighs that could wrap around his neck and pop it in two. She had to go for obvious reasons. He feared for his life. Still another just walked around all day and all night weeping. Kinni could relate to her the most. She didn't know what actually happened to the last one. Kinni believed that her departure had something to do with a dispute over the dowry but she wasn't completely sure. She gathered this information from company that came over, drank and then talked too much. All she knew was that their children took on the negative characteristics of their personalities. The little girl, Janxa, cried incessantly and would break down and fall out when she didn't get her way, which was always. Mandinka husband thought it was cute that Janxa would scream at the top of her lungs instead of simply asking for what she wanted. He'd laugh and laugh and hold her on his knee saying, "What does my little princess want now?" Kinni would have to run and fetch 'whatever,' whether it was in the middle of the day or the middle of the night. She knew that hate was a strong word but she honestly hated the little girl the most, although not one of his children had a kind bone in their tiny little bodies. Like their father, they had an ingrain sense of entitlement which left Kinni running around the house daily up and down two flights of stairs in order to make sure that everything they desired was provided to them post haste. Mandinka husband demanded it. And even if his children were about, he wasn't ashamed of smacking Kinni around when she defied him. Janxa, Jasseh and Jebel would just stand around watching as if it were a show. At those times, Kinni would try her best to maintain her footing and take it as best she could. She tried her hardest not to cry or shriek in pain. She never wanted to give them that kind of satisfaction.

One day after one of these smacking incidents, Kinni fled outdoors in order to get away from all of them, never to return. She made it as far as the front of the house and onto the gravel road a few yards down. There wasn't another living soul for miles. As she discovered, she was in a mansion in the middle of nowhere. There was a huge stone gate that wrapped all the way around the property, which stretched approximately six acres. He had guards stationed at the front and back entrances. These people who watched the house were transients mostly but were loyal to whoever fed them. He paid them two to three dollars a day and never anything on weekends yet they stayed and were happy with their lot in life. One of them stared at Kinni as she exited through the front door. She knew by the bitter way the guard looked at her that she wouldn't get much further had she walked through the gate. She could hear Mandinka's footsteps coming up from behind her, wanting her to come back in for more of the same. She could also hear his children laughing at the abuse that she had just suffered. She hated her life. She hated everything about it. When Mandinka husband approached her, she straightened up as best she could.

"You better stop hitting on me I swear," she faintly warned him.

All she had left was her small thin voice. She didn't know what she might do but if pushed far enough, even she couldn't fathom what she was capable of. She had dreamed day and night about how to murder her own no good father. Mandinka's skinny little body would be a lot easier. Jibril saw that Kinni meant business and backed away from her this time. His advantage was always the element of surprise. He would wait until he could catch her off guard.

"We're leaving soon. Come on," he said while walking back into the house.

"Going where?" she asked.

"To my village," he said with a little bit of a smile.

She wanted to punch his teeth in and especially hated it when he showed them off. 'His village,' she thought. It was a community of shacks surrounded by dirt. The people, although polite, were definitely not trying to keep up with the rest of the world. They did almost everything outdoors. They cooked in an open pit, which was the only thing that didn't taste half bad. They washed their clothes in a basin also outside. Had she known that they were going to his village that day, she never would have eaten anything for breakfast. His village didn't have running water, in fact, there was no plumbing system whatsoever. They used wells and pit latrines, or rather, several holes in the ground should one have to relieve one self. Kinni thought she was going to die the first time she had to go into one of them. The smell alone almost made her trip backward into the nasty, dirty cavity. Then there were the flies that attacked her on every side. The toilet paper or lack thereof was brown and definitely of the recycled variety. She had already survived her father and was just barely but tolerantly dealing with Mandinka husband but that filthy hole in the ground could have been her grave, yet how symbolically appropriate to be found at the bottom of the toilet there in Gambia.

"Why are we going there?" she asked belligerently.

She was sure that if he had time he would have swung at her again but he just glared over at her as if to say, 'later'. He walked over to his crybaby daughter who was only five years-old and whisked her up in his arms. He was tender towards her, doting upon her as a loving father even. Kinni could hardly stand them, these tiresome displays of affection. He was too fickle with his love. He'd sleep with her then beat her within an inch of her life. Yet for her, Janxa, who brought no value to the house except for a mountain of tears, there was nothing he wouldn't do. He brought her to the door and yelled outside for one of the guards to bring the car around. As they exited the house it occurred to Kinni that they were all dressed up. She still had on her housedress, the one she wore everyday all day; the one she slept in every night. She had not bothered with her hair nor washed her face properly since she became a captive. It just never occurred to her anymore. She couldn't remember the girl from Harlem who primped for hours on a simple thing as what earring to wear with what outfit. She had vanished as if she had never existed. Somehow she didn't think that her appearance mattered much as a stranger in a strange land but she would have preferred not to go out in public in such a state. So, she made herself believe that she was just passing through. Whenever thoughts of this place being her real life entered her mind a fear like no other gripped and consumed her. She just couldn't bare it.

She even imagined that a ride somewhere would do her some good. She had no choice but to go, she didn't have the energy to fight and she didn't want another busted lip. It's surprisingly difficult to do anything with one like that and he would kiss her, scabs and all, breaking her cuts open whether they bled or not. So, there she was on a journey with the *family* but the forty-five minute ride took a little over two stressful hours. It was truly miserable. She sat in the back seat squeezed in between the two sons, Jasseh and Jebel. They received the windows of course. Everything about the ride was excruciating and uncomfortable. Although the boys were small in stature they opened their legs wide the way they saw their Mandinka father do. Kinni had compression marks on both sides of her thighs. The boys knew that it annoyed her but that was all part of the fun. This entire experience was degrading on so many levels for Kinni. Then there was the ride itself. Mandinka husband drove the way he did everything without any rhyme or reason but just because he liked it that way. He stopped short every half mile or so jerking the car, lurching forward thereby forcing Kinni's head to fly between her knees often. When they finally arrived Kinni had trouble walking steadily as she got out of the car. She had a cramp in one leg and a twisted ankle on the other.

"What's wrong with you?" Jibril asked and not because he wanted to know the answer.

He grabbed hold of the children and made it seem as if Kinni was acting like a baby while the children were obviously more mature at handling an outing. She would pretend to be asleep for the ride back she promised herself. She spent the rest of the day with a severe headache and her stomach in knots. She would have taken an aspirin if she were back home. However, there in the village whatever remedy these people might have, she was reticent to unearth, some concoction made with the blood of a rat. Who knows? So, she looked forward to suffering through yet another horrific day without any hope of relief.

She must have looked like the walking dead as she followed behind her Mandinka family. The Nadaus laughed and held conversation with practically everyone there while Kinni stayed aloft from the entire goings on. Then when she got an opportunity to depart from them she sat in a remote spot and listened with detached interest. It was inconceivable but, his people believed that she was exactly what she should be as his wife. If she were to mention her dilemma they would have wondered what she was complaining about. It was clear to her that her deplorable manner of dress, the sorry condition of her hair and her general melancholy demeanor didn't deter that notion one bit. She was his new American bride and that alone impressed them. America representing the land of rich and plenty and her Mandinka husband was already rich and had plenty so the match was therefore elevated beyond anything that they could ever hope for. It was hard to fathom but she and Mandinka Jibril were the elite of this community.

The elders treated Kinni as if she were royalty too. They were better to her than anyone she had met thus far and she appreciated their kindness. However, they asked a great many questions, especially about her thoughts of Gambia.

"It's beautiful here, yes?" one elder woman asked.

"Yes," she replied trying to be polite but not to encourage a lengthy discussion.

"Are you happy living in that big house?" she continued.

Kinni assumed she meant as opposed to the shanties that she and her people lived in.

"Yes," Kinni replied again politely and thought that that was a big lie but so what of it.

Although, she was a really nice lady Kinni wanted her to leave her alone but instead she asked more inane questions about her predicament.

"What about the children?" she asked.

Kinni's first impulse was to really lay it out for her, but her cursing alone would have gotten her stoned by the villagers.

"They're fine," Kinni lied through her teeth again, all the while watching Jibril's kids being presented with gifts from various people.

"It's a good day for the ceremony," the elder woman said.

'What ceremony,' Kinni thought. She immediately panicked thinking that they wanted to see her and Mandinka husband jump the broom or something.

"What ceremony?" Kinni angrily asked.

"This is the day that our little ones become women," the elder woman laughed showing all ten of her teeth.

Kinni had no idea what she was talking about and began to think the worst. She wondered if they were going to marry off the little five-year-old too and that's why the family was receiving gifts. It was then that Kinni began to really look around. All of the women, the wives were either cooking something, cleaning something or generally sitting around waiting for their husbands to request something from them. Meanwhile, the men were all seated rather comfortably in wooden chairs smoking cigars looking like fat cats. There was an imbalance of power of major proportions but everyone seemed to be pleased with their individual roles all save her. Kinni was plotting ways of killing her Mandinka husband first then her father directly after.

"What kind of ceremony?" Kinni asked the elder.

"You will see," the elder woman replied with a wink.

Then these musicians came out of nowhere. Kinni overheard someone call them griots. They apparently sang for all types of ceremonies mostly praise songs. Their melodic melodies were soothing. Kinni thought that had she not been there against her will she would have actually enjoyed their beautiful harmonies. When the music began the women perked up even more and started busying themselves with all sorts of prescribed tasks. About four or five of them were standing around a large mortar pot with giant pestles in their hands. They were crunching the heck out of some spices. Kinni noted that most of the men were actually sitting around another rather large pot that was simmering something over an open flame. They were making Happy Tea someone mentioned. The men were loud and seemingly very happy as they prepared this brew. It smelled just awful, even after they poured into it an entire five-pound sack of sugar. Everyone she spoke to told her that it was an acquired taste. There was coly everywhere too being grilled to perfection. Another group of ladies were finishing the cooking of plantains. They smelled truly delicious as did the fu-fu that was being reheated in aluminum foil. Still another set of women hurried all the young girls of this village into one of the huts. Kinni watched and waited wondering what on earth was going on. The thought of the little five-year-olds getting married seemed completely absurd. Why in the world would a man want something that young? She couldn't image what was about to take place and she felt nervous for the girls, even admittedly the one from Mandinka's house, the crybaby princess, Janxa.

A crowd began to gather and they all had their eyes set on that one hut it seemed. Then one by one the girls filed out. Now they all had on white long dresses with nothing underneath. Everyone seemed elated at what was to come next. The knot in Kinni's stomach tightened at the thought of it. The music became electric as the girls pranced around a roaring fire dancing and singing some song whose words were difficult to understand but the gist of it was something about embracing life. The dancing went on and on and on. Then the girls sat in a small cluster and everyone listened to each of the fathers go on and on about their wonderful daughters. When they got around to Mandinka husband he sounded like a typical proud father with enough arrogance to fill a hot air balloon. Kinni just couldn't even look at him. The elder that she spoke with earlier paid particular attention to the bile that Kinni let drip from her eyes for that man. The elder woman had a small grin on her face at its recognition. If only Kinni could tell her the fullness of her hatred. When next Kinni looked over the elder woman pretended she wasn't even there. Kinni began to wonder if the elder woman had endured the same abysmal reality that she had being in Gambia. Though, whenever Kinni looked around everyone seemed to be pleased with their lives. If something was in error, it didn't show. She got to thinking that maybe growing up in Gambia was completely normal for them, and therefore they didn't know any other way. This was natural for them. There's one true thing in life and that's that one can get used to anything. However, Kinni flat out refused to get used to anything there. She had a taste of freedom and she longed to return to it even if it was in a casket.

Directly across from the dancing came another group of elder women. They were highly esteemed and respected. Kinni could tell. For, even the men stopped what they were doing to acknowledge them. They nodded in greeting and made a pathway for them through the crowd. The young girls lined up at their request and followed them to another hut. Then the young girls were evenly spaced around it. Then one of them was escorted in and all of the elder women went into the hut with her. Kinni shifted herself in her chair so she could sneak a look at what was inside. There was a single seat with a missing center just in the middle of the hut. The little girl was placed on the chair and her garments were removed. Then Kinni watched in astonishment as one of the elder women reached around and grabbed a giant knife. Kinni was just about to scream for help when the elder woman she spoke to earlier touched her hand.

"It will be alright," she told Kinni.

Kinni must have looked scared to death because she said it again.

"Really, it will be alright," she repeated.

Then she heard the child cry out in a wail that lasted longer than any note ever held. Again the elder woman told Kinni that everything would be all right. She was dying to ask what they were doing to those kids. They were only little girls for goodness sake. What horror were they perpetrating on these young kids? The elder woman must have recognized her bewilderment because she just started explaining.

"The young girl is placed on the stool first, you see. Then her clothes are taken off. It just makes things easier..." she began.

Kinni must have lurched as to go to the girl's rescue because the elder's hand was on Kinni's before she lifted off the chair.

"...They tie the girl's hands behind her back. This holds the girl in place especially if her arms are wrapped around her waist first. Then two other women hold the girl's thighs apart..." she continued.

Kinni wished the elder woman had stopped talking all together at that point. Kinni had already begun thinking the worst about the entire world. She knew instinctively that it was not something beneficial for the girls. How could it be? They were strapped to a hollow stool. What were they chopping at?

"...Sometimes they use a knife but a razor is better. It cuts smoothly across and before you know it it's gone..." she continued.

The elder woman had a calm voice. There was no emotion in her description of this particular occurrence. Kinni could tell that she was intimately familiar with this subject matter.

"...You really can't feel it. Some of the girls cry because of the blade. It seems enormous at that age but it's not that way once you're my age..." she laughed.

The elder woman reached across and wiped tears from Kinni's face. Kinni hadn't realized that she was crying the whole time. Even after she touched her cheek she still couldn't stop them from rolling down.

"...The cut is made from the clitoris to the small lip of the labia minora. As you can imagine, there's a lot of blood. That's why the cutters place a bucket underneath. When I was younger, there was a hole in the ground. I believe the hole is better because some girls cry when they see that much blood..." she went on as if she needed to.

The girl inside the hut cried and screamed profusely but that didn't seem to spoil any of the festivities.

"...Once it's all stitched up with horsehair, you're done. It hurts for the first few days but then you don't feel anything anymore," she said scrunching her lips together and licking her tongue over the front of her teeth.

The elder woman was so right with that last statement. You don't feel anything anymore.

"Why? Why do they do this?" Kinni naively asked frustrated with what she had witnessed.

"We don't feel anything down there. It makes the marriage easier on the woman, you see," the elder said very matter-of-factly.

Then Kinni and the elder woman both turned and faced the

gathering again. Kinni had no idea what to say to all she had just heard. Then she saw the daughter of Mandinka husband entering the hut next. Little Janxa was smiling from ear to ear as if it were her birthday. Mandinka husband looked on happily waving at her joyfully. Janxa didn't know what she was about to face though she had seen all the other little girls exiting wearing diapers and crying their eyes out. Yet she walked in bravely. She didn't even struggle on the stool. She cried like all the others but not any louder or longer. Once all the cutting was done, each of the girls resumed the gathering as if they had accomplished something to be proud of. All of the women surrounded them and fed them directly out of the pots as little treats. The women kissed them and hugged them tightly. Kinni blushed at their affection towards one another. It was the most she had seen during this entire dreadful journey. It reminded her of her mom and she began to miss her terribly.

As was their custom, all the women sat around at one table with the children, while the men gathered separately at another. The food was served on two huge round metal plates; one went to the men's table and the other went to the women and children. Everyone ate with their hands and, in one of two hands full, the plate was clean. Kinni had watched this routine at the Mandinka husband's home daily but it was quite another thing to see an entire village garble down that much food that quickly. She wasn't hungry after observing that. The elder woman came back over to her and handed her some fu-fu and a long plantain. She knew Kinni so well already, that Kinni was incapable of standing after all she had seen that day. The elder woman smiled at Kinni the way Binta would have when she knew that there was something terribly wrong with her daughter. Kinni wanted her to hug her too and to tell her that everything would be all right.

Then they both looked over and saw Mandinka husband staring in their direction and that thought disappeared like that uniqueness they stole from these women's bodies. Kinni got to thinking that there was a good reason why these women might not want to feel anything. She had had her fill of Mandinka husband. There was nothing pleasant about him and at night she prayed for him to be out with friends or to be too tired to touch her. She felt every iota of him and it was as traumatic for her as what she had just seen those young girls go through. Maybe it was a good thing that they would only have to go through that kind of pain once. There was definitely something to be said for going through this life a little deadened.

Chapter Seven

An entire year had passed and her hatred, revulsion and bitterness had become full-grown. She was disgusted with the heat, disgusted with the rain, disgusted with the food, disgusted with the lack of food, disgusted with his dirty house, disgusted once she had cleaned it, disgusted when the house was empty, really disgusted when there were guests. Her spirit could not be settled. She was so lonely that she felt as if she had disappeared altogether. She was unnerved all the time and her shoulders were raised and hutched in distress whether things were going smoothly or not. Everything had become distasteful for her and she had aged beyond recognition. There were dark circles around her eyes and her cheeks were sunken and pale. Kinni's once beautiful long hair had all been wrenched out by the Mandinka husband, leaving her with bald splotches in the front and back of her head. She looked a fright. Her teeth were yellow and decaying. She was frail and covered head to toe with black and blues. Had she still been in Harlem, she would have been ashamed to go outside but here in hell she looked as ugly as her soul, as decrepit as all the other devils she was amongst. Within this pit of despair she had hardened to where even her very skin was crusted, gray and ashy. She had been through so much that she had literally turned to dust. There wasn't anything about life that she found worth living. Thinking of ways of killing herself had become her daily pastime. It was woven into the everyday routine as one might say, "I brushed my teeth then I slit my throat, then I washed my face, then I jammed a nail in my eye."

She awoke feeling particularly pissed off this day and spat in everything she had prepared for Mandinka husband and his spawn, except for Janxa's food. She began putting all of hers on a separate dish. She figured that having to grow up as a Gambian girl was torture enough. However for Mandinka husband, she blew her nose in his precious fish and didn't even bother to mix it in or pour sauce over it so he couldn't detect her wrongdoing. Part of her wanted him to see it. It would have been the one and only part of her that she gave to him freely. She sincerely hoped this day that he had something else to occupy himself with besides her. She didn't want to be the entertainment that he'd use to kill a few hours. She was particularly un-inspired about life this day for this was the day of her birth. She was turning twelve years old.

Though to look at her she would have appeared to be much more like thirty approaching forty. Mandinka's friends would always say to him, "If you put her on a new dress, she wouldn't look half bad." It was the half bad the stuck in her claw. She was no bigger than his kids and often people mistook her for one of them. She was obviously the bastard child for he would push them forward to greet strangers while she was forced behind to look on ostracized and alienated. On rare occasions sometimes he'd even hold her hand in public and pretend that they were one big happy family. He stopped doing so though because sometimes Kinni would spontaneously burst into tears shaming everyone with her uncontrollable sobs. He'd say, "You're just a disgrace. I cannot take you anywhere." He didn't know how his words bruised her as if he had his foot on her heart crushing it. She was just a child. She hadn't discovered what it really took to stand up to someone boldly without any fear. And admittedly, she did fear him as she did her own father and they both knew it. They each would lord their strength over her and she was too helpless and too weak to defend herself against them. It's ironic but only a weak person would do that to another simply to take what they wanted. In stark contrast, she'd often watch the little Mandinka girl child sit on her father's lap without asking permission. Janxa would just enter a room unannounced, uninvited even when Jibril had guests and she would take her proper seat on his knee. Kinni could never think of doing such a thing with her father. She was just not wanted in that way by him.

For Kinni was born out of the decay of a shattered and wounded soul. Her father had never loved her mother. It was common knowledge. It was an undeniable fact. Matar was, in truth, forced to marry Binta by his mother, Kinni's grandmother. He was dating five other women from his Gambian village when he became of marrying age. It was understood that the next logical step in the progression of his life was for him to be wed. He had completed his schooling at the university, now they were seeking to find him a wife. Matar's mother had long admired Binta's family for this purpose. They were people of means. They had livestock and owned property and a few businesses. She could see that if Matar married into Binta's family it would make for a better deal than any other family in the village. She liked the fact that they were wealthy, sure, but she mostly liked the fact that they were hard workers. She admired their drive. So, Matar's mother and his father offered the customary Kola nuts, which were formally sent by messenger to Binta's house and her family accepted them before either one of the children officially agreed. This custom of gift giving initiated the courtship. Though Matar argued his point of not being in love with Binta and not having anything in common with her, it was difficult to reverse the wheels of some hundreds of years of tradition. Those would have been valid reasons in another culture but in Gambia he would do what was best for the family not just for himself.

"Marry her, son. Look at all the jewels and clothes they have given to us," his mother told him.

Binta's family had sent a dowry that consisted of several baskets full of gold and silver and cash. It was the most wealth Matar's family had ever seen.

"We've just to discuss the bride price and then you will see that everything now will be different for us," his mother promised him.

Things were different. Binta said that Matar didn't look at her during the entire courtship, festivals or even throughout the marriage ceremony. His main goal was to bed her and show the village that there was blood on the sheet. That would act as a bond symbolizing the eternal uniting of these two families. Binta didn't say much about her wedding except that it occurred one typical warm day in Gambia. Kinni had been born out of that abysmal pairing, a mother, who had been raised and prepared to expect a house with furnishing and provisions but not much else, a father, who couldn't wait to move on to his true loves, his next wives. As a child Kinni was treated as such too. Matar didn't have much use for her. Kinni reminded him of Binta, the woman who he was forced to live with for the rest of his life. Sure, he provided for his family but he was never really present in their lives. He was only fulfilling a commitment, a family obligation, a chore, all for which he hadn't a choice except to disown his mother and father. Matar's new family was a burden that he had to bear not a joy which he desired and treasured. Kinni hadn't thought much about that fact until her Gambian experience. Now she was her father and her mother, a person in a marriage where even the lowest of expectations would never be met. Her mother told her that the elders counseled her on her responsibilities of being a wife and mother. She often wondered if they ever told her the secret of how she could be happy with someone who didn't want her. Maybe they said that there was some place deep inside her soul that she could escape to when he decided that his burden was far too great to bear. As Kinni walked along the dirt road to market that day she thought about her mother the entire time. She wanted to hear her voice so badly that she could scarcely think of anything else, for Binta would be the one person in this whole wide world who would wish her a happy birthday.

Kinni snuck a look behind her from time to time. As per usual she'd have at least two guards trailing her to market. Oddly enough, however, they weren't there. It was peculiar that no one was following her this specific day. She wondered why in passing, deciding finally that she wasn't upset about it. Then she kept looking to make sure. It was true. Absolutely no one was there. She, of course, after one whole year, knew their faces well. She began to believe that everyone possibly thought she had resolved to stay in this place, this Gambia, in truth so had she. She hadn't the time to think of a viable way out of Gambia in all these many months. She was completely distracted by chores surely but mostly by her own sorrow. When she was mopping the marble or scrubbing the bathrooms walls, she was forlorn and alone constantly wondering why this was all happening to her. She'd awake feeling ill with worry and dread every single day. However, it dawned on her this day, this obviously special day that she should have stopped feeling sorry for herself a long time ago. For it was only then when she had lifted up her head that she began to see that she was missing out on some very observable opportunities. She stopped just one block shy of such a particular place. It almost knocked her over to think that she had not noticed its significance before. She had learned about such places in school and yet had never determined it would one day be her salvation. Yet there it was for the whole world to see, the United States Consulate building. It wasn't a huge structure. It didn't command the block. It reminded her of a small trailer really but it elated her so. She felt giddy. It made her feel something that she had not felt in months, hopeful. She stood still for several minutes just staring at its entrance. Suddenly, she was nervous with excitement and anticipation. Then she hesitated, thinking of herself as just a minor without any rights save what her parents are authorized to do for her. She thought, 'What can anyone do for me?' In the back of her mind she discerned that the rules of America didn't apply here. Else she could never be married at age eleven against her will. So, there she stood trying to decide whether she should walk into this Consulate place or not. When she looked down the other way to market, she made up her mind once and for all. She was so tired of shopping for her Mandinka family. She didn't want to select another vegetable just to serve it one minute and watch it disappear in the next.

Before she knew it, she was at the U.S. Consulate door. There were two guards keeping watch, one on each side of the entrance. They parted a path for her as she approached.

"United States citizen?" one asked.

She nodded yes. She knew that they wanted her to walk in but she was suddenly hesitant again. Jibril's guards may have been holding watch on her from somewhere in the shadows. She couldn't be too cautious.

"Go to the kiosk," the other said.

She didn't know what he was talking about.

"The big desk, ma'am," he informed her.

Kinni took one long last look behind her then quickly stepped into the building. Once inside she breathed in air in small spurts. Just walking in there had fatigued her for the sheer exhilaration at the mere thought of escaping Gambia. She had conditioned herself to believe it wouldn't happen. She reprimanded herself for having grown so insecure and so afraid within her year's stay.

There were several desks positioned around the room and one large kiosk directly in the center not more than ten steps away. Kinni must have looked confused because a woman rushed from behind her desk and immediately greeted her.

"United States citizen?" she asked brightly with breath smelling of peppermint.

She nodded yes. The woman pointed to another desk and told Kinni to take a seat there. It wasn't long before someone else walked over and escorted her to yet another chair. It was good for them to be so helpful for her feet wouldn't move on their own. She needed all the encouragement they offered.

"You are an American citizen, right?" a very pale white woman asked.

"Yes," she managed in English.

She had been speaking Wolof so much that now English sounded like a foreign language.

"I wish to go to America," she got out while shaking with adrenaline.

"Okay. That can be arranged. Do you have a passport?" she asked.

Kinni heard the words and paused. Then, just like that her dream balloon began to burst. She suddenly panicked. She hadn't thought about her passport all year. Kinni's heart was racing so fast it could have leapt out of her chest.

"Do you have one, a passport?" the woman repeated as if she thought Kinni didn't understand.

"Yes. Yes I do, but...but..." Kinni said and thought to herself that she couldn't remember where she put it.

The woman stared at Kinni waiting patiently for her to finish the sentence.

"I don't remember..." Kinni said and began to cry and hyperventilate.

The woman reached into her desk and pulled out the prettiest flowered box of Kleenex tissue and handed Kinni a whole handful. Kinni knew that she must have looked a sight. Her nose was running and she couldn't stop weeping. She had to once again take courage.

"Do you know where it is?" the woman asked.

Kinni knew that she had to pull herself together. So, she straightened her back and sat up correctly and with that minor adjustment, the woman's question sparked some glimpse of remembrance. Kinni realized that she had never taken it out of her suitcase. When Mandinka husband went searching for it, he probably didn't notice the secret inside pocket. Kinni had her passport and airplane ticket tucked in there and zipped up. Binta insisted that she keep it in a safe place. A smile spread over Kinni's face because the only person who really cared about her, her mom, Binta, had reached across the ocean and given her the greatest birthday present anyone could hope for, her freedom.

"I know...I believe I know where it is," Kinni told her and skipped out into the street with a feeling of extreme joy.

A plan.

A plan.

A plan.

Kinni scurried to market, shopped and got home as quickly as she could, all the while trying to think of a good plan. She ran the whole way back to the mansion carrying three heavy sacks of fruit, grain and fish. Her feet were raw and her arms were sore and weary but she was so excited at the prospect of saying good-bye to Gambia and going home that she could hardly think of anything as pedestrian as her own minor discomforts. However, as she neared the mansion she began to think about how she should act around her Mandinka family now. For the first time in a long time, she was happy, actually happy. Her circumstances hadn't changed, yet she was at peace with the world. She was so transformed that she was afraid that they would somehow notice the change in her and decide to send the guards the next time she went to market. Kinni instinctively sensed that this change in her might just bring unwanted attention. Just like that she was then stricken with a slither of fear. The thought of staying in Gambia forever depleted all the joy from her body. That horrible thought made her doubt that she might someday have any future at all. Now with the hope that she had experienced seconds earlier drained from her, she put on a false armor of calm and marched through the front door.

Not one person lifted a finger to help her nor did anyone nod a head to greet her. She should have known that they would not even notice her at all. She laughed at herself for thinking otherwise, like she mattered. They were so busy adoring themselves that she was nothing more than a fixture really, like a table or chair, except even the furniture was treated better. So, she reoccupied herself with her own agenda. She cooked for them, fed them, cleaned up after them, all the while searching in secret for her suitcase. She vaguely remembered that it was in one of the children's room. She kept thinking about that first day when Mandinka husband sent it flying into one of the rooms along the first floor hallway. She never had a problem with any of them when it came to her entering their rooms. They liked their clothing washed and pressed and neatly placed in their dresser drawers. So she made sure to save the ironing for last that evening. So she could go into their rooms and leisurely poke around. That was the easy part. She walked into one of the boy's rooms first, Jebel, the youngest boy. He had so many toys that she acted as if she was putting them away for him meanwhile searching for her suitcase but she didn't find it there. Then came the little lady, Janxa. She too had a room full of dolls and games but no suitcase either. Their messy rooms proved to be the best way to get away with her hunt. Then came the last room, Jasseh's, the oldest. It had to be in his, she prayed. Kinni looked forward to the same as the rest, a room filled with junk and her cleaning while looking for her suitcase. However when she got to his, it was neat and orderly. She stopped to consider that with this room she would definitely look like she was rummaging through his things. She had to be clever. He had a long closet that stretched across the back wall. He was next in line for Mandinka husband's throne and everything he had showed him as an heir. He had two of the latest of everything. He had two Apple computers each with its own separate desk, just in case a friend stopped by. He had a brand new stereo system audaciously displayed at the center of his bureau dresser with two large speakers flanking it. His room was better furnished and equipped than Kinni's entire house in Harlem and she might have envied him and all that he had but for her singleness of purpose, her passport. There in the corner of that excessive closet stood the black Samsonite–isk case. It was just an ordinary thirteen dollar Wal-Mart special, propped between Jasseh's Le Crosse leather knapsack and his All-Star football collection. He had soccer balls from all over the world prominently exhibited on wire racks. Kinni didn't have to move anything to get at her passport. She thought, "Thank goodness." It was right where she left it, in the inside pocket just below the zipper. She grabbed it quickly and without thinking ran from the room. She didn't want to get caught. The penalty would be far too great.

Unfortunately for her, as she exited she bumped right into Mandinka husband, Jibril. Kinni was terrified. She felt sure he had seen what she had been doing and, unfortunately, she still had the passport right there in her hand in plain sight.

"What's that you got there?" Jibril asked.

Kinni froze not knowing what to do next or where to look or where to turn. He had caught her red handed. Kinni's heart sank. Everything that she had just imagined, dreamed and hoped for in an entire year was about to go up in flames. She was so crushed that she couldn't speak. She just looked at him as if the world had suddenly collapsed.

"I...I was..." Kinni stammered.

Jibril laughed in her face.

"I...I..." he teased mimicking her.

Then he pushed her out of his way and she fell to the floor. Then Jibril simply stepped over her, his foot managing to crush her thumb. As he walked away he gave Kinni some sound advice.

"You need to learn how to talk to people. I thought you went to school in A-mer-i-ca," he joked.

'Yes,' Kinni thought, 'America' and she couldn't wait to return. Suddenly, she was feeling very nostalgic with American songs welling up inside of her, 'Oh beautiful of spacious skies, for amber ways of grain, for purple mountain majesties, above the fruited plain! America! America! God's grace is shed on thee...' Then she thought, '...For the land of the free and the home of the brave.' She could have wept but no more. This nightmare was soon to be over. As she stood back up with her finger stinging in pain, she had an inspired thought. She'd hide the passport in the cleaning shed where the mops, buckets and dust pan were stored. No one would ever think to look in there. They didn't labor in this house; she did. Just in case, she kept one eye on each of them for the remainder of the evening to make sure they didn't stumble upon her hiding place and as the house quieted she couldn't contain her excitement of what lay ahead. She kept thinking that this was finally going to happen, that she would finally be going home. Though she had no idea what to expect, she still couldn't wait to see the City, her city, her beloved Harlem. She longed for all of the little things that she so took for granted. She wanted to go to school again and have homework given to her. She wanted to study with her friends and argue with her mom about curfews. She wanted to ride on the crowded buses and trains and complain that there was no air conditioning along with everybody else. She wanted the smog and the busy taxis racing for customers and practically running people over. She missed it all. Every little nuisance was like poetry to her.

Kinni's rush for freedom was slightly curtailed though as Mandinka husband was waiting for her when she entered his room that night. She was thrilled by one single solitary thought. This would be the very last time. She couldn't describe in mere words how wonderful that truth made her feel. She was transported somehow beyond her own body, buoyant, above any of his cruelty, meanest and his criminal offenses. As he shoved her dress up she couldn't help but to think what he even saw in her. She was never, ever willing to lie with him. She pushed and hit and cried every single time. Then she slept on the floor beside his bed and prayed that he or she wouldn't make it through to see another morning. By all accounts she was not someone he should have wanted around, feeding him and his children food that she had prepared. Yet there she was for an entire year dealing with all the intricacies of every aspect of their lives. Jibril and his family were definitely sleeping with an enemy and had Kinni been older, he would have woken to find her stabbing him or worst. It was time for her to leave. He had no idea that she was saving his life by departing. He grunted and moaned like a wounded dog and never ever spoke to her while he was ramming his penis into her unyielding vagina as if this was strenuous and exhausting. He sweated and looked pained by it all. Again Kinni wondered why anyone would desire this type of arrangement. She cursed him with every breath she took and even tried hard not to swallow the same air he expelled. She loathed every part of his body interacting with hers. It was as if he were contaminating her with every stroke. She always thought of him as something creepy like a slug oozing and clinging to dirty, filthy surfaces. It couldn't have possibly appeared as if she liked him in any way and yet, there he was inside of her, enjoying the feel of her. She couldn't for the life of her figure out why.

Chapter Eight

Two long days later, market day, Kinni was at the Consulate door once more. This time she ran to the kiosk and the same woman who she spoke with earlier that week happened to be there to meet her.

"I have it," Kinni shouted loudly before the woman had even gotten a chance to say hello.

The woman smiled.

"My name's Mrs. Chapman. What's yours?" Mrs. Chapman said reaching over and shaking Kinni's sweaty hand.

"Kinni, Kinni Bragia," Kinni said proudly handing Mrs. Chapman her ticket to freedom.

Mrs. Chapman looked it over in a scrutinizing way then escorted Kinni to her desk.

Once they were both seated Mrs. Chapman asked, "Tell me, Ms. Bragia, what is it you want me to do for you again?"

Kinni was immediately taken aback by that question. It seemed so out of place for someone to actually be asking her what they could do for her. She felt tears welling up inside of her and tried for dear life not to allow them to surface. Then she thought very deliberately about an answer.

"I wish to leave Gambia and..." Kinni began wanting to blurt out just how much she wanted to leave Gambia.

"Do you have family here?' Mrs. Chapman asked.

Instinct propelled Kinni to say yes. Yet as she pondered the question, she realized that family was not a factor for her in Gambia. Family didn't seem to matter anywhere with the exception of her mom, but especially not in Gambia. After her father and his dictates, she had a new version of the word family that had preoccupied her mind for the past several years. Thank Allah, she was hesitant to share her horrific theory on the subject with a complete stranger. She didn't realize it but Mrs. Chapman was as much family to her as was anyone else. So she resolutely said no. She told her that she had no one she could call family in Gambia not to be a complete liar.

"Okay," Mrs. Chapman went on with a slight curious tilt of her head, "So, what would you like then?"

"I would like to go back to America," Kinni told her firmly.

"Okay, do you have an airline ticket, any money? What brought you to Gambia originally?" she asked.

Kinni was afraid that she'd be asked these questions and knew that if this woman was going to help her that she would have to tell her the truth. She finally decided that in the telling of her story that she would make it brief. She felt so ashamed and exposed with the telling that she could barely stay seated in her chair.

"I was sent to Gambia by my father a year ago. He told me that I would have to take care of my sick grandmother. I know, I know she is a relative but…" Kinni couldn't breath for the sadness at the thought of even her grandmother deserting her.

"Go on," Mrs. Chapman told her, "Continue," making it seem as if that fact didn't matter.

"…I got here, to find this man, a stranger, waiting for me…" Kinni paused.

The idea of calling Mandinka husband a man and not a monster made her feel as if she were diminishing his impact on her life, made her feel as if this was the bigger lie she was telling.

"…He said, that he was…" she paused, "…my husband.

It was not at all how I imagined it would be."

"These things never are," Mrs. Chapman interjected then persuaded her to go on.

"You see, he beat me severely every day. Both of my eyes have closed shut for many days at his hands. Then without so much as a band-aid, I was made to cook and clean for him and his children night and day as if I were a slave...but I was treated worst than a slave..." she paused again just thinking about Mandinka husband and it made her stomach churn with anger.

There was so much more to say about the daily torture that she didn't know where to begin. "...Now, I am done," Kinni told Mrs. Chapman sternly, "I am done."

Kinni just looked at Mrs. Chapman for a long while without saying a word. She wondered what Mrs. Chapman must have been thinking of her. Perhaps that Kinni was so young. Maybe Mrs. Chapman was thinking that Kinni was just a child. Kinni looked down at Mrs. Chapman's hand very casually staring at her ring finger. She had a small oval shaped diamond wedding band on it that she moved around slowly in a twisting motion. Then Kinni glanced down over at her own. Her hands were ashy and peeling from the amount of water she placed them in for daily washing and cleaning.

"He doesn't know that I'm here," Kinni went on, "If he did, he would probably beat me and drag me back to his house."

Kinni did begin to cry at this point but not as a child, rather as a woman determined.

"I am not going back," Kinni told Mrs. Chapman, "I will never go back there."

Mrs. Chapman reached into her desk drawer and pulled out her beautiful box of Kleenex tissues. She handed the box to Kinni and told her to keep it.

Then Mrs. Chapman pulled out a stack of forms. She told Kinni that she had to sign a few of them then she explained to her what help she could offer.

"I'm very sorry about what happened to you. I know that this has not been easy for you. I do know one thing for sure though…things will get better. Mark my words. It was very brave of you to come here like this. You did something that most people would never do…you stood up for yourself. You took your life into your own hands. That's very, very brave," she said over and over again, "That's very, very brave of you."

Mrs. Chapman regretted to tell Kinni that nothing in Gambia happened terribly fast. She told her that she would have to contact the United States Consulate and that they would have to send an answer. Then she would have to have them issue a plane ticket and so on and so forth. Kinni couldn't help thinking that that was an awful lot of work for just little old her. Then Mrs. Chapman said something that Kinni would never forget.

"It's my pleasure to help you," Mrs. Chapman said.

Then she dialed someone on the telephone and told Kinni that the call wouldn't take long.

"Yes, Auntie Lula, it's me, Dorothy. Yes, yes, fine, thank you. Listen, Auntie Lula, I have a young lady here who needs some shelter. We don't really know. It might be longer, it depends. Have you got room? Excellent. Excellent. Twenty, thirty minutes? Do you have the real pretty ones? Excellent. Yes. Traditional, no vows strikes again. Yes. Yes. Thanks. Bye now," and Mrs. Chapman hung up.

She stacked the papers together, stapled them and then turned to Kinni and took her hand.

"You're going back to America, young lady, but first I need to put you up for a week or two maybe longer," she told her sweetly.

"Thank you," Kinni said through tears she couldn't stop from flowing if she tried.

"Can you handle that?" Mrs. Chapman asked.

"I can handle anything," Kinni said not even realizing how much truth she had spoken.

Mrs. Chapman and Kinni drove about an hour outside of town to a place similar to Mandinka husband's village. All Kinni saw were trees and huts along the way. Out of the car window she counted about twenty shanties lined up in a row approximately a foot or so apart. It had started to rain and the road turned into a thick soup of mud making all the huts lean over to one side. Mrs. Chapman stopped just shy of getting the tires stuck and they walked the rest of the way to one of the larger shanties. By all appearances it looked like a miserable day. However, Kinni wasn't thinking about the weather conditions. She wasn't thinking about the bucket bath nor the pit latrine she saw out of the corner of her eye either or the issue of the Gambia's poor plumbing condition in general. Nor did she ponder what the accommodations would be like for her for the next several weeks, or months. She didn't think about the fact that she had no money or clothes or that she was only equipped with the breath in her body, which wasn't all that adequate. She didn't think about this woman either, Mrs. Chapman, of whom she had just entrusted with her life, or that she was no more than a stranger. Mrs. Chapman was someone that Kinni had told a story to, and who had believed it instantly. She didn't think about the fact that Mandinka husband would be searching for her at the market and all over town. She never allowed herself to linger on the many weapons his guards would carry as they spread out across the countryside on their manhunt. She didn't think about the many police that Mandinka husband had wrapped around his finger and how they would jump over hoops to find her for him. No, those many thoughts did not occupy her mind. It was as if she had stepped remarkably back into her own skin after one long year apart from it. Regardless of all the obstacles that she now faced, she was going home and nothing, absolutely nothing could stop her from smiling about that.

Mrs. Chapman and Kinni stepped into the oddest looking shanty Kinni had ever seen and thereby fittingly into a whole other world. A very heavy set woman jumped up and eagerly greeted them as if she hadn't had company in a long while and welcomed the interruption.

"Dorothy, how the heck are ya', girl?" she said hugging Mrs. Chapman very tightly.

Then she reached over and without much warning grabbed Kinni. Kinni could smell her perfume and nothing else. Kinni's face was pressed against her ample bosom. She was enveloped between fleshy mountain clouds and admittedly very snug and secure. It reminded her of her mom's hugs.

"Sugar, I'm so happy to meet you," she said over and over again talking to Kinni as if she were an adorable toddler.

Kinni could tell by the woman's bear hug that she meant for her nothing but the best. She supposed that Mrs. Chapman told her something about her with their own little social worker code.

"My name's Lula but I want you to call me Auntie Lula, okay sugar?" she said with a most enduring smile.

Auntie Lula sat back down looking like mother earth herself. This Hawaiian beauty had the entire shanty decorated as if she were still there in her native land. There was grass skirted around all the tables and covering the holes in the walls made in the shape of rectangular windows. And from roof to floor, it was adorned with wooden craved hula inspired ornaments and cups and saucers with all kinds of uplifting sayings on them and intriguing symbols. It was altogether colorful and inviting. Kinni couldn't believe that a shanty could be so transformed and personalized. She had only seen the ones at Mandinka husband's village that all pretty much resembled the other with a barren, wasteland array. Not with Auntie Lula's, however, she had decided to bring some life into the place and it had a flavor all of its own, unique and wonderful. Kinni liked her immediately.

"Dorothy and new little friend, if you don't sit down I will be insulted," Auntie Lula shouted at them joyfully.

Mrs. Chapman and Kinni plopped ourselves into the nearest seats. They were cushioned and comfortable just like the room just like its owner. Auntie Lula poured them a drink of some concoction and gently forced it into their hands. Mrs. Chapman looked into her glass scrutinizing its contents, same as she did with Kinni's passport. Kinni was thirsty and swooshed hers back with all haste. It was sweet and bitter at the same time and totally refreshing. Auntie Lula's smile grew even wider after Kinni drained the glass and held it out for some more. Auntie Lula anticipated that and poured Kinni some more instantly.

"Guava's my favorite too. You are going to love it here. We have several girls here about your age and you can help me with my translations. I hear you speak Wolof," she said with a wink.

Mrs. Chapman took a little longer to finish her drink. In fact, she politely placed it down on the table once she got a whiff of its smell. Auntie Lula just grinned and shuffled some paperwork around on her desk.

"All right, let's see now. Your birth name is Kinni Bragia. What a lovely name for a very lovely young lady," Auntie Lula said turning towards her.

Kinni couldn't help but smile back and blush.

"Now, we have a few rules here for everyone. You like rules, right?" she said without waiting for a response, "Number one, no swearing. We do not use profanity here. Also, everyone must pick up after themselves. We do not have a maid service and really, can you see me doing everybody's laundry? And one more thing, and this is very important..." she leaned in real close to Kinni as if she was about to tell her a secret, "Everybody calls me Auntie Lula...but you already know that, right? Right?"

She laughed and laughed and her belly hopped up and down and danced from side to side. To anyone else she might have seemed a bit ridiculous but to Kinni she was like an angel. Kinni decided that she liked Auntie Lula a lot. Mrs. Chapman giggled some too at the sight of Auntie Lula billowing over her chair.

"Dorothy, you know how I am? You know," Auntie Lula said to her friend and then looked at Kinni, "We're going to have a good time, you'll see."

Mrs. Chapman got up and started signing some of the paperwork that Auntie Lula had just been fumbling with.

"Don't forget to sign this one, sugar," she told her, "That one keeps food on the table."

Auntie Lula got serious for a moment as she perused every document carefully. She kept silent making sure that everything was in perfect order.

"Auntie Lula, did I make any mistakes this time?" asked Mrs. Chapman.

"Sugar, you are spot on, as usual. Mistakes? You have the intelligence of a scholar and you know it," Auntie Lula told her.

Once every single page was combed over by Auntie Lula she turned to Mrs. Chapman and handed her a box.

"All right now, you know the drill. The one nearest Auntie Lula then as time goes by...well you know," she said giving Mrs. Chapman instructions.

Mrs. Chapman accepted the small box in a routine manner and without a single word, stood up.

"Ms. Bragia, it's time," Mrs. Chapman told Kinni.

"Time? Time for what?" Kinni asked suddenly afraid that

they were going to send her back to Mandinka husband's house.

"Sugar, it's time for you to go to your new home," Auntie Lula told her.

Auntie Lula heard it in Kinni's voice that she was worried. Kinni thought that this was all they could do, a nice drink and a hearty laugh but she was so much mistaken.

Mrs. Chapman escorted her right next door to another shanty, her new home. It was perfect to her too. It had a cot pushed up against one wall and a few chairs against another. There was a small stool between the chairs, which could be used as a desk or table. On the bed was some clothes stacked and folded neatly.

"Are those for me?" she asked Mrs. Chapman.

"I didn't know your size but I believe those will fit," she informed her.

"I don't know how to repay you," was all Kinni could think to say.

Mrs. Chapman just smiled.

"I wouldn't take your money, honey," she told Kinni.

Then she placed the small box on the bed and began exiting outside.

"Oh, I don't know how long it will take before we get your ticket back to the States but you're welcome to stay here as long as you like. It's not much, I know," Mrs. Chapman said with a sigh.

Kinni looked around the room again. Even if she hated it and thought it looked like a jail cell, she would have loved it still.

"It's great, really. Thank you so much," she said wanting to say so much more but the tears were working their way up into her eyes and she hoped that Mrs. Chapman could tell that she was overwhelmed with indescribable gratitude.

"You're welcome," Mrs. Chapman said while leaving, "I

must get back to the office now but I will return to check on you from time to time. You're in good hands with Auntie Lula, though. Oh, and you can open that box if you like."

With that she left. A few minutes later Kinni could hear her honking her horn and Auntie Lula shouting her good-byes over the pounding of the rain. Kinni looked around at the clothes Mrs. Chapman had brought for her, the bed, the tattered but clean chairs, the little wooden stool, the sawdust floor and the tiny box now within her hands. She hadn't even realized that she was holding onto it. It had a smooth surface and it smelled really nice like fresh cut flowers. She opened it slowly wondering what more could these beautifully generous people, who knew her no more than a complete day, possibly give. She gently lifted the top. There in the box was a bright yellow card with her name on it. It was the card that had a lovely scent. She opened the card to find a hand-written note which read:

> *Kinni,*
> *You are precious to us and we welcome you into our home. There is no danger in this place only peace. We'd like you to think of this place as your home for as long as you like.*
> *Sincerely,*
> *Auntie Lula*
> *Gambian Mission*

She read the note three times before placing it down onto the bed. Then she smelled the most heavenly of aromas coming from the remaining contents. She looked inside to find an array of different flavored toffees all individually wrapped in wax paper. She couldn't help but smile. Then she gobbled up as many she could open. This was becoming a wonderful belated birthday. Then she placed her head on the freshly washed pillow and slept more soundly than she had in years.

Chapter Nine

Suddenly, that next morning, Kinni shot bolt upright in bed. She couldn't remember where she was, half expecting to see Mandinka husband, Jibril, right beside her barking orders as was his customary practice. She was sweaty, her hands clammy and she was considerably terrified. Same as every morning in Gambia, she was not herself but forever bound to a nightmare. It took her eyes several moments of blinking before she began to focus on the small wooden stool adjacent to the bed propped against the wall. She didn't recognize it at all. Then slowly, very slowly she began to remember the shanty she was brought to in the pouring rain the night before with Mrs. Chapman and Auntie Lula. Her heart stopped galloping apace and she calmed herself down. She was ashamed at the amount of fear related residue her recent past life had left her with. She didn't relish the idea of being in a constant state of peril upon waking each morning, but that was the price of all she had been through. She would forever shutter and shake as if she were coming down from a chemical dependency. She wanted her life back but realized that that would be a physical as well as mental makeover. It dawned on her and she began to let the idea sink in that her mind would take much, much longer to mend and heal than her body.

"Breakfast! Breakfast!" someone shouted from outside of her doorway.

Her stomach was in a constant state of hunger whilst in Gambia. Gambians didn't eat much or she should say as much as she was accustomed to. In other words, she was starving.

She hurriedly grabbed one of the new dresses and changed into it. It was similar to the one she had worn for a year but it smelled of lilac and it was soft and comfortable. As she was admiring it, there was a knock on the door opening.

"Decent?" Auntie Lula asked.

"Yes," Kinni replied.

Auntie Lula walked in carrying a large box, which she placed on the bed then she sat down in one of the chairs by the wall. She was out of breath.

"I've been up early and this is the first time I'm sitting all morning," she said, then excitedly she said, "Well, go on, sugar, look in the box."

Kinni immediately jumped upon the bed and took a peak inside the box. After the sweets and the lovely dresses, not to mention the card, Kinni was excited at the thought of more presents. She saw a stack of freshly washed white towels within and a toothbrush, shower cap and a few other toiletries and feminine products.

"I hope you like them. You sleep well?" Auntie Lula asked admiring the great big smile upon Kinni's face.

Kinni shook her head yes about the sleeping part. She hadn't even noticed that she was smiling from ear to ear. She jumped up and hugged Auntie Lula for a very long while.

"I know, I know, sweetie," Auntie Lula kept saying.

Auntie Lula gently unraveled Kinni's arms from about her neck and helped her stand back upright. Again the tears were flowing without warning or pause. Auntie Lula hoisted herself off the chair and began to exit.

"You coming?" she waved at Kinni.

And Kinni scurried happily behind her.

"I want to show you around. It's not much now but I think you'll find it to be homey. I want you to meet the others too.

Come on now," she told her perceiving that Kinni was suddenly hesitant to be introduced around.

They exited out into a brightly lit morning. The sun had dried the ground and everything seemed particularly pristine, rejuvenated and fresh. As Kinni looked over the shanties to the countryside beyond, she thought, honest to God, that she was seeing Gambia for the very first time. It astounded her how green it was and how delicious the air smelled. It was really beautiful. She hadn't even noticed that before.

"These are the bathrooms," Auntie Lula showed her.

There were outdoor shower stalls with heavy-duty curtains surrounding them.

"The water pressure is just okay but you can get a good lather with the soap I gave you," Auntie Lula further informed her.

Some of the other girls were making their way out of their shanties and following behind Auntie Lula and Kinni.

"Morning," Auntie Lula shouted out to them.

"Morning," each of them replied.

They looked the same as Kinni, young and lost. One of them ran right out and having seen Kinni, a new face, stepped up and greeted her immediately.

"Hi, I'm Uzuri, pleased to meet you," she said.

"I'm Kinni, pleased to meet you, U-zer-i," Kinni reached out her hand to shake Uzuri's but Uzuri drew Kinni towards her and hugged her same as Auntie Lula did the night she arrived.

"I can braid your hair like mine if you want after chores," she told Kinni.

Kinni was afraid to even think about what her hair must have looked like. Uzuri's hair was neat and clean and in long corn-rolls evenly spaced lengthwise upon her head. Kinni's was most probably in a deplorable state of knots mixed with dirt and dust.

"Uzuri is our little beautician around here," Auntie Lula

informed Kinni all the while looking proudly at Uzuri.

They finally had arrived at a large sized shanty and everyone filed in. The room had tables lined up cafeteria style with long wooden benches on each side. The girls took what looked to be assigned seats for they each went directly to their places. Auntie Lula took her hand and pointed Kinni in the direction of an empty spot.

"Here you go," she told her.

Kinni looked up once she was seated and realized that she was directly across from Uzuri.

"This is Kinni," Uzuri announced to all the other girls at their table.

Then they all started saying hello one by one and giving Kinni their names. Kinni couldn't remember any of the names and desperately wanted to because they all seemed so nice. It made her remember her friends in America who were probably wondering where she had been this past year. She wondered what lie her father could have possibly told them. Then she recalled the one he told her. Auntie Lula sat not too far away and once she did everyone immediately held hands with the girl next to her leaving the aisles clear.

"Our Father who art in heaven hallowed be thy name…" they all recited.

Kinni had heard the prayer before but still wasn't completely sure how it went.

"…Thy kingdom come, thy will be done on earth as it is in heaven…" they continued.

Their voices sounded like music.

"…Give us this day our daily bread and forgive us our debts as we forgive our debtors…" they went on.

Kinni hadn't really listened to the words before and liked what she was hearing. Although the word 'forgive' stuck to her like a wedged splinter beneath a fingernail. Kinni believed whole heartedly in retribution. The one thought that pulled her through her year with Mandinka husband was the knowledge that one day she would have her revenge on him and her father. She felt sure that Allah had preserved her life for that very reason.

"...And lead us not into temptation but deliver us from the enemy...Amen," they concluded.

As the amen's rang out across the room, several girls stood up and began serving everyone else. Each girl got a plate from one girl then a fork from another. Then another girl filled their plates with bread and another with fruit. The servers worked together proficiently, as if brilliantly choreographed. Everything was timed and accurate. Auntie Lula just smiled widely admiring their poise and obvious skill. She was the proud momma of all her girls and Kinni knew that she would be endeared to her forever.

After breakfast Uzuri gave Kinni two distinctly different kinds of tours of the place. She told her what was what but more importantly who was who.

"That one there is pregnant. She won't talk about who the father is either..." Uzuri said pointing to a tiny little girl of about ten.

The young girl appeared to be a little frightened around all the other girls.

"...That's Bini right there, she's my girl..." Uzuri said pointing to a girl who had this wonderful arrangement of braids atop her head.

Kinni could tell that Uzuri's handiwork had struck.

"...And that's Teri. Teri, how's it going?" Uzuri asked a rather tall lanky girl.

Teri turned and hugged Uzuri.

"Girl, how's it going with you?" Teri shouted back at her.

"This is Kinni right here," Uzuri introduced her.

Teri went to hug her too. Evidently it was something that they all did. Before she knew it, she was hoisted off her feet and in the arms of another complete stranger. She wondered if that's why the pregnant girl looked a little intimidated.

"She's a little, little thing, ain't she?" Teri asked Uzuri about Kinni.

"Yes," Uzuri agreed, "She is."

Once Kinni could feel the earth beneath her feet again, Uzuri gently pulled her over to the bathroom.

"Kinni, I'm afraid that this is all yours today," and she pointed to the stalls.

Uzuri had a very sorrowful look on her face as if it was not her choice at all for Kinni.

"All the new girls get this chore, Auntie Lula's orders. She says that it makes them humble or something like that," Uzuri told her.

Kinni didn't mind cleaning the stalls. She looked at them carefully and other than the smell there didn't seem to be anything terribly difficult about them. She had done a lot more cleaning than that back home and definitely more at Mandinka husband's house. Kinni figured she'd be done with them in no time. However, as she looked around all the girls began to migrate pass her with sympathetic stares and words of encouragement.

"It's not that bad when you hold your nose, like this," one girl told her while pinching her nose between her fingers.

Others just shook their heads from side to side empathetically. Auntie Lula walked over carrying some additional cleansers and a bucket of water in her hand.

"Here, you're gonna' need these," she said handing Kinni an all-purpose cleanser and a rag and placing the bucket by her feet.

"Aunt-ie Lu-la, I really don't mind cleaning the bathroom. Back home I would have to do far more than this. I cleaned the whole house top to bottom everyday plus went to school," Kinni told her wondering what all the fuss was about.

Auntie Lula just shook her head and laughed.

"I know. I know," Auntie Lula said, "We do this every time someone new comes in here. It's kind of a right of passage."

"And don't throw the water out when you're done," shouted Uzuri running up the pathway to greet someone else.

Kinni didn't understand what either of them meant and she didn't even bother to ask. She just took the cleanser and starting wiping and scrubbing everything down. It wasn't difficult at all. She looked around and saw all the girls hard at work in their individual work zones. Some were raking leaves into piles then placing them in big heavy-duty bags. Some were picking up laundry bags that were left in front of each shanty and bringing them over to another shanty that had the word wash written on a cloth hung above it. She could see some girls within washing clothes in these huge basins. They were all singing as they worked lovely melodies that were in perfect harmony and sounded as if a full band were accompanying them. Once Kinni finished most of the stalls, she placed the cleansers to the side and started strolling around to get a better look at everything now in the light of day. Uzuri saw her and joined her for a walk.

"It's nice here," Uzuri said.

"Why not throw out the water?" Kinni asked her.

"Hot water on the earth burns the ancestors. Just let it cool first, that's all," she instructed.

"Really," Kinni replied, "...ancestors...", she said thinking of the many superstitions the Gambians had.

They walked some more along the dirt road together.

"How long have you been here?" Kinni asked her.

"Oh, I've practically been here my whole life," she said, "Well, not really..." she confessed, "...but a very long time now."

She had a tearful look on her face.

"I'm not telling the whole truth. I just came not too long ago," Uzuri said.

Then she looked off into the hills and meditated on something from her past. Kinni could tell that she didn't want to really delve into it, which made her want to hear it all the more.

"My mother died..." she said tearfully and her voice trailed off.

That was not what Kinni had expected to hear.

"It was either here or join the army," Uzuri said.

"Can women join the army?" Kinni asked naively.

"Kinni, women don't join the army. The men take them for, well it's sorta' like for their nasty entertainment," she said very matter-of-factly.

Kinni understood something about that. The lust of men had been in her life for a very long time. She had times when all she thought about was killing them all one by one. She was the wrong person to speak to about such topics.

"My sister was taken and I have not laid eyes on her since. I was lucky people have told me. I hid beneath the house by the garbage and the chickens. I was outside feeding the animals when they came to my house. They snuck up like they were conducting a raid or something. Anyone who did not cooperate, they simply killed. They just stuck the blade of an ax into my mother's stomach before anyone knew what was happening. I saw my mother fall to the floor with this stunned look on her face. My little sister watched them do it too and she just

QUEEN KINNI   87

screamed the whole time. I was too shocked to move…" she said.

Kinni didn't quite know what to say after all that. To look at Uzuri, Kinni would have never imagined that she had gone through anything that frightening. She seemed too pleasant and kind, too unmarred by life's tragedies. Kinni thought that if she were in America that something like that wouldn't have happened but then again she had been through some horrific stuff there too. The great ocean in between had not stopped evil from traveling.

"…I will look for her one day soon. I'm making friends who can help me do just that. I miss her, you know. She's the only real family I've got. My left eye keeps itching, which means that I will see her again very, very soon. I doubt if she's handling things well where she is. She was always the delicate one in the family. She was afraid of the chickens for goodness sakes. That's why I was feeding them that…..." she said with a small giggle and then her face went cold.

What does one say after such a story? Uzuri had a future awaiting her that seemed totally ominous and utterly terrifying. This was a real horrifying life for which she herself seemed too delicate for the undertaking. Kinni couldn't imagine having to fight an army for anything. While Uzuri seemed resigned to her fate as if there wasn't anything else she longed to do in life. She wasn't thinking about the things that Kinni and her friends back home would dwell upon, like becoming teachers or going to the prom. Kinni had endured a lot while in Gambia for sure, but Gambia was not her home. She could just pack up and leave. And she was looking forward to doing just that. She was going back to the States and seeing her little sister and brothers and finishing high school. The most difficult thing she had to look forward to was her father's rules and fighting him off of her should he want a repeat performance of his disgusting endeavors. Uzuri, on the other hand, was looking forward to fighting a band of rogue warriors who had no respect for life in order to get her sister back who undoubtedly would have been through hell and near death's door the entire time she was with them.

"Do you have any idea where she is?" Kinni asked Uzuri.

"I believe that they have settled along the border of Senegal. It is not that far away. They would want to be ready in case the other factions came along from the east to overtake them. At least that's what my contacts tell me," she said.

Uzuri seemed too young and childlike to be talking about armies and such. Kinni would have laughed the entire conversation off as ridiculous if it hadn't been for where she was in this place, in Gambia. It was entirely possible that Uzuri would create her own army and defeat the ones who kidnapped her little sister. She seemed confident as if she were the commander of an army already and no doubt brave enough to fight the good fight even if it meant to the death. Kinni berated herself for thinking that she didn't expect to see Uzuri live through this ordeal.

"I'm ready to do what I must and I have some who are willing to do the same. I'm ready," Uzuri repeated with resolve.

Kinni could tell that she was too. Just then another girl who Kinni hadn't met walked over to say something to Uzuri secretively. They whispered for a few seconds in very hushed tones. Kinni couldn't hear any of what they were saying. Uzuri just nodded her head in agreement.

"Thanks, Bisi. I'll be right there," Uzuri told Bisi.

Bisi walked away obediently to her shanty.

"I've got to go. See you later. I'll do your hair, okay?" Uzuri told Kinni and scurried off after Bisi.

Kinni wondered what they had discussed but then she was distracted by Auntie Lula introducing what looked like another new girl into the group. Teri passed by while Kinni was walking back to her shanty.

"They're going to move you over one," Teri informed her.

"Why?" Kinni asked, not that she had become so fond of hers.

"The new ones can be a bit suicidal...not you, you know...just some of them, you know..." she said trying not to offend her, "Auntie Lula likes to keep an eye on them because they've been through so much, you know," she went on, "That's why your space was so empty."

Kinni honestly didn't know what she was referring to. Her shanty had a bed and chairs. Kinni thought it was totally perfect. Teri must have saw that Kinni wasn't following and pulled her over to hers.

"Look at mine," Teri said gently pushing Kinni into her shanty.

The first thing Kinni noticed was the two plush reclining chairs propped up against the wall and the beautifully wooden carved ottoman with the soft leather top in between. The shanty was painted too. It was green with a burgundy trim.

"Wow!" Kinni shouted.

"Nice, right?" Teri said jumping onto her bed and stretching out upon it.

"It's real nice. I love it," Kinni told her.

"Yours will be like this too after a month or two here," she grinned.

Kinni didn't have the heart to tell her that she had no intention of staying in Gambia that long. Suddenly, the shanty curtain flew open and Uzuri came in angrily until she noticed Kinni standing there admiring the place.

"Teri, where have you been?" Uzuri asked Teri modulating her voice from a harsher to a softer tone.

Teri straightened right up. Kinni almost thought that Teri was saluting Uzuri. Then they both ran out together into Bisi's shanty.

"I was showing the new girl my digs," she told Uzuri.

"But we've been waiting for you. You know we only have a few minutes before…" Uzuri told Teri and their voices faded out as they hurried away. Kinni had no idea what they were up to and as the new girl she would not find out, she was sure, for a long time or until they felt completely comfortable with her.

Chapter Ten

Just as Teri had told Kinni earlier, she was moved over one shanty down in order to accommodate the new girl. She had thought about what Teri said about some of the new ones being suicidal. Particularly since this new one was a mousy little thing. She could see why Auntie Lula wanted to keep an eye on her. She didn't say a word to anyone not even to Auntie Lula whose warm personality seemed to be able to draw anyone out. Apparently, all she wanted to do was sleep. Auntie Lula practically dragged her to dinner that evening and then sat her close by in order to watch over her. As soon as the girl saw the food she gobbled it down so fast that even the Gambian girls who ate their food traditionally quickly stopped and stared. The poor thing was starving. Auntie Lula kept right on eating as if nothing seemed unusual even though everyone had paused to watch the show that the new girl was putting on. Seconds later, the plate was completely empty. The new girl had food everywhere around her chair and her face. She looked like a five year-old all messy and unashamed. Then she shot straight up out of her seat and ran back to her shanty. She was of course the talk of the place after that. No one could think of anything else to say and everyone wondered what had happened to leave her in such a state. Having been in Gambia a year herself, Kinni could imagine that it was probably something devastating.

"Kinni, why don't you show the new one around?" Auntie Lula asked Kinni.

"But...I...what...", Kinni stuttered.

She barely knew the place herself and doubted strongly that

she was the right person for this particular task.

Uzuri immediately walked around the table to Kinni.

"She likes giving people difficult assignments just to see what they're made of, you know," Uzuri told Kinni.

"I don't think I'm ready for this one. You saw her right?" Kinni sheepishly asked.

"How could you miss her? She reminds me of someone," Uzuri said.

"Who?" Kinni asked.

"Me, when I first got here," Uzuri replied and walked back around the table to finish eating.

Kinni lazily walked over to the new girl's shanty after supper. She had no desire to escort an obviously distraught girl around who was obviously in need of a mental professional. All the while she thought about what Uzuri had told her. Auntie Lula may not like what she's made of, she thought. It wasn't that she didn't have compassion for the poor girl it was just that she wasn't good at talking to people. Her mom was the only person that she ever really talked to and trusted but lately she hadn't that luxury. She was so out of practice for goodness sake. She knocked on the door-frame. She didn't hear a sound from within so she knocked again this time harder. Again. Nothing.

"Can I come in?" Kinni asked.

Again. Nothing.

"Hello! Hello? Hello!" Kinni said sing-songy.

Auntie Lula passed by Kinni who was leaning into the shanty straining to see if the girl was even in there.

"Her name's, Shauna," Auntie Lula told her and kept right on walking.

"Are you sure she wants to see the place?" Kinni asked in desperation all the while wanting Auntie Lula to say that this would keep until morning.

Kinni was thinking that if the new girl didn't want to be bothered then everyone should simply respect her wishes, the fact that that worked out in Kinni's favor notwithstanding. Auntie Lula didn't bother to answer. It was clear that this child was getting a tour by Kinni whether either wanted it or not. Kinni finally decided that she had to show Auntie Lula that she was worthy of all her kindness but more importantly that she could handle this. She leaned in again and this time called out the girl's name while entering the shanty at the same time.

"I'm coming in," Kinni said pulling back the entrance curtain and unadvisedly stepping across the threshold.

When she walked in she didn't know what to expect but she was surprised none-the-less. She looked around the entire shanty and didn't see Shauna at all. So, she retreated back outside to make sure that she was in the right place. She could see on the right Auntie Lula's bright colorful décor beaming blindingly. She was in deed at the right one so she stepped back inside and looked around again. As she scanned the room she could see that nothing had even been touched. The bed was still freshly made, the chairs hadn't been moved and everything was as clean as when she had left it that morning. Kinni stood frozen in the middle of the room thinking that she heard something just to the right of her. She looked over the bed and there she was, Shauna, all scrunched up into a little ball and pressed as far as she could go into the corner. She didn't stir at all in Kinni's presence. She had her head between her knees and she was sobbing quietly. Kinni sat down on the bed and just looked at her for a long while not really knowing what else to do.

"Are you all right?" she asked her politely.

Shauna didn't respond. She didn't even seem as if she knew Kinni was there. Kinni didn't know whether to walk over to her or to touch her or what. Lately she had been the one usually balled up crying somewhere. She kept thinking what she would want someone to do for her during those times when nothing seemed to comfort. She was coming up short because after leaving Mandinka husband other than a few sleepless nights, he was a faded memory for her now as was the pain she'd suffered. Just a day or two away from his house and she was already becoming her old self again, just like that. He didn't deserve anymore of her tears. She actually had to think back to those lonely times, when she wanted her mom around saying comforting words. Then it hit her.

"Everything's going to be all right," Kinni told Shauna as if by rote, whether she truly believed it or not.

At that, Shauna's sobs grew louder. So, Kinni reached over and pulled her up upon the bed. She stretched her arm around Shauna's shoulders and allowed her head to rest on her chest.

"Everything's going to be all right. Everything's going to be all right..." said Kinni repeatedly while rocking Shauna back and forth as Binta had done with her, and as if she knew what the future held for Shauna.

To her surprise Shauna responded as if what she was saying was the absolute truth. Kinni prayed to Allah that her words were true for Shauna's sake and for her own. Kinni looked over and saw the present Auntie Lula no doubt gave to every new girl who entered this mission. She grabbed it and placed it into Shauna's hands.

"Open it," she told her, "It's a gift."

She was hesitant at first but then seeing the sincerity in Kinni's eyes, Shauna pulled the flap and finally looked inside the box. Pushing the note aside, a big smile spread across her tiny face and she immediately opened three of the toffees and at once ate them without the slightest care. Her entire mouth was sticky with sugary powder as was her hands. She absolutely loved them.

"Very good," Shauna said in perfect Wolof.

"I know," Kinni responded back, also in Wolof.

Shauna's face lit up when she heard Kinni speaking Wolof. After that night, Shauna followed Kinni around wherever she went. Everyone began calling Shauna Kinni's little sister.

Kinni had been at the Gambian Mission two whole months when Uzuri first extended an invitation into her shanty. Kinni considered it to be an honor. Uzuri had been there longer than most and everyone respected her. She told Kinni to come over right after chores and she would braid her hair. Kinni couldn't wait to have it braided by Uzuri because for one, it would finally look like something and secondly, because she was afraid that if she didn't do something to it soon, the rest of it would fall out, no thanks to Mandinka husband. As per usual, Shauna had finished the stalls and was on her way over to help Kinni clean the dishes. Kinni had been upgraded from the stalls, leaving Shauna to be initiated. The stalls were, although easy for Kinni, the hardest job there. Auntie Lula figured that a person who can clean up after everyone is a person of good character. Auntie Lula had had some in the past who would not lift a finger to assist anyone else at the shelter. This was her test, so-to-speak. If you could clean up other people's bodily waste then you were a worthy new addition to the place. If you couldn't or, worst yet, wouldn't, apparently you were escorted to the nearest road. Kinni really began to like Auntie Lula when she heard that. That's why the girls all passed by to see who had bathroom duty. They wanted to take a peep at you before they didn't see you ever again. Kinni was so glad that she had passed the test. She had nowhere else to go.

"Did you need my help?" Shauna asked her.

"I'm all done, thanks," she told her as they both approached Uzuri's place.

Uzuri greeted them at the doorway.

"Shauna, I'm sorry," Uzuri waved Kinni inside only while blocking the path for Shauna.

Shauna took the obvious distinction well and didn't let on that she even knew it was a rejection.

"Maybe another time, okay?" Uzuri gently told her.

Shauna walked away promising that she would come see Kinni later. Kinni yelled out to her okay but her breath was totally taken away by what she saw once she entered Uzuri's shanty. It wasn't the décor so much as the number of people who were already there. It was observable to her all of a sudden that Uzuri wanted her there for more than just grooming purposes. Teri waved at Kinni and offered her a seat next to her on the bed. Kinni bewilderedly squeezed through the crowd and sat down beside Teri. Kinni sunk into the fluffy, soft down mattress. Hers was comfortable but it was definitely a bargain variety. When she turned she could see that practically everyone else had brought in their chairs.

"Hi," was all she could think to say to the group.

She hoped that their gathering wasn't about poor little Shauna, seeing as she seemed to be the only one not invited other than Auntie Lula.

"Okay, now down to business," Uzuri became solidly serious once she turned around.

Bisi handed her a stopwatch that everyone could hear ticking through the silence in the room.

"How much time we got?" Uzuri asked her.

"About fifteen," she warned.

"Okay, let's get right to it," Uzuri said to the group at large.

Kinni just sat quietly same as everyone else and figured that someone would eventually tell her why she of all people was invited, rather tricked into coming.

"Kinni, I heard that you are going back to America soon," she said more as a statement than a question.

So, Kinni just slowly nodded yes, gathering that these girls knew a whole lot more than they let on about what was going on at the mission.

"I hoped that maybe I could, that is, that we could persuade you to do us a little favor…" Uzuri asked.

Kinni didn't quite know how to respond. She felt a little ambushed.

"It's nothing illegal or anything like that," Uzuri assured her.

"Yes, it's nothing like that. We promise," Teri added.

"We would never do that to one of our own," Bisi threw in.

Even with their seemingly sincere reassurances, Kinni still didn't want to do anything that would jeopardize her exodus from Gambia. Pure and simple, she was ready to go home. She felt that she had been through enough to even deserve a trip back home. Besides, she had unfinished business to take care of. She had a score to settle and she was looking forward to making that dream a reality. She had certainly not forgotten the injustice that her very own father had done to her and she wouldn't let his crime go unpunished. Whenever she felt a slither of discontent over her situation in Gambia, she always thought of the sweet revenge that awaited her in America. The thought of killing him was what kept her going the entire time she was away from her home. She didn't want to get caught doing some no doubt petty crime in Gambia that would land her permanent residency there.

"I don't know…" Kinni stammered.

"Let her know what it is before asking her if she's gonna' do it," spoke mousey little Bisi very demonstratively.

Uzuri sat on the bed and lowered her head.

"Okay. You are right. Let's tell her what we'd like then we'll see if she could help us," she said to the girls but mainly to herself.

Kinni could tell that Uzuri was proud and didn't like asking people for help. She would rather be the person doing the favor or telling someone what to do. Uzuri was a natural born leader. Kinni believed that Uzuri was one of the first Gambian females she had known who was taking charge of her own life. She really admired her for that but she couldn't allow herself to get tangled up into something that would hurt her chances of leaving Gambia for good.

"Well…you see…" she faced Kinni, "We have a contact there in the States, at the U.N. His name is not important right now. If you do us this favor I will tell you who he is, of course. Anyway, it's been hard to contact him because all mail is reviewed. Sometimes we speak in a version of Wolof but it's hard to explain everything. He has not understood three of our last letters. We need someone…."

"…Someone in the States right?" Kinni interrupted.

"…You see our problem. If we show you the language, since you speak Wolof, you can show him, then…" Uzuri shrugged, "…It wouldn't be hard for you to learn it."

"…Then he will know what you are talking about, right?" Kinni asked her but everyone answered her with a single head nod.

Kinni understood their problem but she still had some questions about the variation of the Wolof language and thought that maybe they were all being unreasonably mistrustful about someone reading their mail. She of course couldn't be sure but Auntie Lula didn't seem the type to check under the beds for monsters. It sounded a bit like a suspense movie drama or something.

"You probably think that we're paranoid, right?" Uzuri asked as if reading Kinni's mind.

"No, no," Kinni lied feeling exposed.

"Well, we cannot take any chances. I told you of my situation…" Uzuri gave Kinni a knowing stare, "…well each one of us here has a similar story."

That part of Uzuri's implore gave Kinni a lump in her throat. She looked around the room and took a measured glance into each girl's face. They seemed to have this peculiar numbness that saturated the ruddiness of their beautiful skin. She recognized this image immediately in each of them. It was how she looked for that past year. She had crawled into herself and the only thing that stuck out for the world to see was a raw, pale empty covering. She saw in them what she had glimpsed of herself whenever she passed a mirror and caught her reflection – death. It was the death of unimaginable dreams, the death of futures that didn't include killings and rapes and servitude. It was the hollowness and loneliness of children whose parents had died in the most horrific ways right in front of them. They were shell shocked devoid of any sense of self-esteem or self-worth. They were the living dead and Kinni was definitely one of them. Once again she was asked to be brave about something that she felt sure she couldn't. Once again she braced herself for the challenge and accepted it as part of the journey.

Chapter Eleven

'The land of the free and the home of the brave' was finally, blessedly in sight. Kinni could see the runway lights from the window seat that Mrs. Chapman graciously got for her. She would never forget her or Auntie Lula's kindnesses, two strangers that embraced her and took her in as if she were family and had cared for her in a way that she had not seen in her entire life. She cried when they all said goodbye and for several hours during the plane ride she couldn't stop the tears from coming down. It took the last month of her stay in Gambia before she realized the beauty of it all. It was definitely within its people. The Gambian Mission girls all hugged her one by one. Shauna especially wouldn't let her go. She asked Uzuri to take care of Shauna for her. Uzuri immediately put her arm around Shauna's shoulder and pulled her in. They each had a special place within Kinni's memory that seemed to be sutured with unbreakable thread. Though she wanted to see and hear from them again and even gave her address for each of them to write, she had no desire to ever go back to Gambia. Gambia was a bitter sweet symbol now. It represented betrayal, loneliness and prison for her. It represented Mandinka husband, Jibril and his bratty children and how they all had taken advantage of her during her time of captivity. She didn't quite understand how not even one member of that family ever thought to give her the smallest touch of grace, that she could care for them in such a constant way and never receive a single thank you. Doesn't a servant deserve at least a lowly pat on the back once in a while? She would never forget them either but not fondly. She would think of them with bitterness and resentment, forever longing to see them suffer in a most egregious way.

As the plane taxied round, Kinni's heart literally leapt in her chest for joy at the sheer simplicity of seeing an endearing familiar place, America, her home. She couldn't wait to feel the soil beneath her feet. She actually understood the saying 'kiss the ground' because she was tempted to do just that as the plane came to a halt and the travelers were told to prepare for exiting the aircraft. Kinni grabbed her one nylon bag that Auntie Lula gave her, which she had placed in the overhead bin above her seat, and descended out onto a land that she thought she would never lay eyes on again. It was a pristine clear day the kind that delivers so much exquisiteness that the mere acting of seeing it brings about life. Every seemingly insignificant thing she saw had poignancy for her. She loved the fact that there were telephone booths lining the airport. In Gambia she had longed to just call home from time to time and was never given that small indulgence. She loved the bathrooms with twenty different booths, and running water from actual taps and mirrors waist high to the ceiling. She loved the newspaper stands with all the different varieties of books and magazines, and the many candies and other treats. She hadn't read anything since her Gambian experience and realized now how much she missed it. She just stood and stared and marveled at it all including the mechanical doors that slid open for her as her foot touched the threshold mat before the exit. The smell of the city hit her in a visceral way. She had remembered it and could recall that smell anywhere. It was as if her entire body knew the place not just her eyes. She was home. She was home. She was finally home. She felt as if she were experiencing a miracle. Freedom and well-being engulfed her and she knew that she would never be a slave to anyone or anything ever again. Those days were solidly, resoundingly over and she would do whatever she had to, whatever was in her power so that she would never have to endure that kind of cruelty at the behest of another human being.

Kinni knocked on the door and rang the bell at the same time. She missed her mom terribly and was dying to see her and her little brothers and sister. She had vivid thoughts during the eight-hour flight and forty-minute taxi ride about their jaws dropping at the sight of seeing her come through that door. She was so excited at seeing the shocked look on everyone's face that she actually shook with anticipation. Then she heard heavy footsteps coming towards the door. Kinni's heart was in her hands with glee for she knew that it was none other than her father. No doubt coming to see who could possibly be disturbing his rest at this ungodly hour of the morning.

"Who is it?" he shouted from behind the closed door.

Then Kinni saw an eye pressed against the peephole followed by the two latches on the door being turned and twisted open. The door swung wide with a jerk. There Matar stood with his mouth stretched broadly and his eyes bulging at Kinni in a sort of horror.

"Kinni?" he asked frozen with shock.

Kinni made sure that she looked better than she had before she left. She had on one of the new dresses Mrs. Chapman had given to her and her hair was styled with beautiful long extensions thanks to Uzuri. The expression on Matar's face was priceless. He was beside himself with curiosity and wonder.

"Matar," Kinni said with a forced smile, "I'm back."

She wasn't about to call him dad or father or anything except by his first name or else devil. Then she pushed right pass him because she could see Binta beaming with joy from behind his hideous back. Binta snatched Kinni up into her arms and held onto her as if she would never, ever let her go. Then they both cried until there was nothing left but smiles.

"How? What? I can't believe it. I just can't believe it. My baby's home. My baby's really home," Binta cried.

Then she smiled and hugged Kinni some more.

"You look so good, girl! Look at you! Matar, look at her," Binta asked her husband to see his daughter.

Matar looked at Kinni with a smirk that hadn't faded from his face since she walked in.

"How? We didn't even know. How did you get home? How's your grandmother?"

Binta and Matar both hurled questions at her. When she didn't answer any of them Matar began to look at her suspiciously.

"So, you're back home…to stay?" Matar asked with emphasis on 'to stay'.

Binta grabbed her and pulled her towards her again.

"Let her alone. It's four o'clock in the morning. We can find out the details tomorrow, I mean today but later. Later," Binta told Matar.

He backed up ever so slightly but his inquisition was far from over.

"Does your husband know?" Matar asked in a very accusatory manner.

Kinni pretended that she hadn't heard him. Though, her very soul was filled with all kinds of aggrieved emotions at his mentioning of the word husband. He, her conniving father, had decided to declare that she had a husband. Binta and Matar could see the anger in her for they both took a few steps back as she recoiled her fists and glared at Matar until her eyes were just a slither.

"She does not need to talk about all that right now. My baby's home. My baby's home. You look so skinny. Did you eat at all while you were there? How's grandmother? Did you see her while you were there?" Binta asked.

Kinni nodded to a few of her questions, yes or no but she didn't want to delve into any of the details about her stay in Gambia. As far as she was concerned it was over and done with. And she would sooner die than go back there.

"Who gave you the money to get back here?" asked Matar while locking the front door and obviously sulking over her surprise return.

Kinni realized that her father must have thought that he was through with her for good and that he probably, unbeknownst to Binta, secretly never wanted to see her again.

"I have my ways," she replied mysteriously on purpose.

"Your ways, huh? What might that be…you stole money from him and then…" he yelled at her.

"Stop! Stop! Please," Binta broke his stride.

So, determined was he to find the specific factors of her departure from Gambia, that Kinni thought she was on trial. Though she thought it very funny watching him squirm on account of her non-responsiveness. It was obvious to all three of them that he didn't want her back in his house but Kinni could care less. She didn't have any place else to go and she would stay until she was good and ready to leave. She had grown up over that past year and a half. Matar had no idea the woman he was dealing with now. Plus, she was physically stronger in case he thought he was ever going to lay another hand on her again. She looked forward to him trying and her chopping it off, whatever part of him touched her, that is. She thought that it was so typical of him to believe that she had stolen money from Mandinka husband in order to escape. In retrospect, perhaps she should have thought of that while in Gambia but contrary to her father's low estimation of her ethics, she was never a thief.

"Can't you see she's hungry after such a long trip?" Binta cautioned Matar in every effort to change the subject.

Matar was so intent on getting to the bottom of her apparent wrongdoing that he was unrelenting.

"I don't really care. I just want to make sure that everything is all worked out. You know that," he told Binta as if they were discussing a secret.

And by 'all worked out' he meant that Mandinka husband was not looking for any additional money from him on account of their so-called arrangement being abruptly severed.

"I have to call him," Matar told Binta, "You know that."

"Well, can't it all keep until after breakfast? That should be all right, right?" Binta asked Matar.

He nodded rather obediently for someone who never took a single request from a woman seriously save his mother. Kinni saw fear in Matar's eyes. She realized that that wasn't the type of phone call he really wanted to make when all was said and done. He just needed to make sure that he wasn't on the hook, that he had done everything he could to make things right. Binta went straight into the kitchen and began cooking as if it were nine a.m. Kinni went right into her room to place her bag down.

"Your brother's in there now," Matar proudly told her.

"Well, he'll have to go back to his own room now won't he, Ma-tar," she snapped at him.

"Kinni, come help me in the kitchen," Binta interjected just as Matar was about to give Kinni a good cursing out for among other things calling him by his first name.

Kinni could feel the anger in him. It was hot and prickly radiating off his dull skin. He was determined not to make any of this easy for her and she was determined not to care what he thought. As long as her mom was around Matar knew that he couldn't go but so far. Kinni went into the kitchen and Matar went into the living room and sat down in his reclining chair. He was resolutely wide awake and no longer in the mood for sleeping. Kinni had, it seemed, forever interrupted that.

Kinni stepped into the kitchen and saw Binta sitting at the table just smiling away from ear to ear.

"Kinni, my baby," she gestured for her to come and join her.

Kinni walked over and she hugged her again. Binta's sobs filled the middle of Kinni dress.

"How was it?" Binta asked quietly as not to alert her husband.

"Difficult," Kinni simply told her as not to worry her.

Binta nodded in a blank stare as if she knew exactly what Kinni was talking about.

"I do not love him, mom...but you knew that," Kinni said bluntly.

Binta nodded again with a distant vagueness as if her core bore witness to those words.

"I left because I just couldn't take it anymore. I was not treated well the whole time I was there," Kinni said all the while not wanting to really get into the heart of the matter. However, she knew that she had to at least give her mom some kind of explanation. Kinni began to cry but this time looked away and grabbed some napkins from the center of the table to dry her eyes. She didn't really have any more sad tears for this unfortunate time in her life but just those of joy. She wanted to celebrate, dance on Jibril's grave, and shout ecstatically through the streets. She was no longer troubled by anything. She was home and there to stay.

"Did he tell you to leave?" Binta asked.

"No," replied Kinni.

She could now see that Binta was dying to know everything about it as much as her father. And, although with Binta, Kinni was willing to tell a bit more, she didn't wish to upset her at the same time.

"We didn't get along, mom. He was angry with me the whole time and I could never just talk to him or say anything that was on my mind," she said still not wishing to divulge too much. She didn't want to scare her mom or make her even more depressed.

"Did he ever hit you?" Binta blurted.

"Everyday," Kinni replied automatically without even thinking.

With that Binta stood up and hugged her again. This time gently as if Kinni were ever more fragile. Kinni so desired to tell her mom that her life was like hell there but more importantly that she would never stand for that kind of treatment from another man again. Binta released Kinni and placed her in her seat and began cooking breakfast.

As Binta prepared breakfast, pancakes, Kinni's favorite, they both could hear Matar whispering to someone on the telephone. Kinni and Binta both guessed that he just couldn't wait for Kinni's version of the story and just had to know for himself. Kinni was right because directly after hearing the receiver slammed down he marched into the kitchen looking meaner than she had ever seen him. Binta blocked him just before he stomped over to Kinni.

"Can't it keep?" Binta said to him in a soothing tone.

He kept on walking over to Kinni and then without warning reached up to slap her across the face but Kinni caught his arm on the down swing. Binta stood there astonished. Kinni glared up at him with the same amount of intensity that he was flinging in her direction. Binta stared at both of them in shock but mostly at her daughter who was holding tightly to her husband's arm. Matar couldn't move it in any direction.

"I will not be hit on ever again. You got that?" she told him sternly, "Get used to that. I'm here to stay and there is nothing you can do about it."

"I'll change the goddamn locks. No child of mine is going to tell me what I can and cannot do in my own house," he shouted, snatching him arm back and lowering it.

"I'm not a child anymore that you can beat up on!" she shouted back waking up the whole house.

Deebal, Jumu and Sara were now entering the kitchen, at first startled, then beaming smiles at Kinni. When her little sister, Sara, came and gave her a hug, Matar finally backed off realizing that he was out numbered. Everyone else was genuinely happy to see Kinni. So, he had to let the excitement of that moment pass before he could fight with her over Jibril. Kinni was actually looking forward to it.

"Damn," he said turning on his heels and exiting the kitchen.

She could see her mom smiling as he left. There was this energy amongst the rest of the family that couldn't be squelched for several months. As far as Deebal, Jumu and Sara were concerned, Kinni was their big sister who had just come from abroad. They marveled at that fact and flung question after question at her somewhat relentlessly. Kinni loved it. They treated her like a hero returning from war. Little did they know how much truth was held within their innocence.

Chapter Twelve

"You look good, girl! I love it!" Saundra told her.

"Yeah, girl. That child put a hurtin' on yor' herr," Michelle told her while pulling at it to make sure the extensions were firm.

"What are you trying to do, pull them out? Stop! Stop!" Kinni told Michelle while backing away from her at the same time.

"'chelle, you're nuts. Her hair looks really nice. What are you jealous or somethin'?" Trese pulled Michelle off of Kinni.

Then Michelle and Trese got into their usual fight, the one over absolutely nothing but would last for several days.

"Who you callin' jealous, jealous yo' self," Michelle barked at her.

"Am not," barked Trese right back at her.

"R 2!" screamed Michelle as if speaking loudly would win the argument.

"Cut it out you two, gees," chimed in Saundra.

"Am not."

"Are too."

"Yo' mamma's a ho!" shouted Trese.

"Yus ah playa hatin' 'cause yor daddy's paying our rent!" shouted Michelle back at her.

"Yo' mamma's cleaning our toilet."

"Yo' mamma is our toilet."

On and on it went as the sun set in between the monkey bars and the broken chain linked swings. The reflection of the rays dancing off the metal reminded Kinni so much of Gambia that she actually got lost in the simple splendor of it. It wasn't as if she missed Gambia, it was just those last few days there at the mission, where its essence began to shine through.

"Am not. How can you say that to me?" Trese asked.

"Are too. Are too. Are too!" Michelle told her.

"Children...children...stop already. You're giving me a headache," Saundra yelled at them with a snigger.

Saundra turned toward Kinni to confer about their behavior but Kinni wasn't paying any attention to either of them. Kinni was too preoccupied following the movement of the sun all the way down to the chess and checker tables. A few elderly men were having their own championship tournament, equipped with shouting over each other and cursing each other out. Apparently one of them had been cheating and the other could no longer stand it. As Kinni watched them she also couldn't help but see Devon. Everyone called him Dev for short. He was blacker than anyone touched by the Gambian sun. He had dreadlocks that stretched way down pass his shoulder blades. He always wore them up in a tied knot and off his statuesque face. His skin was so smooth and even it seemed to be carved out of onyx. He was with the same group of guys that she'd always seen hanging around him whenever she was at Marcus Garvey Park. None of them had jobs or ambition. They just sort of hung around the park day in and day out. They seemed harmless enough but she would never want to owe any of them money. She looked over at her three best friends. Though Michelle and Trese's argument had gotten completely out of hand and Saundra's screaming at them to hush was equally annoying, she was so happy to be in their company. It might have been boring to anyone else but Kinni had longed to be right there, school out, crashing in the park with her friends and no worries, no more Mandinka husband.

"Can you believe those two, Kinni? Kinni? What are you

staring at anyway?" Saundra asked her.

Saundra followed Kinni's vacant stare over to the tables where Devon was now sitting all by himself. He was actually looking at both of them who had these bizarre expressions on their faces. Saundra and Kinni turned away as quickly as humanly possible as not to make him think they were interested and went back to the business of watching Michelle and Trese, still screaming at each other without taking a breath.

"Why you got to say something like that? I was just telling her that her hair looks good," Michelle told Trese.

"Whatever," Trese said, sounding tired of their little spat.

Soon after, Michelle and Trese simply got up and left saying that they were both hungry and thirsty. Kinni stayed. She could have sat on that bench all night. She had gotten used to not eating very much from her year in Gambia. Besides, she didn't want to go back home and have yet another argument with her father. Kinni had grown so tired of having that same old battle over and over again. Without fail Kinni was always to blame for whatever ill occurred in that house. She was exhausted of his relentless chiding, reprimands and screaming at her.

As she thought about all the reasons not to go home, she looked up and saw Saundra waving good-bye to her too.

"If I'm going to be by myself..." she said waving and smiling.

It was true. Kinni's mind was elsewhere. She truly was happy to be with them but she was a little bit preoccupied, but not only with her father's tirades. She was also secretly admiring Devon from afar. Once Saundra reached the gate, Devon approached as if on cue.

"What you do to your hair, girl?" he asked her.

"Braids, nothing special," she said coyly.

"It looks nice. I like it like dat. It makes you look like an African queen," he told her, "Queen Kinni."

"I bet you say that to all the girls," Kinni said smiling.

"I'm not like dat," he said sitting down next to her.

"Sure," she said.

"Really. I don't even have a girlfriend," he said.

"I don't care," Kinni lied.

He pulled at Kinni's hair, teasing her.

"Little girl, I like your pigtails," he joked.

She liked it when he played with her like that. Though she didn't think for one minute that he was actually interested in her. She wasn't quite his type. She had always seen him with these light skinned girls who wore blouses that looked like a scarf covering their ample busts. Besides that the Gambian sun had fried her to a crisp shade of blue black and she was as skinny as a rail.

"I noticed dat you don't like goin' home. What's up with dat? You can tell me," he observed.

"You think you know me now, huh?" Kinni asked.

"No. No. I'm just sayin'..." Devon said, "...Really, what's the story?"

"There is no story," she said trying not to tell him all of her business.

"Parents?" he asked.

"Pa-rent," she said.

"Father?" he asked.

"Yeah. It's no big deal though," she said being bold.

"Yeah. Yeah," he rightly said as if he didn't believe her.

Then he ran his fingers down her braids. She playfully pushed him away.

"Look, I didn't mean anything by dat. You know me. I ain't tryin' nothin', ya' know. I just like your hair," he told her.

He even moved away from her in an attempt to make sure that she knew he wasn't trying to crowd her. She liked that about him. He was a decent thug.

"Well, my pops died when I was only eleven but before he did he made sure to kick my ass on a regular. I remember dat she-it too. He said it'll make me tough," Devon said with a smirk.

"Yeah," was all Kinni could offer.

She would never, ever tell anyone what her father did to her. She thought, 'If only he could die too.' People like her father don't die though. They keep right on living, creating as much havoc and chaos as possible.

"If ever you needed somethin'...you know...I could help you out," he suggested, "You seem cool and all like you might need a little help from time to time."

Then he reached into his pocket and pulled out a one hundred dollar bill.

"Here. Take it," he said pushing the bill into her hand.

"I can't take your money, Dev," she told him.

"Why not? It's not good enough for you?" he asked.

"It's fine. It's just that...well, I don't know," she said not wanting to finish the thought for fear that she might hurt his feelings.

"You don't know what?" he asked refusing to take the money back.

"I don't know, does this mean I owe you something now?" she asked him.

"You have a real low opinion of me, don't ya'?" he asked.

"Well..." she didn't want to insult him or anything but who just gives money away?

"Keep it, really," he said getting up and leaning over her to make his point.

"So, I don't owe it back?" she asked him.

"Consider it a welcome home gift. I missed you," he told her.

"Really?" she asked blushing.

"Really. I'm not the jerk you think I am. Look we friends, right?" he asked her.

"Right," she said nodding yes.

"Well, look if I had somethin' that I knew you needed then as a friend I would just give it to you, right, seeing as you needed it, right?" he asked.

"Yeah, I guess," she said with a shrug.

"Well, I know that you're too proud to ask for money. So, as a friend, I just gave it to you. Dat's all," he said.

"Well…" she began.

"Well what?" he joked leaning into her.

"Well, I guess I'm gonna' have to take it then. I don't want to lose you as a friend," she joked right back.

"Good," he said sitting back down right next to her.

Then they watched the two elderly men exiting the park. They were still discussing their most recent chess match trying to determine who actually won.

"Look…" Dev began, "…if you prefer earning your money, I know how to make dat happen too."

"I ain't no prostitute. So, you can just forget that!" Kinni yelled tossing his lousy money back at him.

The crumbled bill fell into his lap.

"No, no, no. Nothing like dat, boy…" he said offended picking up the hundred and putting it on the bench between them.

He could tell that he hurt her feelings. So, he picked the money back up and now folded it gently into her hand.

"Look, I'm on your side. I know how you could make a quick five hundred bucks without doing more than one easy hour's work. Dat's all I'm sayin'. Trust me. I would never be into somethin' nasty like prostitution. Dat's just not me," he said as if he were apologizing whilst feeling slightly offended himself, that she could think so low of him.

"Oh, really…five hundred dollars and I don't have to get undressed?" she asked.

"Not unless you want to but I wouldn't advise it," he laughed.

Kinni stared at Devon for a minute to see if he was being sincere. He did seem like he was. He did give her the hundred without her even asking. He did seem to know things about her without her having said a word.

"What exactly would I have to do…in case I liked the idea of making some money, that is?" she asked without committing herself to anything.

"Just deliver some merchandise. No big deal," he grinned.

"That's all?" she asked.

"That's all," he replied with a glimmer in his eye.

It didn't seem terribly complicated. It reminded her of Uzuri and her United Nations' contact. All Uzuri had her doing was passing notes along. At least with Devon, she could make some money in the process.

"So, bring what to who?" she asked.

"So, you are interested in bettering yourself after all?" he joked.

"Well, I do need a few things. A girl gets hungry now and then," she said.

"Meet me here tomorrow and I'll tell you everythin'. You down?" he asked.

"Yeah. Yeah, I'm down," she said trying to sound tough.

Then he walked out of the park and left her sitting there alone, one hundred dollars richer. She remembered walking home thinking that she really did need some money to get some new clothes. Even before Gambia when Binta would go shopping for the kids, her father flat out refused to give Binta enough to get Kinni anything. Every single one of her brothers and her sister got new shoes while she received a twelve-dollar pair of skippies from DeeDee's. She was happy to have them but the way she walked, hard on her heels, they didn't last two weeks. She looked down at the hundred. She was going to take that money and get some new shoes and maybe a pair of jeans and some t-shirts.

When she got home, Binta was in the family room putting together their million-dollar piece puzzle. They had been working on that thing for about three years. She had started up again now that Kinni was back home. It was their way of bonding and enjoying each other's company.

"Kinni, where you been all this time?" Binta asked, "Come help me with this thing."

"Park," she told her.

"There's some chicken in there," Binta said.

Kinni went straight into the kitchen and flipped the lid of the pot on the stove. It smelled delicious. Kinni so missed her mom's cooking. She immediately took two giant spoons full and clopped them into a bowl. Binta walked into the kitchen and joined her.

"How was school?" she asked.

"Good. It was nice to be back," she said.

"How's 'Chelle and the other girls?" Binta asked.

"They're fine…fighting as usual," she said.

"You know, they used to come over while you were away?" Binta informed her.

"Really? Why?" she asked curiously.

"They missed you," she said flatly.

"Really? What did they do while they were here?" she asked.

"Help me around the house...stuff like that," Binta said.

"Man, I had no idea." Binta really shocked Kinni with that bit of information.

"Kinni, we all missed you," Binta said with tears in her eyes.

"I know. I missed you too," Kinni confessed.

"Kinni, I never wanted for you to go. You do know that, right?" Binta blurted out.

With that declaration she stood up trying not to face Kinni as she spoke.

"Sometimes things are out of my hands, you know," Binta cried.

Kinni stood up too and put her arms around Binta.

"It wasn't easy for me to let my baby just go away like that. You have to understand. It was just not easy. I worried about you all the time. I couldn't even call. I wasn't allowed to," she hugged her.

Then they both heard the lock turning on the front door. And they both knew what that meant. It could only mean that Matar was home. They wouldn't be finishing their little puzzle that night. They would have to save their hugs and tears for another evening. They wouldn't be able to finish their quiet intimate discussion. They would both wash up and go straight to bed, Kinni to hers and Binta with that man, Matar Bragia, Kinni's father.

Chapter Thirteen

She took a taxi all the way up to 165th Street. Devon insisted that she do so. He said that it would be quicker and that he didn't want her to be late. He had a thing about punctuality. So, she hailed a Livery cab and told the driver that she needed him to wait for her. Again, Devon said it shouldn't take more than one hour round trip. He said that he wanted to make sure that her parents wouldn't have to come looking for her. She didn't have the heart to tell him that it would just be her mom should she tarry. During the ride she couldn't help but think about how Mandinka husband denied her the simple courtesy of a two-dollar cab ride, even with her arms full of groceries, to feed his skinny body and that of his children. When it stopped in front of the house, number Three Twenty-seven, Kinni didn't know what to expect and she suddenly became fidgety. She was as nervous as she could be but even more-so once she stepped out onto the curb. She was about to really do this and the implications attached to this transaction started flooding her mind. She thought about jail time, about possibly getting into some altercations with god knows who. There before her was a typical brownstone and not at all in a bad neighborhood but it seemed like the perfect place for a crime, unassuming, bland. It was just a bit too quiet for her. Her hands were too sweaty for her to hold the package in them. So she shoved it into her knapsack and slung it over her shoulder.

"I'll only be ten minutes tops," she told the driver.

"Ch-ess," the driver replied in his best English.

They had initially discussed the fare. So, the driver knew the details. Kinni did a lot of pointing and waving her hands to indicate you stay while I go. Now she just wanted to make sure he understood. He was Senegalese and his second language wasn't English but Creole. She then turned away from the security of the taxi and climbed the seven stairs up to the front door. She didn't like the fact that there was nowhere for her to run in case this whole thing went down terribly wrong. She had no idea what was in the package but she did have sense enough to know that whatever it was it wasn't legal. Who would pay half a grand for a delivery? She saw the way messengers dressed with their cheap nylon running pants and ripped wind-breakers. She doubted very strongly if they were paid as much for their vanilla envelops and letters.

The door opened abruptly just as her fist was about to knock on it.

"Yeah," said this baritone voice from behind its swing.

"I need to speak to Big Mi...?" Kinni said combining a statement with a question.

Before she could get his entire name out, the door swung wide and the most enormous man she'd ever seen in her life stood in its frame. Kinni's head stretched up to his face and then all the way down to his huge feet. Then she slowly scanned his gigantic body all the way back up again to his head. He was so big that his body covered the opening of the entire doorway and then some. He was so tall that he had to stoop in order for her to see his face and he looked fairly uncomfortable doing so. Kinni's head was directly level with his crotch. And that was big too.

"You like what you see?" he asked.

With that comment, she really didn't know where to look. She was so unglued that she thought she was going to pee in her pants. She suddenly realized that she had no idea what she was dealing with. This man could lift her with his pinky if he wanted to and knock her completely out just by blowing hard. Sure she was frightened but she knew better than to let it show.

"I have business with Big Mike and nobody else. You got a problem with that?" Kinni asked craning her neck so she could look him dead in the eyes.

He backed up a little. She could have sworn she saw him smirking.

"What do you little girl want with Big Mike? What you say…biz-ness?" he asked suspiciously.

"Do you know where he is or not?" she asked rudely but meanwhile embarrassingly scared to death.

"Don't get your panties all in a bunch unless you want Big Mike to iron them out for ya'" he said showing off his sparkling giant gold and white teeth.

He didn't look half bad when he smiled but his sheer size made him intimidating nonetheless.

"Are you Big Mike or what? I got other stuff to do today," Kinni lied with a huff for effect.

She had to get home preferably in one piece because she had a biology exam the next day to study for. She had only seen the tough girl act done on television and was desperately trying to remember how it went. She wasn't sure if she looked confident or like a toddler playing in her mommy's make-up and high-heels. Either way she prayed that all of this would be over quickly like Devon swore to her it would be.

"Alright. Alright. So what if I am Big Mike? What of it, sweetheart?" he asked.

"I got something for yu' and, I'm not yo' sweetheart," she told him while pulling her backpack off and reaching into it.

"Hey! Hey!" he said with a start while whipping out his

Beretta.

It was tucked inside his belt, which was straining to contain his belly that honestly hung out and over towards his knees. The gun, though big, didn't scare her at all even when he shoved it in her face. She attributed that strength to the incident with her father. Anyone who seemingly only wanted to show it didn't necessarily want to use it for shooting.

"Get that damn thing out of my face," she said slapping it to the side.

He grinned at her and stood down.

"You got gusts, gal. You could have gotten killed," he said putting his gun back in his pants.

"I doubt it," she sneered.

His fat swallowed it back up to the point where she couldn't make out even the smallest part of the weapon.

"What you got for Big M...i...k...e anyhow?" he asked, "No weapon, right?" he ducked and dodged playfully behind his hands.

"You thought I was trying to take you out?" she asked him.

He nodded sheepishly yes. She realized something very valuable then. If someone like Big Mike could be scared by someone like her then intimidation really might not have anything to do with strength or size.

"It's entirely possible," he replied.

"I bet a big guy like you doesn't have any enemies," she told him still shaking with fear herself but feeling a little more in control of it.

He laughed a lot when she said that. Then of all things he hugged her like they were old friends. Except his embrace felt more like a headlock. If it weren't for the fact that he seemed extremely genuine with his fondness of her, she would have reached down into his pants and pulled his own gun on him.

Though he probably would have thought she was just kidding at that point too.

"Who you with anyhow?" he asked her mischievously leading her into the fowler of his house.

He kept walking in but Kinni refused to follow or go any farther. It was a safety issue with her. She wanted to be able to see daylight at all times. The front door was staying open and she wanted to have at least one foot on the outside of it.

"Dev," Kinni said.

"Alright. Alright. You don't have to come in," he said making his way to the couch and falling down onto it, "Dev said you were feisty but he didn't say just how much."

"So you are Big Mike then?" she asked just to make doubly sure.

Devon said that the first rule in delivery was to make sure you have the right person. He said that people have gotten hurt or even killed by messing up something as simple as giving the package to the wrong person. Kinni took the package out of her bag and Big Mike immediately reached for it though he couldn't get to it because he was having difficulty lifting off the sofa.

"Huh, huh, huh…I need to see some I. D. first," she told him.

"Huh? I.D.? Dev has trained you well," he said pulling his wallet out of his breast pocket and thumbing through it for his driver's license.

"Unlike those other little hoodlums who, by the way, I would never let step foot in my kingdom…" he said with his arms open extending out showing her his living room, "…you know how to handle yourself."

She scanned his living room just to be polite. It was all right. He did have one of those humongous widescreen TV's, not a plasma but nice, and a kick-ass stereo duplex. Other than that, there was the sloped leather couch from his body weight lowering it to the floor and the empty Chinese food containers covering every other surface. Kinni smiled anyway and made it seem as if she was impressed. Then she studied his driver's license in the same way Mrs. Chapman would have were she in a similar situation. She began to understand the importance of getting certain things right the first time. She didn't want some goon after her on account of her impatience. She studied it so hard that it was almost as if she were memorizing every single number and letter.

"Wow, I feel like I'm getting busted. You're not F.B.I. are you?" he laughed.

She handed it back to him and then she handed him the package. He took it and placed it on the coffee table without even looking at it. Then he reached into his shirt pocket and pulled out a wad of bills. He didn't look at those either. He simply handed them to her. And she counted it right in front of his face.

"You might have trust issues. I like that about you," Big Mike grinned.

It was all there as Devon had promised too, five thousand dollars all in crisp clean hundreds. Having concluded their business, Kinni then turned around and started to make her exit.

"Don't tell me, Dev told you to make a fast getaway, right?" he laughed again but this time more heartily.

He was right though. She was told to get out of there quickly and no one had to tell her twice.

"Don't you have time for a quick bite or something?" he asked making an attempt to get something for her but still having some difficulty getting off the couch.

She thought it was nice of him. Though, she had no intention whatsoever of playing houseguest to Big Mike. Before he knew it, she was in the taxi again with the Senegalese and heading for home. It took several blocks and a few avenues before her hands stopped shaking and her breath became steady and normal. Her stomach felt queasy and she was sure that her heart literally halted all together. Other than that, she was pumped out of her mind. The adrenaline coursing through her veins was like youth serum. It was a wonderful drug to her body. She felt so alive, so happy, so rich. The whole world seemed brighter and better all of a sudden. She loved her City again. She was flying so high it was difficult for her to see the ground. The whole transaction took about fifteen minutes and it seemed so easy. Before the taxi came to a complete stop at the entrance to Marcus Garvey Park, Devon ran up to greet it. He opened the car door for her then haphazardly threw some money into the cabby's window.

"You didn't have to do that," she yelled at him.

"Don't be silly," he said escorting her out of the cab, his palm in hers.

The Senegalese driver tried to give Devon his change but all he got was the slamming of the car door.

"Keep it!" yelled Devon back at him with a wave good-bye.

The driver showed them his pearly whites together with enough 'Tank ku's' to fill a large tub. Devon and she grinned stupidly until the driver peeled off still waving as if they were his family. She was pleased with Devon for having tipped him so generously. She wouldn't have made such a grand exit from Big Mike's had it not been for the driver waiting patiently for her at the curbside. In so many ways Devon was proving to be unlike any man she had ever met. He was like a puzzle for her, completely sure of himself but without being cocky or mean. That aspect of him took her totally off guard. Can a man be such? She hadn't known any that could be gentle and calm yet remaining by all accounts a man. And he was like that with everyone, young, old, male or female. All of his male friends and associates gave him respect but he never begged for it or kicked the crap out of people until they hadn't a choice but to honor him. She had never met a man who actually got high praise by earning it.

"How'd it go?" he asked her gently letting go of her hand.

"Good," she said smiling from ear to ear.

Then they walked into the park and sat on one of the benches. She was still too excited to speak.

"You say 'good' as if I'm supposed to understand that," he shrugged.

"No…no…I mean…it went just fine," she told him pulling out all of the hundreds and placing them on his lap.

"Nah, nah, girl. Those are yours…" he said putting five of the hundreds back into her bag, "…You earned it."

Kinni smiled like the Senegalese driver, wide and gleeful.

"How was Big Mike?" he asked.

"Big!" she told him.

He just laughed.

"He needs Jenny Craig or something," she said seriously.

"I keep telling him that but he just says that he'd just eat her too," Devon joked.

Kinni couldn't move for the desire of not wanting that moment to end. She had been through so much and felt like she was being rewarded for all she had suffered.

"You gonna' buy me dinner with all that cash?" he asked.

"You hungry?" she asked shuffling her bills.

"Are you asking me out?" he asked curiously.

With that suddenly she awoke from her dream state. She hadn't realized that he was flirting with her until that moment.

"No!" she shouted disgustedly.

"Why not?" he asked in a pout, "You don't like me or

something?" he gently inquired.

She didn't know what to say to him. He was like a god to her. She would have had all of his children if he asked her to right there in the park but secretly she really didn't think that she was good enough for him.

Chapter Fourteen

"Mom, 'chelle invited me over to her house for dinner, okay?" Kinni bold faced lied to Binta. She even had the nerve to call her from Devon's cellular while they were still in the park and with his help concocted a little story that would get her out of returning home that evening.

"Okay, but I made lamb stew," Binta said trying to entice Kinni, "Matar won't be home until real late."

Kinni loved the way Binta made it with loads of buttery potatoes and succulent choice chunks of lamb. Ever since Kinni returned from Gambia Binta had promised that she would prepare some especially for her. Kinni was almost tempted to tell Devon that they would have to dine together another day. Yet there was something tugging at her to go out with him and to see what he was all about finally. She only really knew him from their after school moments in the park, which were glimpses in between chats with her friends. Although she realized that this longing to get to know him better might have just been the new found wealth that she was experiencing at his hands. She wasn't quite sure. So, she told her mom to save her some stew and handed Devon back his phone. He slipped it on his hip like a gun slinger and hailed a cab.

"What are you in the mood for?" he asked.

"Food," she told him.

He laughed when he realized she was giving him a serious answer. A taxi stopped for them and Devon made sure to hold the door for Kinni while entering. Plus, he remained the perfect gentlemen throughout the entire ride. She had always loved the

City at night and sought it as an opportunity to be awed once again by the sights. While Devon made a couple of calls getting daily reports from some of his other couriers.

"Jay, yeah it's me. Who did you think it was?" Devon asked some guy.

That was followed by him saying yeah about ten more times before hanging up and calling his next contact.

"Sorry about that," he said to Kinni finally putting the phone away, "I just needed to see something, you know."

"It's okay, Dev," she told him.

They got out downtown in the forties on Broadway. The bright lights and the people and the smells of food everywhere hit her immediately. There was an excitement there and it seemed as if everyone was engaged in enjoying life. She and Devon went into a restaurant she had never heard of called Houlihan's. She thought that it was wonderful but of course she had nothing to compare it to. She had never been to a real restaurant before in her life except for the one that her father was trying to lease so he could open up his own. Devon requested that they get a booth. When one became available, Kinni slid in while he remained on the outer edge. He had a way about him that was so non-threatening. She liked that, having been around so many men who just pushed and shoved her around, she preferred his more relaxed style. It was refreshing to see that he didn't want to crowd her insisting on being right next to her. The menus were already at the table and they were huge. She liked variety but really found it overwhelming. She thought that it was too much to read.

"You should try one of their soups. I heard you saying that your mom made stew tonight," he suggested.

He was nice that way, remembering something about her tastes. She made a mental note of his attention to details. He was right too. She had the clam chowder, which was delicious and then she had a turkey burger, also delicious. He had steak and potatoes and a glass of wine. He offered her a glass but she was too high already on life. She was having a superb time just being with him and listening to him tell funny stories about the people he'd known in his travels. She divulged a little more about her to him too. To her surprise, he already knew about her Gambia trip and her marriage and practically everything about her thanks to Michelle. Michelle never could keep other's people's business to herself. He didn't pry though. Kinni could tell that he wanted to know even more about all of it, especially about the husband.

"What was he like?" he asked her gingerly.

"Skinny and rude," she answered.

"Was he rude toward you?" he asked.

"Every gotdamn day," she answered.

"Did he…fight with…you…?" he asked sensitively.

"If you're trying to ask me if he hit me…then the answer is yes. Yes, he did," she interrupted.

"Well, I wasn't trying to pry or anything like that, you know. It's really none of my business really," he said and then got very quiet.

Kinni liked that about him that he didn't push. She had to admit that everything was still very raw for her on the entire subject of Gambia, Africa. She had only been back in the States for a few months. There was no life as usual for her either. Kinni's father barked even louder at her or about her on a regular basis. If he had it his way she would be at home every hour that she wasn't in school same as before the Gambian experience only worst. The difference now was the way she reacted to it all. Now, she routinely bended the rules to the point of breaking, just for the hell of it. She flat out refused to be cooperative unless her mom personally requested that she do so. His opinion meant nothing. His presence meant even less. She was finally her own person, determined to get out of that house as soon as she was old enough to be on her own.

"You hit him back?" he asked with a smile knowing damn well the answer.

"Every chance I got," she grinned.

Being with Devon was so unique to her. She felt like a lady out on the town with a grown man, a real man. She was so tickled at that fact that she giggled a lot, possibly too much. She should have had some wine just to shut her up a bit and mellow her out. He seemed to enjoy her quirky frenetic company though. He just grinned and waved his hand at her as if his side was splitting from so much laughter. She was completely serious with her answers to his questions but he thought the bluntness of her delivery made them all seem hilarious.

"Well, I've been out of the country but never to Africa. What was that like?" he asked keeping the conversation going.

"It was hot mostly. Towards the end, though, I actually began to enjoy it, you know, met some new friends, had some laughs, stuff like that," she said.

From the second floor of the restaurant, they had a perfect view of the street below and from time to time Kinni couldn't help people watching. New York being the type of city that always had all kinds of interesting people coming and going from all walks of life. They both laughed at quite a few who either had too much make-up on or at a few older men tip-toeing around with women obviously half their age.

"You sure you don't want some of this?" he asked while generously pouring some of his wine out of his glass and into hers, "I'm not really a drinker."

"Okay, just a little. We wouldn't want it to go to waste," she smiled.

He put the equivalent of a large gulp into her empty water glass. Wine wasn't anything new to her. She had had some before at home. Her mom would give the kids a sip on special occasions or on holidays. Her father would nastily say to Binta that she could give to all the kids except to Kinni because he thought Kinni was more likely than the rest to become a drunk. Of course, Kinni from then on was determined to prove anything he said about her wrong out of sheer spite. But the truth was she really never had a taste for spirits, until that night with Devon, that is, when he poured some for her. It made her feel special. She was honored that someone like him would even take her out. And then to wine and dine her so, she was a little overwhelmed by his unaffectedness. It seemed to her that he could have any woman of his choosing and for the life of her she just couldn't figure out why she was sitting across from him that night.

"Do you do this for all your couriers?" she asked coyly.

"Yeah, me, Jay and Paulie and Jun-bug like a little candle light now and again, ya' know," he joked.

Kinni had to laugh because Paulie, although nice, probably had never changed clothes ever. He always had on a particularly baggy pair of faded jeans whenever she saw him. Jay spent most of his time in and out of jail and Jun-bug is so-called because he liked to eat bugs. Enough said.

"That would be pretty funny," she told him.

"Are you saying that you want to be my new 'courier'?" he asked.

"Well..." she smiled.

"You would make a good addition to the family," he said.

"How so?" she asked as if she was on a formal interview.

"Well, you know, you're young but you're smart. We need

people who know how to handle themselves. I don't like it when people try to act tough knowing that they can't back it up, you know. If you're carrying, that's one thing but if you don't have no back-up, then shut the f- up, you know," he said, "'scue my language."

"Well, I'm already a courier," she revealed to him.

"By the way, we call them runners. Couriers are messengers and ya'll ain't delivering no message, you know what I'm sayin'?" he corrected her with a grin.

"Well, I'm sort of a runner already," she told him.

"Who for?" he asked suddenly more alert.

"Well, remember I told you that I met some people in Gambia…?" she asked.

He nodded yes still with this really puzzled look on his face.

"…Well, they have me sending messages to this guy at the U.N.," she told him.

He leaned back in his seat and placed his hand to his chin, in thought.

"You into some real world class espionage, ain't cha'?" he asked.

"Sud'en like dat," she joked but he didn't crack a smile.

Instead he just studied her for a real long while. Then the broadest of smiles came across his face.

"Do you know what's in these notes? I mean for all you know it could be something about terrorists or something like that," he asked.

"Of course I know," she answered proudly.

"Do you mind me asking what they're about? I'm just curious, girl. You got a lot of mystery about you," he asked.

"Well, you can ask all you want but just 'cause you're buying me dinner don't mean I have to tell you nothing," she told him point blank.

He laughed so hard and so loud that he nearly fell off his chair when she said that to him. He was still laughing when a waiter rushed over to make sure that everything was all right. Everyone in the restaurant turned to see him with this big fat grin on his face. Even she had to chuckle a bit but made sure that she kept her face somewhat serious. She wanted to make it clear to him that he was not dealing with some little African girl from the boon docks but a born and raised Harlem, New York bad-ass. He leaned up in his chair and matched her serious intensity.

"We might be able to really put something together, me and you, you know…" he said as he shook his head up and down in thought.

"Put something together…?" she asked.

"Yeah. The way I see it is that my business is doing fine but I wouldn't mind having a little of that global th'ang, you know what I'm saying?"

Chapter Fifteen

Kinni awkwardly stood in the doorway waiting for some sort of sign as to whether she should enter or not. She wasn't sure if it was going to come from something he said or something contained in the vestiges of her own heart that would lead her farther into his apartment. In all her experience, she had never been to a man's apartment with the intension of staying the night. She was apprehensive about the whole thing even though they had already established that they were just interested in sleeping.

"You're letting the flies in," he told her.

She sniggered a little and wondered where her head was in the first place for accepting his invitation and worst yet for lying to her mother. She painstaking closed the door all the while thinking that if need be she could still simply get up and go home. She had taxi money. Heck, she had several rides worth. So that was not an issue. She had a key, thanks to her mom, and she could just sneak into bed without waking the house.

"I got beers and water! What's your preference? I'm having a beer myself," he called from the kitchen.

"…eer," she tried to confidently say but the word beer landed squeakily at the entrance of which she was still wavering in front of.

"What you say?" he asked entering the living room and slipping an opened ice cold Budweiser into her hand.

He had already kicked off his shoes and dropped himself into his favorite chair before she took a single step. As he leaned back Kinni lightly tiptoed over to a hard wooden upright chair and finally sat down.

"You comfortable over there?" he factiously asked her.

She nodded yes all the while thinking that she shouldn't start out by lying to him seeing they were destined to be good friends. It wasn't her style to do so. So she quickly jumped up and strolled over to the cushy sofa.

"I thought so," Devon told her with a grin forever playing the host.

He clicked the television on and started flipping from one sports news cast to another with the universal remote. Kinni thought of her father and how he would do the same thing after a long day. However, she wouldn't hold that particular similarity against Devon. He had already shown to her that he was nothing whatsoever like her father. Eventually Devon turned, faced her and smiled.

"You want to see something?" he politely asked.

With that Kinni began to warm up to him again. She was thoroughly impressed with him all evening but that act of kindness struck a significant chord with her. She was rarely if ever asked what she wanted and never from the mouth of a man. She thought hard about the number of people who ever asked her her opinion on anything. She could only come up with her mother and Mrs. Chapman and one or two teachers down the line. It began to scare her that Devon was vastly becoming one of her favorite people. Yet she wanted to keep that particular secret to herself and just smiled back at him.

"How about something funny?" she asked while sipping beer too quickly for her own good.

He was kind enough to pretend not to notice as she spilled some down her blouse. Then they sat watching Nick at Nite's, *The Honeymooners*. Each time Ralph Kramden opened his mouth so did Devon with a boisterous laugh.

"I love that guy," he would say through tears of laughter.

Kinni felt too self-conscious to even laugh with him. Suddenly as if she hadn't noticed, she realized again that she was actually in Devon's apartment, just the two of them, alone. She didn't quite know what to do with herself. Her insecurities were budding like spring roses. Instead of watching *The Honeymooners* with him as she should have been, she scanned her eyes around the room and tried to see as much as she could of the apartment. It was small but she had to give him respect on how neat and clean it was, that is, for a man. She didn't have any confidence in men being able to actually pick up after themselves. Every area of his place reminded her of him from the milk crate holding up the television set and the sparse furnishings of the kitchen with just a small round wooden butcher-block table and not much else. It seemed as if no one really lived there. She giggled.

"What you laughing at?" he grinned.

"Man, you need some furniture up in here. I know you making money. Where's your stuff?" she asked with a head roll and much attitude.

"What, you don't like the place?" he leaned back eying her playfully.

"It's al-right," she shrugged looking around at the bare walls.

"I know. I know. It's not like I ever invite people over, you know," he confessed.

She was dying to ask him if that number of invites excluded females as well. She had already observed that of all the rooms, the bedroom was the most fully furnished and had the most lived in look. It was equipped with a mahogany sleigh bed, mounds of soft pillows with a satiny mauve colored quilted blanket, obviously a woman's touch.

"Like I said, I don't have a girlfriend," he repeated significantly observing where she was staring.

"I wasn't asking," she assured him.

He squinted out a smile in her direction and she pretended that the laxative commercial was more interesting than what he had just said. Meanwhile secretly she wanted him to like her, not the way all of the other men in her life did, but like someone who would dare to take the time to get to know her. She wanted him to respect her and to listen to her. She wanted her no's and her stop's to have some meaning that went beyond a typical man's physical lustful needs. She wanted her voice to somehow touch the man's heart and brain and remind them of what her words meant.

"I think I should go home," she told him rising up off the sofa quickly.

"Did I say something wrong?" he asked surprised at her sudden retreat.

"No. No. I just think that it's getting late and I know I said that I would…but…" she continued while walking toward the door.

Devon jumped up and reached for the doorknob and turned it open for her.

"Look, if I said something that was out of line, I'm sorry," he apologized.

Kinni paused recognizing the sincerity in his voice. She felt at once foolish for letting her own internal dialogue and past horrible experiences get the best of her.

"Listen, Kinni, excuse me, Queen Kinni, I really and truly am tired. I just want to wash my face, brush my teeth and go straight to bed…forgive me, to sleep," he told her walking away from the open door, "You can call a cab if you want, number's on the fridge or you can sleep on that sofa there. Anyway, I'm going to bed. I'm tired."

With that, he left her teetering between the hallway and his foyer. He went into his bedroom and closed the door.

"Turn off the TV before you leave, 'kay?" he asked her from behind the closed door.

Kinni knew that there was something about everything that had transpired that night that would forever change her perception of men. She would have to take another look at the long list of hated ones and remove Devon's name from it. She couldn't believe that she had misjudged him so. She just figured that every single man she would ever meet would be her father or her Mandinka husband. She slowly closed the door, took a deep breath and walked back over to the sofa. Once she wiggled her behind all the way to the back of the cushion, she began to realize that Devon was the exception. She didn't have the energy to contemplate that maybe in this entire messed up world of hers that there was even the remotest possibility that he might be the rule and all the others were exceptions.

The next morning came as a shock to Kinni. She awoke in a cold sweat. Her dreams still haunting her. She saw a plane landing at JFK airport. At the gate stood Mandinka husband and two of his most trusted guards. They flanked him and escorted him out into the street. Before she knew it, he was at her school waiting at the front door for her to exit the building. She stepped outside of the school door to find him laying in wait for her. At that point, the dream ended abruptly. She shot up from a deep sleep drenched and fearful.

"You alright?" Devon asked coming to her aid.

He reached out to hold her hand and she jerked away in a panic.

"Yeah," she told him, then realizing what she had done added, "Sorry."

He tried not to let it show but her rejection was heart felt. She immediately jumped up and followed him into his kitchen wanting to quickly smooth things over. He placed a cup of tea in front of her.

"Dev…sorry," she told him again.

He understood that she didn't mean any harm and accepted her apology with a shrug.

"I just had a bad dream is all," she said smelling the most heavenly food, "What you making?"

"You like pancakes?" he asked.

All she could do was smile. She once again had no idea why she was giving him such a hard time. He was quite possibly the nicest person she had ever met let alone the fact that he was a man. She knew that she had to make it up to him somehow for her painfully obvious brush off.

"Yes. Yes, I do like them," she said, "Thanks."

"You don't have to thank me, Queen Kinni," he joked, "I'm here to serve you. Besides pushing my hand away means you no longer have use for your lowly servant."

They both had to smile at his charm and wit. She loved the fact that he wouldn't hold her momentary craziness against her. He placed two pancakes in front of her and blew on them to make sure that they weren't too hot. She comically brushed him away.

"See, now that's yet another way you can dismiss me without saying a word," he smiled being truly amused with himself.

"I'll give you a word alright," she warned him.

"Listen, youngster, you need to get your butt to school," he reminded her.

At that she quickly sought out a clock.

"Oh, my God, I'm gonna be late," she fretted.

"I'll call you a taxi. Not to worry," he said dialing the phone.

"I don't even have time to wash up or anything," she said

embarrassed.

Devon handed her a wet paper towel to clean off her face.

"You look great. Ah, youth," he joked, "Look, your chariot is gonna be here in a minute. So, eat up and get going," he said to her then bowed.

CHAPTER SIXTEEN

From then on Devon's apartment became a regular hide out for Kinni. She stayed over at least three days during the school week and even managed to wrangle a couple of weekends out of her parents. They, of course, didn't know where she was in reality going, having told them time and time again that she was at a friend's. Though her father tried his hardest to find out the truth of the matter at her sudden need for sleepovers, he was met with some clever lies at the hands of all of Kinni's friends. Michelle told him when he happened to call her house looking for Kinni that they had a special project to complete for science class. When he asked to speak with Kinni, Michelle informed him that she had some of her mother's famous chili and would be indisposed for a while. Trese was even more convincing when she told him that they couldn't get through the mountain of geometry homework given them and speak to him at the same time. Matar would hang up the phone and pout thoroughly unwilling to be out smarted by a bunch of teenage con-artists. He knew that if Kinni ever said that she was going to Saundra's house for the night, that he would finally catch her in her lies. Everyone knew that Saundra was a terrible liar. Matar politely asked her one day how was school and Saundra gave a rather painful detailed account of her day, equipped with her lunch meal selection, as to be as completely accurate in her description. She was an admittedly forgetful person who preferred to always speak the truth. She was the most helpful around his house when Kinni was in Gambia, so Matar knew her character pretty well. Unfortunately for him, Kinni also knew the caliber of her character and never ever said that she was going to sleep over at Saundra's house.

Matar was so convinced that Kinni was lying that one day he decided to follow her over the Michelle's house to see for himself. Kinni walked the long ten blocks up from One hundred and Twenty-fifth street to One hundred and Thirty-fifth street. She had no intention, of course, of actually going to Michelle's but for the taxi she saw trailing her that particular evening, she decided to stay the supposed course. She wasn't sure who it was crotched in the back seat of the cab but she could see that whoever it was had asked the driver to tail behind her very slowly. She was the only one on those particular blocks that evening, so this occurrence stood out. Also, she recalled noticing that her father was getting ready to go out as well while she was packing her overnight bag. His back and forth behavior struck her as being odd but she didn't pay it much mind. He kept pretending that he was forgetting something before leaving each time she made a movement toward the front door. She thought it peculiar as she observed his movements and lingered a little longer in her room to see if he would indeed leave out before her. She had become extremely sensitive to people following her from her Gambia days. She decided that like Mandinka husband, her father would go to any length to make her life a living hell and that she best keep the true nature of her business as far away from him as possible. She walked ever so slowly up St. Nicholas Boulevard toward Michelle's house that evening. Devon's apartment was all the way over on Adam Clayton Powell's and quite a walk away but she decided to see just how far her father would go, for she knew in her heart that it was indeed him following her. The Livery cab he was hiding in dragged along the street at quite an eerily slow pace. Kinni grew increasingly upset when it would pause in the middle of a block and wait for her to cross the street before proceeding forward. As she neared Michelle's and would have to confront her friend's mom or dad if Michelle wasn't at home and make up some lie to gain entry, Kinni began to feel physically ill. She had already missed her opportunity to run and thereby loss her stalker. At least if she tried to run, she could tell her mom that some strange taxi was following her and she ran the streets of Harlem trying to get away from it. She'd be sure to get her father's attention, and weep a little for dramatic effect. Fortunately, she had some luck that evening. The Livery cab was so unhurried that it blocked up a street that had cars trying to pass who eventually blew their horns until the cab was forced to speed up and ultimately turn around the corner. Kinni knew that she finally got her chance to run and so disappeared into the Projects as the taxi made a long journey around a congested, evening rush hour New York City block.

She was breathing heavily when she entered Devon's apartment. She and Devon were merely business partners but Kinni had her own key to his place. She found it so peaceful to come in and be able to hear her own thoughts instead of her father's loud brandishing on what she'd recently done wrong or equally overpoweringly loud television recalling all the horrible news it could find in the City. She preferred the silence. Her grades had actually improved since her nights over at Devon's. She knew that it was the serenity of his place. Though she had a revelation as to why her father and Mandinka husband ultimately struck the deal that they had to marry her off. They were exactly the same, possessive maniacs. She could just picture her father lifting her up off the curb and forcing her into the taxi same as Mandinka husband did when she arrived in Gambia. She was mad enough to return home just long enough to curse him out then leave again but knew that that would only bring too much attention to her home away from home. Being at Devon's house was her salvation, her retreat. She had to protect it. Otherwise, she would have taken one of the many weapons that Devon insisted she carry and charge back to her father's as fast as her little feet could take her. She'd decide whether she'd actually kill him or not once they stood toe to toe. Deep down she knew that for her mom's sake she'd probably never follow through on it.

She was glad that his apartment was quiet when she entered. Devon had already told her that he would be home late noting that, unlike his girl, Kinni, his boys needed his full supervision. Devon thought it easier this way that Kinni have her own set of keys in case he was delayed when she got out of school. Kinni loved it. It was her first real taste of freedom. It was exhilarating to the point of being unnerving sometimes how good it all made her feel. However, in the back of her mind, she knew that it was only a matter of time before she'd self-destruct in a buddle of insecurities. She knew that the entire time she was with Devon that he was so much more larger than life. Half the time she expected to find another girl in his apartment, cooking for him or washing his briefs. She caught a peak at him in the shower, innocently, but noted that he was a deep shade of brown all over. Kinni had two major problems with her current situation, her increasingly nosey father and her swelling desire to be more to Devon than just a friend. She began to think of her crush on him as some kind of force far greater than her own will. Everything about him was magnetic to her and try as she might to hate him as she had done with every other man in her life, Devon continually surprised her by shattering the mold of the typical, egotistical male. As she walked into the living room, there was a note left for her on the coffee table telling her to go and look in the refrigerator. She smiled upon opening it to find a container of lamb stew with the name, Queen Kinni, written on it. He had gotten it from an African restaurant in Brooklyn he took her to one day, called Keur N'Deye. She couldn't stop talking about their dishes on the ride back to Harlem and indeed for the next few weeks could hardly speak on anything else. She skipped over to the microwave and allowed her joyful giggles to spatter out of control as it warmed. She was in trouble. She was falling for Devon in a monumental way.

She had to stop herself from jumping excitedly as the front door opened and Devon walked in.

"Honey, I'm home," he joked walking straight into the kitchen and kissing Kinni on the cheek.

She tried to stand still when he brushed against her although all the hairs at the back of her neck sprouted to attention. They were like an old married couple without any of the intimate details. Devon stuck his finger into her stew and tasted it, while she grabbed another bowl and spooned some of hers out for him.

"How'd it go?" she asked him.

"The usual. Big Mike wants more, more, more," he said.

"He's gonna have to pay more, more, more," she said.

"Says the white boys like the new stuff better than that old she-it, you know. Stuff like that," he told her.

"You want me to see what I can do?" she asked.

He lifted up from the table and went around to her, placing his arm around her shoulder.

"Look, you're good and all but I don't like you talking to those cats, you know. They talk about meth and she-it. Blacks don't do meth and ludes come on. They're not all together, all together. Know what I'm saying," he said twirling his finger around indicating that he thought them to be a little crazy.

Then he reached into the kitchen cabinet and pulled out two nine millimeters and two silencers. He started taking each one apart and cleaning the barrels and the inside of the chambers. Kinni watched him do this hundreds of times but this time was different. He already had his favorites on him. She wondered why he was preparing these two new ones. She knew better than to ask.

"Look here, eat up cause we got some work to do tonight," he informed her.

"Not too late. I've got school in the morning," she said with a laugh.

School had meant very little to her lately. She was just trying to keep the peace at home with her mom at this point, who wanted her to graduate. Devon was already an expert in her mom's handwriting and had taken Kinni out of school for weeks at a time. According to Kinni's school at Devon's hands, Kinni had had every kind of flu and stomach virus known to man.

She and Devon took a taxi out to Jamaica, Queens that night to see a guy named Rex. Rex was a gun running hustler of twenty-three years of age with already more than twelve years experience under his belt. He started right out of grade school using the Forty Projects as his main headquarters. He was known for two very serious focal reasons, he was insane and he outlived all ten of his predecessors on account of them coming up missing and never being found again. The story was that he would have them train him then he would permanently have them removed from their post. And everyone who knew anything about him knew that he had something to do with their sudden disappearances. He would all but say that they died at his hands. "Let's just say 'dat he had 'dat comin'", he'd say rather wickedly to those in his employ when someone who was mentoring him hadn't been heard from in a while. Though the only proof of his involvement were those very chilling words from his very own mouth; everyone swore that he was, although a charming murderer, nonetheless, a murderer. Anyone who valued his/her life would never say a word against him for they might suffer a similar fate as his forerunners. Devon was greatly interested in going into business with him for one equally self-serving reason, greed. Though he had Harlem sewn up with crack and was expanding overseas thanks to Kinni's connections at the U.N., he wanted to make his money really work for him. His purpose for meeting with Rex that night was to persuade him to add drugs to his catalogue of wears. Kinni would follow Devon anywhere and yet had some reservations upon meeting Rex. His reputation was like that of a dark cloud hovering over all of Queens. Kinni could feel his evil from the inside of the car as they taxied over to his townhouse, an evil that began to suffocate her even before the musty outside night air hit her face. Devon slipped one of the nines into her handbag as they exited the car. She turned to him and gave a stare as if to say that she was paranoid too.

Rex's house was wholly nondescript. It blended in perfectly with all the other houses on the dreary tree lined block but Kinni could tell that nothing good could come out of Rex's place. His bushes were overgrown and the grass or lack thereof was brown from dehydration. Even when Devon introduced Rex to Kinni, her opinion didn't change from the low estimation she had already formulated.

"Rex, Kinni," Devon presented one to the other.

"Yeah, yeah sit down," Rex mumbled inaudibly nodding over at the most broke down couch Kinni had ever seen.

Kinni had been in shanties that looked better than any of the furnishing of Rex's house. She just couldn't understand how he could have millions of dollars and live in a pigsty. She wanted to ask him but instead decided to keep one eye on Devon and the other on the nearest available exits. Two barely clad women walked into the room and slithered into the love seat that Rex now occupied. He placed his dirty hand on one of their thighs then the other around the other's neck. Kinni began feeling completely uncomfortable, which was only a hair's breath away from what she originally felt upon entering his house. Devon tried to pretend that he didn't notice any of it. He was firmly familiar with men who wanted their guests to believe that they were like celebrities.

"Hey, can we talk, man?" Devon asked him indicating that they should have their conversation in private.

"These my women. They know somethin' 'bout mie bizness. Talk," he told Devon.

The two women wrapped their legs around Rex and kissed him about his angular unshaved face. He twisted himself around and slobbered his fat lips into each of their mouths one slow jerky kiss at a time. His long dark tongue shot out like that of a poisonous snake and he literally forced it down their throats. They seemed to enjoy it, though Kinni could tell that they were faking it all the while for his pleasure. Their actions were mechanical and seemed rehearsed. There was something in their groans of enjoyment that simply didn't ring true. She giggled at the discovery of their pretense and gave a forced cough in order to cover it up. Unfortunately, Rex had noticed it. His sharp eyes shifted meanly over towards Kinni in recognition.

"What you want, Dev? Talk. I ain't got all nite," he barked at Devon in response to Kinni's noticeable disrespect.

"Hey man, I was thinking that maybe you and I could get

something going, you know?" Devon told him.

Rex pushed each of his treasured vixens off of him and made them sit on the floor at his feet. Kinni rolled her eyes to the ceiling in disgust.

"Look man, I don't like people showing up at mie' hoause in the middle of the nite. You thank' we can do somethin'"? Somethin' like what?" he asked rather hostilely.

Rex didn't acknowledge Kinni the whole time but both Devon and Kinni knew that his sudden angry behavior had everything to do with her repugnant grimaces at how he was treating his women. It was obviously a sore spot with her that could not be squelched.

"Linda, Car'ol…" he said titling his head for them to exit into another room, "…get lost 'sa minute."

Kinni was so happy when they left that she didn't know what to do with herself. Their presence made her very distracted and emotional. Neither reaction was appropriate while doing business with Mr. Rex. Rex gave her a nasty retaliatory glance then looked back over at Devon.

"Well, look, man. I give you much respect" Devon said trying to butter him up though he was feeling increasingly repulsed by him as well.

He wasn't a prude or anything like that he just didn't like to ever mix business with women. He had witnessed in his own experience that it always released the most volatile, unstable nature in men. He was also very cautious and didn't like a bunch of extraneous people hanging on his every word.

"What 'bout her?" Rex asked Devon indicating that Kinni should also leave the room.

He wasn't aware of the fact that Kinni wanted to leave the entire borough so badly that she could hardly sit still.

"'Kay," she said standing to scurry outside.

"She's not my lady, man. She's my best runner," Devon informed him.

"No she'it?" Rex said with a small grin.

Kinni slouched a bit to give him the full bad-ass effect. Rex finally nodded in her direction thinking that her discomfort of his women had been because she was really one of the boys. He treated her differently after that pronouncement. He gave her a tad more respect, not much more but his attitude towards her was much improved from that point on. When he turned to get a cigarette, Kinni used that moment to put her hand around the nine millimeter within her bag in case he turned on her again. She couldn't help herself. She had a bad feeling about guys who were so easily intimated by girls. She didn't like them and she definitely didn't trust them.

"So…you want to put some of your she'it into mie' mix, huh?" he asked Devon while lighting up and taking a few drags.

The smoke quickly filled the room choking off any available air.

"Yeah, man. Look, the way I see it, you got people and I definitely got people…why don't we expand together, you know," Devon explained.

"Expand, huh?" he asked Devon.

Devon nodded his head while shooting a little wink over at Kinni.

Before either Kinni or Devon could say another word, Rex had a thirty-eight pointed at Devon's heart, then he shifted his waist and pointed it at Kinni's head. She couldn't breathe at all for the processing of what was happening. Kinni and Devon realized that Rex was just going to kill them both right there in his living room. She realized that that was probably why the place was in such shambles. He probably killed quite a few people right there in that very stifling room. Then he pointed the weapon once again in Devon's direction.

"I really don't know which one of you to do first," he grinned like a hellion.

Kinni could tell that Devon wanted to reach for the gun he had tucked within his pants but by the time he'd get to it, Rex would have killed them both at close range. Kinni allowed her fingers to stretch around along the barrel of her gun. She hadn't the time to discern whether Rex was serious or not with his proposal. Then slowly, very, very slowly she pointed it out in Rex's direction while it was still safety tucked in her purse. It was tough getting her finger around the trigger, but she was determined to get at least one bullet in him before she died in this surreal empty way. She figured that she might have to stand eventually if she really was intent on shooting him. She really didn't want that to be the case. She hadn't the skill for killing. She wasn't a marksman and had only fired a weapon once at Devon's place. He insisted that she practice and made her shoot a twenty-two into a pillow. In truth she had absolutely no desire of shooting Rex but if she needed to defend herself, what other choice did she have? She couldn't believe that they were just going for a drive, same as usual, to do some business only to end up with this apparent nut job. She tried her hardest to look directly into his eyes, same as with her father when he pulled a gun on her. She could tell the outcome as if her father's eyes were truly the pathway into his soul. She decided to try the same technique on Rex. Rex's eyes were jet black and glistened with the intensity of still water. She suddenly, fearfully made the scary discovery that Rex was much harder to read. She knew with absolute certainty that Rex was not arbitrarily threatening them. He had every intension of making good on his threat. Kinni realized this doom and desperately wanted to warn Devon in case he thought otherwise. She, unfortunately, would never get that chance. Rex gripped the handle of his weapon and pulled his index finger slowly towards himself. Kinni felt as if everything was happening in slow motion. Rex's gun was waist high and stretched out directly in front of Devon's chest. She could hear Devon's heart racing as he shifted his weight in order to dodge the bullet that was all too quickly about to explode from Rex's gun chamber. Devon flew off the chair managing to hit the floor as the bullet slipped into the cushions and ripped a gnawing hole in the fabric. Before Kinni knew it, the barrel was now pointed at her skull. Unlike Devon, she remained completely still. All the while Devon scrambled reaching within his pants for his nine. As he was setting up his shot, Rex suddenly keeled over on the sofa with a thump. Devon immediately upon seeing Rex's slack body, turned and looked at Kinni, who simply sat very calmly within her seat as if it was just a normal evening outing again.

"Kinni, you all right?" Devon asked while watching her and quickly nudging Rex's body to see exactly what had just happened to him.

Then he slowly moved closer to the sofa and could then see a small patch of blood on the back of the seat. He turned slowly towards Kinni again.

"Kinni…" he said in a whisper realizing something significant about her silence.

Then he witnessed the smoke coming out of her bag. Then he noticed her hand within the bag. He quickly boosted her out of her seat and whisked her towards the door.

"Not a word. Let's go," he told her.

They ran three blocks in silence. When Devon hailed a passing taxi by standing in the middle of the street to stop it, he practically lifted Kinni's stiff limbs up and carried her into it. Then he smiled the whole way back to Harlem.

"You saved my life, girl," he told her as if he wanted to cry.

Kinni was in a state of shock. She was so glad that Devon put a silencer on that gun because she didn't think she could take the noisy blast of it on top of everything else that had just transpired. It was simply unimaginable for her.

"You think he's dead?" she asked Devon innocently.

Devon shook his head yes checking that the driver wasn't paying close attention to their conversation.

"I hope so," Devon replied.

Chapter Seventeen

Kinni dropped her bag on the coffee table and walked straight into the bathroom immediately upon entering the apartment. To her utter surprise and shame, she was not unhappy with the result of her actions. She didn't really recognize any penitence in her person for what she had done to Rex. The only thing she currently felt was hunger as she had not finished her stew when Devon announced that they had somewhere to go that night. Other than that she just felt a little dirty and grimy from being in Rex's filthy house. She was level headed, even-keeled and as steady as a rock. Devon snuck a few curious glances in her direction as she maneuvered to and fro gracefully throughout his domain. He already had enormous respect for her but after that night's events, he was positively smitten. She was his hero. She had single-handedly managed to save them both and although he believed that underneath her calm exterior she might actually be a bundle of nerves, she didn't let that side of herself show. She was as cool as a summer breeze. She slipped into the shower stall and allowed the whole episode to wash itself away down the drain into the intricate sewers' matrix below her beloved, Harlem. She knew that there was no turning back now. She was officially a drug running cold hearted gangster. It didn't quite live up to the images that she had seen portrayed on television. She'd seen the videos where the street gangs were all gathered together living the high life and thanking the universe that they had lived to see another day. She had no such delusion. This life for her was hard work and a paradox, filled with exhilaration and terror at every turn. It was the type of life that required quick thinking and even quicker responses. One had to be sure footed and ever ready to do whatever was necessary in order to survive. She absolutely loved it. As with the first time she acted as Devon's runner, she was completely renewed with fervor. That was only partly due to killing Rex. What really consumed her was the intensity of having to fight for her life and blessedly win the battle that made every aspect of that moment captivating. She knew beyond a shadow of a doubt that she was justified in shooting Rex. She knew that if she hadn't, he was going to kill them both and for no apparent reason, other than the fact that he simply didn't like them or possibly he liked Devon's idea but didn't need either of them to fulfill it. She just kept telling herself that it was either Rex or her and Devon. As the water trickled down her sides and swirled around her ankles, she recalled with blow by blow clarity other times in her life where she was in mortal danger, where it was either going to be her or her opponent. Her senses had been so sharpened by her other experiences that she knew there was good reason she had accompanied Devon that night. It was then that it dawned on her that she was his protector. As she had been so many years for her mom, she was forever playing that role. As with her mom, she wasn't sure if she was equipped or skilled enough, but nevertheless, there she was acting as guardian in the face of unspeakable harm.

As she stepped out of the bathroom, she strolled past the kitchen to find a huge sundae placed in the center of the table. It had vanilla, chocolate and strawberry ice cream, fudge, whipped cream and a cherry on top. She smiled.

"You went back out?" she asked Devon who was seated in front of the television set halfway finished with his own sundae.

"There's some nuts in the fridge if you like yours like that," he told her.

She lifted hers from the table and sat in the living room with him. They both seemed cozy and relaxed. Kinni had no desire to speak on the day's events and neither did Devon. They were quite content to just sit and enjoy their sundaes at eleven-thirty at night. Kinni loved the fact that Devon made her feel so comfortable. She could never do anything this remotely satisfying at home. With her father about, the only relaxation came to her at night while she was asleep, that is when she was not beset with nightmares, or when he wasn't at home at all. At those times she could become one with her own thoughts and remember happier times with her mom and with her brothers and sister, times that were special even. They would play endless games of tag, slipping and sliding throughout the house in nothing but their socks. Her mom would toss her onto the sofa and tickle her until she cried, 'uncle.' Kinni's stay at Devon's reminded her of those moments when she wasn't fighting her father over every little thing. Despite the present circumstances and with everything that had transpired in her entire life, this was the best she had ever felt.

"My girl," Devon said with the broadest of smiles.

Kinni loved it when he spoke sweetly to her. She was a sucker for it. His lips poked out in the form of a kiss. He had slipped out of his shirt and shoes and sat across from her now in nothing but a loose fitting t-shirt and jeans. She gathered for the first time in her life why they called them muscle shirts as his pectorals flexed and contracted effortlessly. His smile wasn't the only thing that was completely captivating about him. Kinni had to look away as he licked his lips over his spoon and his teeth sparkled so beautifully that she felt a flutter within her belly. She knew that their adventure that evening had heightened every aspect of their lives. They had crossed that invisible divide between simply existing and actually living. Every fiber in her being was alert and sharp and ebullient. It was as if she became plugged into a power switch. She was full of energy and vigor.

Devon felt it too. He was positively on fire. He was so pumped that he knew he wouldn't be able to sleep for at least several hours if at all.

"Hey, you want to catch a movie or something?" he asked her.

"Boy, you crazy. After everything that happened tonight, you want to go someplace else?" she asked him steadily shaking her head in disbelief.

He shrugged realizing that maybe his suggestion sounded better in his own head.

"I forgot that my girl has to go to school tomorrow. Damn, I like that she-it 'bout you. You're smart," he grinned.

"Yeah, I'm smart enough to know not to get up off of this here couch. You're on your own, buddy. Sorry," she told him.

"You have ice-cream all over your mouth," he stood up pointing at her lips.

Then he walked over and without so much as a warning, passionately started giving her little love bites all around her face. Kinni sat very still and allowed him to touch her. She instantaneously sunk into the exhilarating sensation of it as if she had been waiting for it her entire life. It was such a warm, eager, consuming embrace that it caused her to stop breathing momentarily. Her belly flipped over again and she could feel her knees melting like ice into the floor. As she slipped practically off the sofa he caught her and held her around the waist within his strong arms and pulled her tightly into him.

"I got you, baby," he whispered.

And the sound of his deep voice rippled inside her ears causing her to shutter with delight at the tenor of it.

"You comfortable?" he asked holding her.

She felt as if she was suspended in mid-air as his grasp tightened so he could make sure that she didn't fall. She loved him she told herself and yet didn't feel safe enough within to give herself fully over to her own desires. She kept thinking that they were a perfect fit all tangled up and locked in their loving clinch. The entire moment was whimsical and other worldly. She had never experienced a kiss such as this with its intensity and yearning and the burning sensation that roused every nerve. His kiss was hypnotic and all consuming. She knew that if he stopped, she would topple off the earth never to be heard from again. She longed to be with him, to touch him all over, to forever be tied and knotted up to him. She began to kiss him back. Devon perked up at the idea of Kinni coming on to him. He suddenly realized that she might actually like him as much as he liked her. She was just his type. He liked girls who had a good sense of themselves. Kinni had shown him that she could definitely hold her own. Every time he thought about her saving his life by blowing away Rex, his kisses took on such depth of meaning that they both felt transfixed. He was falling for her and she was spiraling right down alongside.

"Girl, you got beautiful lips," he moaned.

"You too," she moaned.

"How'd you get so damn sexy, girl?" he rhetorically asked.

Then he lifted her up and placed her more firmly onto the sofa.

"Is that okay?" he asked totally concerned with her comfort.

"I'm fine. How about you?" she asked equally concerned with how he was doing.

He licked his lips, picked up her hand and kissed it as if she were royalty. Then he kissed every inch of her arm. Kinni remained still against the cushions and allowed him to do so, all the while thinking about how strange she felt receiving this kind of treatment from someone as gorgeous as Devon. She had to fight against feeling completely intimidated but that just added to the excitement of it all. To her utter dismay she then suddenly became altogether self conscious, with him staring down on her and admiring what he saw. Seeing this transformation, Devon paused once he was face to face with her.

"You don't look so good. You all right?" he asked her gently.

"It's nothing," she told him.

Then she rolled into a standing position, pulled herself together and brought her empty ice-cream bowl into the kitchen and placed it into the sink.

"You don't have to do that now," he called after her slightly disappointed that their kissing session ended so abruptly.

"I know. I know...but..." she started and he came to join her in the kitchen.

"You alright?" he asked maintaining a respectable distance from her.

"Maybe it's just all this excitement tonight, you know. I'm...I'm...just a little more shook up than I thought," she said not really believing herself or what she was saying.

"Well, that's understandable. Kinni, what you did tonight, well, it just took a whole lot of guts. Half those idiots on my payroll wouldn't get me a cup of water if I were dying of thirst unless I was giving them something in return..." he moved in closer to her, "...but not you. You jumped right in there without any hesitation and did what you had to do without fear and saved us both. I'm so proud of you."

He reached over and kissed her on the cheek while her hands were still stuck in the sink rinsing her dish. Then he turned and walked into his bedroom and gently closed the door behind him. Devon could tell that their love making was over and he was not the type of man who would push a woman into doing anything that she decided she didn't want to do. He would tell anyone who'd listen that his mother raised him much better than that.

As Kinni heard his door close she forgot about the dish and became lost in thought steadily trying to make peace with her self. She just kept thinking, 'I killed a man. I killed a man. I just killed a man.' All at once she was emotional. As much as she had longed to do something like that to her father and to Mandinka husband, now that the deed was done, it didn't sit well with her. She watched the suds die out and couldn't help making the correlation that that was precisely what had happened to Rex, that is, after the effects of the bullet sunk into his flesh. She knew that she didn't have any choice. She knew that she could be in her grave instead of him. She knew that what she was beginning with Devon would have never happened had things not turned out in their favor. She knew that ultimately not even Rex's very own mother would miss him and yet that didn't alleviate this brand new phenomenon, remorse. She couldn't understand why but she actually felt sorry for the man, this man Rex. Ultimately, she didn't want to be the one responsible for anyone's demise. She decided that after all was said and done, that no matter the circumstances, no one really wins, including the survivor. She felt cold all over and couldn't shake that weary chill regardless of how warm it was in Devon's apartment. She didn't believe in hell but felt sure that she might be fated to go there with this latest episode in her life. She hoped and prayed that Allah would be merciful considering she had no other choice but to shoot first.

Chapter Eighteen

Kinni lay on the couch with her eyes wide open. Unbeknownst to her, Devon was doing the exact same in the next room. It had certainly been an eventful day with all that occurred at Rex's and they were still feeling the after effects but they were also still reacting to the consequences of their ardent kissing. Kinni couldn't stop thinking of Rex's demise interspersed with her longing to be with Devon. Devon too thought a little about Rex and how disappointing it was to discover that he was evil-unleashed, but it was Kinni's smell all over his body and the taste of her mouth on his lips that had him counting ceiling tiles that night. Kinni had her legs draped over the back rest and her arm dragging the floor unable to cool herself from the heat rising up within her loins. She was restless and tossed herself about several times in every effort to get comfortable. She had twisted around six rotations before she finally sat up and began looking out of the apartment window. Harlem was awake as usual with those who loved to sit out on their stoops all times of night and converse until dawn. She could hear groups of teenagers strolling by in packs carousing and reveling spiritedly down the block together with the after-dinner crowds looking for watering holes. If New York was the City that never slept, Harlem was the section of town doing its share to perpetuate that myth. Kinni thought about abandoning the entire idea of sleep for the night and just staying up watching whatever was on television. Devon had cable, so she thought surely she could find something interesting. Before her hand reached the remote, Devon was out from behind his door and standing right beside her. He didn't say a word but just took her in his arms and pulled her towards him. His lips pressed against hers gently and his body welded into her deeply. The warmth of him, the caress of him, the scent of him, the feel of him all excited her and lit a flame like none other she had ever encountered. He was delicious and so enthralling that she felt certain that she might keel over at any minute. He definitely knew what he was doing because he touched in such a way as if he had known her body. Yet never once did she believe that he was being inappropriate or grabby. He lifted her off the floor and carried her into his bedroom all the while with his lips fastened to hers. She admired his dexterity and the ease at which he maneuvered them both through his apartment. She felt as light as a feather and completely comfortable inside of his capable arms, one of her favorite parts of his body. She had always stared at them from afar even before she knew his name. They'd flex and contract even when he was simply speaking to someone and they always shined as if he were dipped in smooth creamy chocolate. She had secretly longed to be wrapped within them and swallowed up by his prowess and strength. She was glad that he swept her up because as he kissed her she felt sure that she would faint within his grasp. The atmosphere in his room was ripe with the energy of his passion. It was soaked in his musky, manly smell that she got a whiff of once and now was forever in rapture of.

When he placed her on his bed, she had the sensation that her feet would never hit ground again. He made her feel something that she had never in the arms of any other man, feminine and desirable. His very presence evoked security and an unequivocal mastery of that moment in time which stood still then spun round atop its axis. It overwhelmed her with pride to think that someone like him, beautiful in every way, liked someone like her. He took his time undressing her. She allowed him to do so, practically begging him to do so with her eyes and her heart. That was also a new revelation, that she could want a man and not loathe the sight of him, the touch of him. This too sent uncontrollable ripples of joy up and down every single inch of her body. He nibbled at her skin and caressed so lovingly that she felt altogether special and dare she dream, loved. There was nothing like it in her past to compare it to. She was without definition and utterly speechless.

"You're so beautiful," he whispered softly to her.

It hurt her to even look at him, so enamored was she and swelled with actual fear at how gorgeous she thought he was. Whenever she took the courage and peaked directly into his face, chiseled to perfection by God and bronzed by the sun, she would burst into a blush that even made him giddy at the sight of it, which in turn made her feel deeply vulnerable.

"I'll only go as far as you want," he mentioned and paused to await her response.

She yearned with her entire being for him to just ravage every inch. She wanted him to swallow her whole and leave nothing left but marrow. Her limbs were all aflame and he was the only one who could sooth and calm her wanton passion.

"I'm okay," she offered with what was left of the air in her lungs.

Everything in her was yielded unto him, Devon. He could have done anything he wanted to her that night. She wouldn't have minded at all.

Yet out of sincere respect for her, he paused once more.

"We can just curl up together and sleep, you know," he said.

"Is that what you want?" she asked pointedly, practically nude and drenched with perspiration.

"It's not what I want, baby…" he leaned in and kissed her,

"...I'm talkin' 'bout what you want."

She didn't know what to say to that comment. It was so far from what she had heard her entire life. Could he actually be concerned about her health and well-being? Was he expressing some type of interest in her that was even beyond what he himself desired? She could see for herself that he was greatly into their love making and that he was tempted and longed for her as much as she did for him. What got to her though was his undeniable restraint. Never in her life did she believe a man was capable of holding back, especially not at this point. She had been thrown down and raped and pulled apart by men who couldn't stop if their very lives depended upon it. Was Devon more of a man than the rest? Did he possess that gene that persuaded a man to forgo his own needs for the sake of another? Kinni honestly did not think it at all possible and for a brief moment couldn't believe her own ears.

"You want to stop then?" she questioned him bewilderedly.

He sat down on the bed beside her and took her face in his hands.

"If that's what you want...yes," he simply said reassuring her.

Kinni sat shocked as he kissed her ever so sweetly. That's when she knew in her mind beyond a shadow of a doubt that she was going to have him that night even if *her* life depended on it. They were going to make love no matter the consequences. In fact, she knew that she was going to make love for the first time in her life and that thought thrilled her. She grabbed hold of his clothes and slowly started disrobing him. As she slid his pajama pant legs down to his ankles and gently nudged his thigh with her head, he was glad that he had waited for her response. She was no longer the little girl, shy and bashful. She was the woman now in complete control of what she wanted and how she wanted to receive it. She pulled him down upon her willing body and kissed him greedily upon his open mouth.

Chapter Nineteen

Big Mike, among others, were very unhappy about the new order of things. It was bad enough when Devon came up to see him, but when he and Kinni paid him a visit, it was down right impossible. Devon was forceful and demanding as per usual but Kinni was clever and a tad scary for Big Mike. Word had traveled quickly that she was the gunman behind Rex's sudden departure. No one in their right mind missed Rex save Linda and Carol, and that was only because their primary vocation was pleasing him and keeping his house. In return they received free room and board and three square meals a day. Big Mike looked over at Kinni paying particular attention to her hands and where they were placed. The rumor was that Kinni tricked Rex into thinking that she liked him meanwhile placing her hand into her handbag and setting up her shot through the nylon all the while aiming like a professional marksmen at his heart. Big Mike shivered at the thought of it.

"You cold, man?" Devon asked him.

Big Mike shrugged off Devon's question and kept one eye at all times on Kinni's digits.

"Nah, nah…just hungry, you know," Big Mike joked.

"Too much of a good thing isn't good for you," Kinni chimed in.

"Yes, Miss Kinni," Big Mike said out of utter respect for her and a smidgen of fear.

"Miss?" Kinni asked.

Big Mike shook his head yes affirming that from this day forward she would be Miss Kinni.

"I call her Queen Kinni," Devon told him.

"Would you prefer Queen?" Big Mike seriously asked her.

"Devon, stop. Big Mike, he's just kidding," she told him.

Big Mike felt uneasy and just wanted both of them to leave. His trust in them was completely shaken and nothing could persuade him otherwise. He just wanted to conduct their business at hand and save on the jokes and new titles and anything else.

"Look, Big Mike, I want you and Kinni, excuse me, Queen Kinni to meet the shipment on Friday night. I've got some other business in the Bronx, kay?" he explained to Big Mike.

"What about Ousman? I told him that I, that we would have some more for him this Friday," he asked Devon.

"Look man, that's what I'm talking about. Ousman will have to wait until we pick the she'it up now won't he. How much he need anyway?" Devon asked him.

"My man's selling like crazy in Gambia to the soldiers there. The girl, uh, U-serri, well she distributes it somehow without any problem. Now, the order's thirty instead of fifteen," Big Mike informed Devon and Kinni.

"It doubled?" Devon asked him.

"Yeah, man, thirty pounds," Big Mike said with a grin, "He says that they can't get enough of the stuff down there."

"Uzuri writes him directly?" Kinni asked.

"Yeah. I think they have something going, you know. Like he's trying to sponsor her, something he said. I don't know," Big Mike told her.

Kinni just looked at him puzzled, not that she didn't understand what he was saying but for the revelation it inspired. It implied that Uzuri had abandoned her sister's rescue effort for the sake of her own career in crime. Somehow she couldn't believe that someone so dedicated to a single cause could suddenly just leave it. She believed that Uzuri was forever haunted by her sister's captivity and her mother's death. Kinni thought that possibly Big Mike had gotten it all wrong and that Uzuri was using the drug running as a means of funding her army still. At least that's what she wanted to believe.

"You sure about that, Big Mike?" she asked him.

"'Bout what part?" he asked her.

Kinni just sat still wondering what he could possibly know about the intimate details of the Gambian women. She figured that eventually, somehow, she would have to ask Uzuri herself.

"You two cool with that?" Devon asked them both about the arrangements.

That Friday Kinni and Big Mike stood at the dock overlooking the east river. It was a perfect place for their rendezvous, as there was never anyone around. Redhook, Brooklyn with its many dark, dank old shipping buildings and limited residential dwellers, made it easy to go sight unseen for days at a time. Everyone had heard rumors of someone buying up the entire shoreline and erecting condominiums, at fifty-five million dollars per unit, for years. However, the only people who frequented that area were artists in need of loft space and the homeless. Kinni and Big Mike literally waited casually for their ship to come in. It was going to be a small fishing boat Ousman told Big Mike earlier that week. Each pickup required a different boat and a different location. This was done as to not attract the attention of the Coast Guard, who almost never harassed the recreational fishermen. Even after the events of terrorism in New York City on September eleventh, they hadn't experienced a single search. Ousman told Big Mike that the trick was to have the boat smelling so bad of dead fish that no one really wanted to go near it let alone board it.

The fishing boat approached, engine turned off and a two man crew. Kinni recognized them immediately. The putrid odor alone was enough to make her lightheaded. She knew it was them by that signature stench. Devon referred to them often as mutt and Jeff. She stood waiting for them to dock considering which was which, whether Jeffrey was Jeff or mutt or whether Malik was mutt or possibly Jeff. Jeffrey was a mix of Irish, East Indian and Black and was therefore more mutt than Malik, who haled from the Ivory Coast. He spoke fluent French but preferred to speak home-boy instead. He wore anything and everything American, denims sans belt hanging down to his knees, Converse sneakers, high tops, of course, a small fade in his head and a diamond stud in his ear. By all accounts, he looked more American than most Black Americans. Yet when he opened his mouth, a beautiful French accent came out, which made everything he uttered appear peculiar coming from someone who looked like a straight up gangster. He also knew everything American. The latest songs, especially the rap songs, which were always in his IPod, which he had on him at all times. He could be counted on to know where all the latest, hippest parties were too. He was better informed about the latest goings on in New York than the New Yorker magazine, particularly those pertaining to the young urban Black American male with tons of disposable income and nothing important to do with his time.

"Where to tonight, Malik?" Kinni asked trying to make this entire transaction pleasant, friendly and most of all fast.

It took Malik a few minutes to dislodge the speakers from his ears. Then he had to re-groom his hair to its originally puffy height.

"Big Daddy Cain's in town. So, you know where I'll be," Malik told both Big Mike and Kinni with a knowing wink.

"How you get tickets?" Big Mike asked him.

"Tickets? I don't need no tickets. Cain's my boy," he said while securing the boat.

Jeffrey jumped out before it was safely alongside the wooden post. Malik rolled his eyes at him.

"Jeff, man…what's wrong with you?" Malik yelled at him.

"What's wrong with me? I'm getting out. You got a problem with that?" Jeffrey snapped back.

"Man, you're the one with the problem."

"Can we do this, please?" Big Mike yawned at both of them.

Jeffrey looked as if he had more to say on the subject. Malik mumbled beneath his breath something that sounded a lot like jerk, referring to Jeffrey.

"You're the jerk, man. You got problems," Jeffrey told Malik.

"Guys. Not tonight. We all have to do this and then get on out of here. It's not like we're having a picnic," Kinni informed them all.

All three men practically stood at attention when she spoke. Both Jeffrey and Malik knew Kinni well and what they didn't know their wild imaginations made up. She had been dropping off to them for about six months, which in the life of crime was the equivalent of approximately a year and a half. They knew that she was Devon's girl and that alone scared them. It meant that she controlled him to some degree. They also knew that she protected him and even went as far as to shoot Rex for him. This made them particularly uneasy around her. In their minds she was crazier than Rex, which was in street language an extreme compliment.

"Yes, Miss Kinni," Malik respectfully replied.

Big Mike snuck a quick glance at Malik, acknowledging that he felt exactly the same about Kinni, slightly terrified. Meanwhile Jeffrey darted his eyes at Malik also thinking that he was sucking up as usual.

"Malik just wants to hurry so he can go kiss Big Daddy Cain's behind," joked Jeffrey.

"What you say to me?" Malik asked Jeffrey leaning into him trying to intimidate him.

"You think I'm scared of you?" jumped Jeffrey up into Malik's face.

Big Mike sucked his teeth and glared at both of them. Kinni hadn't noticed this sort of behavior from them before. She decided that it was mostly annoying. She wanted to in all honestly get back to her man, Devon, who she couldn't stop thinking about no matter where she was or who she was with. The fact that she was conducting some of his business made it all the more poignant. Devon didn't trust anyone else to do these drop-offs like he trusted her.

"Boys. Boys, this is getting old. Can't you do this later?" Kinni said with a hint of tiredness in her voice.

At that, Malik shoved Jeffrey out of the way and grabbed a heavy duffle bag from the boat. It too smelled of rotting fish.

"We're gonna' have to think of a better way of making this happen," Kinni said pinching her nose.

Malik reached into his pocket and pulled out a fresh plastic bag. He handed it to Kinni so she could re-wrap the smelly package into it.

"S..uck u...p," mumbled Jeffrey under his breath disguising it with a cough.

Big Mike chuckled while handing Jeffrey a nylon sack. The transaction was complete. Malik glanced over at the open empty, quiet river. There wasn't any sign of life at all. Then he looked at the Redhook streets. They too were deserted. It was the perfect meeting, no interruptions, no cops, and especially no witnesses.

Chapter Twenty

Kinni opened the front door to her house half thinking that her father would be there to greet her with a where have you been shake down as that had become one of his trademark hellos. She promised her mom that she would help her around the house that weekend although she secretly longed to be with Devon instead, especially after everything that had transpired between them. Binta was anxious and greeted her as soon as she walked in.

"Kinni, that you?" Binta asked walking into the living room.

Kinni didn't have time to stash the cash within her backpack. Devon assured her that it would be all right for her to hold onto it provided she had it for him in a day or two. Kinni thought to simply push it underneath her bed when she got a moment. She'd told herself that once she locked her room door that it would be safe from prying eyes.

"Yeah, mom," Kinni replied.

"What you doing coming home so late, girl?" Binta asked slightly on edge.

"I had a lot of work to do," Kinni answered shrewdly yet now puzzled by her mom's shaky voice.

"My Lord, what kind of work they give you kids in that there school I just don't understand," Binta said almost angrily.

Then Binta scooted her into the kitchen before Kinni could put the bag away.

"I know you must be hungry. That skinny little Michelle looks like her mother doesn't feed her at t'all," Binta said with an indignant wave of her hand.

"Mom, mom, I'm not hungry, really," Kinni told her while

pulling her over to the table and sitting her mom down.

They sat silently for a few moments. Kinni could always tell no matter what was going on when there was something amiss with her mom. Binta was fidgety and restless, which was never her normal state of being. Plus the house was, by Binta's standards, practically in a state of shambles. Kinni had noticed that right off. There were pillows and sheets strewn all over the living room and Binta shockingly still had dishes in the sink. Kinni stood up, pushed up her sleeves and immediately started washing them. Binta simply sat with her head in her hands.

"I have something to tell you," Binta began shyly, tentatively.

Kinni continued to wash the dishes. Then when Kinni finally turned around Binta was in tears. She rushed over and hugged her.

"Mom, mom, what's wrong?" Kinni asked.

Binta couldn't speak at all for the sobs. Then there was a sound in the hall. Someone was walking down the hallway. It didn't sound like Matar thought Kinni. She, at first, assumed it was one of her brothers or her sister but there was something different in their gait.

"Did you two have a fight or something?" Kinni asked Binta referring to her father.

"No," Binta told her, "It's nothing like that."

Before Kinni could ask another question, an unfamiliar woman walked into the kitchen. She had on pajamas and slippers and her hair was disheveled from sleeping. Binta straightened up immediately.

"I see you finally decided to clean the kitchen," she said out of the corner of her mouth while heading toward the refrigerator.

Kinni gave Binta a curious stare. Binta just waved her off.

"This must be Kin...Kinnu?" the stranger rudely asked.

"Kinni," Binta corrected her.

"Pleased to know you. I'm Claudia," Claudia said offering Kinni her limp, high yellow hand.

Kinni shook it out of habit but could immediately tell that she wasn't indeed someone she'd be pleased to know. It was her mom's reaction to this Claudia person that made Kinni suspicious. Yet each time she looked over at her mom, Binta just sat stubbornly mute as if every breath was drained from her body.

"I'm the new wife," Claudia said with a giant smirk upon her face.

Kinni just stared at her all wide-eyed and bewildered as Claudia drank orange juice directly out from the Tropicana carton. Kinni held up her hands in disbelief as Binta merely leaned back in her seat and shook her head affirming that what Claudia told her was true. Kinni seethed with anger. She hated Claudia immediately and her father once again proved that her dislike of him was well justified. She couldn't believe that he would go and marry another woman. Claudia made wife number four.

"Did you know he was getting married?" Kinni asked her mom as if Claudia wasn't even in the room.

"Why would she know? She's no longer the re-al wife anymore. I am," Claudia informed them both with an air of superiority and a stamp of her foot.

Kinni eyed her sharply then turned again to Binta, but once again Binta didn't make a single move. Kinni noticed that Claudia put the juice back into the refrigerator and couldn't be bothered with wiping off the top.

"You two better get used to there being a new lady of the house around here," she said sauntering over to a kitchen cabinet looking for something to munch on.

Kinni was all too willing to drag her by the hair, take her

outside and push her head into the pavement but Binta suddenly stood up and blocked Kinni's path to Claudia.

"You looking for something, Claudia?" Binta asked her ever so politely.

Kinni suddenly noticed the additional lines upon her mom's face which seemed to have grown there overnight. Kinni thought that she looked at least five years older than she just had a few weeks ago. Kinni wasn't sure if it was the unexpected pregnancy or the obviously troublesome new wife but she feared for her mom's well being at this point more than getting a hold of Claudia. Binta's once beautiful olive skin was now green and pale and she hunched over as she walked and tired easily doing the simplest task of reaching into the cabinet. Kinni realized that she had been absent far too long. These were major changes for the worst not the better that she had completely missed. She felt all at once ashamed for what had been occupying her time.

"I'd like some potato chips, please," Claudia answered Binta gruffly.

Binta turned very slowly and paused before speaking.

"We don't keep those kinds of snacks around this house," she told Claudia firmly.

Claudia turned on her heels in a huff and began to leave the kitchen. However, as she stepped on the threshold she turned around again.

"Things are going to be different around here now that I am the lady of house. I expect to have what I like in the cabinets from now on," she practically shouted at Binta.

"Now you wait a damn minute. Who the f- do you think you are?" Kinni shouted and rushed to stand toe to toe with Claudia.

Claudia was not about to let a mere child jump in her face and curse at her. She lifted her hands and shoved Kinni back as hard as she could. Kinni, who was thin from all the running around she'd be doing, slammed into the kitchen table. Binta went to see if Kinni was hurt but before she could reach her, Kinni was up in Claudia's face again shoving her right back.

"Don't push me! Nobody pushes me around!" screamed Kinni.

"Why you little piece of she-it! Who do you think you are?" yelled Claudia while slapping Kinni across the face.

Kinni swung at her with all her might. And her fist landed squarely against Claudia's temple. Claudia buckled but did not fall, though the blow was powerful. Claudia stood her ground and growled at Kinni.

"I'll let Matar take care of you, you little bit-ch," spat Claudia.

When she turned to leave, Kinni lunged at her and jumped upon her back bringing Claudia crashing down to the floor. Kinni immediately grabbed a hand full of her hair and commenced pulling it out from her head. Claudia screamed and shrieked like a wounded animal. Binta hesitated a moment or two before coming to Claudia's rescue. Meanwhile, all the other children awoke rushing to see what all the commotion was about; only to find Kinni being dragged off of their new mother, Claudia, who now had tears in her eyes and scratches upon her face. Kinni was angry enough to pull away from weak, frail Binta and go at Claudia again but something within her told her not to. She realized that as Claudia stood up and slowly walked back to her parent's room that her fate with her father had once again been sealed. All of her hard work of avoiding him was now at a resounding end. He would undoubtedly do his utmost to kill her for sure this time. Claudia sashayed away like she was Scarlet O'Hara in "Gone With the Wind." Her hips practically hitting the hallway walls as she glided through the apartment. She was a beautiful looking woman and Kinni had noted that fact upon seeing her for the first time. However, now that they had gotten to know each other a little better, she thought her to be ugly and vile.

"Well…" was all Binta could say sitting once more at the kitchen table with her eyes drifting off someplace other than her home or Harlem.

She was tired and worn and frustrated with every aspect of her miserable life. Soon Matar would come home and the fighting would really begin, and of this she was certain.

"Ya'll go on to bed now. Shoo, now, go-on," she told her children and they scurried to their several rooms, each feeling slightly uneasy as if a storm was heavily looming over their heads. None was more perplexed than Kinni. She knew that she had stepped in it this time and had no one to defend her either. She knew that Binta was with child and suffering from the pains of such, therefore, wouldn't render much help once Matar came in wanting to slam her against a wall or something equally as horrible. She also knew that he had just been waiting for such an opportunity, as if he needed a reason to beat her or threaten her with his gun, or worst.

Kinni followed suit with the movements of everyone else in the house and went to her room lugging her backpack with her. She had forgotten about its contents and about all of her other extra curricular activities. Mutt and jeff were a faint memory, as was Big Mike. However Devon was the one she longed to be near. She wished that she and Devon were married and that she wouldn't have to stay under Matar's roof any longer, abiding by any of his rules. She crashed down hard onto her bed, unaware herself of how tired she actually was. Being a runner was hard enough without having to come home and fight with some strange woman in her own kitchen. She knew deep down that the only thing that was keeping her in that house that night was her mom and her younger brothers and sister. Her siblings seemed to have adjusted quite nicely to the goings on in that house; they marched back to their rooms without a single whimper. They were accustomed to the middle of the night fights together with all the yelling that would take place in the near future. Kinni was still gripping the backpack as she stretched across the bed longing to leap into a taxi and go over to Devon's. She missed the silent, peaceful, cozy atmosphere there and the way she could be herself within his place. Mostly, though, she missed him and the sweetness of his breath, his caresses, his smell, and especially the way he held her in his arms. With both her eyes closed she imagined that she was still there wrapped in such an embrace barely able to speak or breath and loving the comfort and familiarity of it. Her body warmed at the thought of it. Everything else began to fade like whispers in a crowded room, she was forever lost in remembrance of him.

She awoke an hour later with a start. As was predicted, Matar was standing over her screaming.

"Get the f- up, I said!" he bellowed with his hand raised ready to strike her.

Kinni heard footsteps behind him. It was Binta making her way towards them. Kinni would find out later that Matar had pushed her down onto the sofa when he heard from Claudia what had happened.

"Don't hit on her," yelled Binta though her voice sounded thin and whiny.

Kinni moved swiftly out of the way of his first blow. His huge hand missed her and went sailing down onto the mattress. Kinni smiled causally until she saw that he had picked up her backpack. She started to yell for it back in a panic but something told her to play all of this very coolly. So, instead she got up from the bed and stood still waiting for his next move. Matar threw the backpack onto the floor. Binta was already at the door wobbling and holding onto the doorframe. Claudia rushed up behind her and forcefully squeezed herself through the door causing Binta to stumble farther back. Once Claudia was standing next to Matar, her courage seemed grander, definitely more puffed up.

"You little b-itch," she spat at Kinni.

Kinni continued her frozen stance, loathing both Claudia and her father. Everything about them seemed so ignorant to her. She would have loved for them to just take a trip somewhere together far away from normal folks. They could have their little romance and leave the rest of the family out of it. She couldn't understand why her father never simply abandoned them all. He obviously lacked anything remotely resembling love for any of them. Why else would he insist on taking so many other wives? And although only two of his wives lived in America, he made frequent trips to Gambia to see the rest, without the accompaniment of his family. Else he'd speak to each of them often on the telephone right in front of Binta. Kinni found it thoroughly disgusting.

"Why aren't you two on your honeymoon or something?" Kinni rudely asked.

"You b-itch!" screamed Claudia.

"Shut your smart mouth," Matar shouted at Kinni.

"Well, what are you gonna' do to her?" Claudia calmly asked Matar, "She's a disrespectful, low life maggot."

"Wait a minute…….." Binta jumped in to stick up for Kinni.

"No one asked you, Binta," Matar sneered at Binta.

Binta stood holding her belly and leaning over.

"Mom, you all right?" Kinni asked her still remaining on the opposite side of her room far from Matar's reach.

"Yes...Yes...baby...I..." Binta spoke in spurts, "...I'm...fine...."

Kinni desired to shove both her father and Claudia out of the way but they seemed eager to throw her down and trample her under foot.

Then Matar started searching through Kinni's chest of drawers.

"Let's just see what your no good daughter has been up to all this time," he suggested sifting through her clothing searching for contraband or anything incriminating.

Kinni didn't move. She knew that he'd eventually make something up if he had to whether he found drugs or money or whatever he was looking for. In truth, she couldn't remember if she had something tucked away or not. She hustled out of Redhook, rushed home and everything she was carrying was dropped about the house wherever she was standing except the backpack that was now on the floor by Matar's foot. In some ways, she didn't care whether he found something or not. She had already decided that she wasn't going to stay in his house any longer than she had to especially not with this Claudia character around. This whole situation was getting to be completely out of hand. Now that she had Devon, she knew that she finally had a refuge. Her only worry was her mom. Deep down she knew that she would eventually have to come back and get her out of his house too. Money was good. She imagined that she could even possibly set her mom up in her own apartment not too far away from her and Devon, but that would be far in the distant future. Right now she had her father to deal with.

Matar looked down and remembered the sack he had placed on the floor. He went into it feeling around the side pocket with his gigantic fingers.

"I wouldn't be surprised if this little b-itch had a gun in there. She looks like she belongs in jail," Claudia said gruffly as if she looked to nail Kinni to her own bed and pummel her with a brick.

Matar didn't find anything except pens on that side and started to open the other side. Kinni knew that that was probably where she hid the money. Yet, she still didn't make a move but stood rigidly against the bed. Binta strolled calmly over to Matar and snatched the bag out of his hand. He quickly reached around and smacked Binta with the back of his hand. At that, Kinni leapt across her bed and swung at Matar with all her might. She toppled Claudia accidentally while seizing hold of Matar's arm and hitting him all over his face.

"Don't you hit my mother!" she yelled over and over again while swinging wildly.

She couldn't control herself. She couldn't contain her emotion. She wanted to kill him. Before Kinni knew what was going on, Claudia was all over her back, scratching her face and hands trying to pry her forcibly off of Matar. Meanwhile, Binta was all over Claudia trying to pull her off of Kinni. Binta struggled finding it difficult with her plump belly in the way. Claudia pushed her and Binta went sailing into the door, tripping over the bed and hitting her lip upon the metal door saddle. Kinni saw her go down out of the corner of her eye and immediately paused from her strikes upon Matar's face. Matar used that split second to hoist her off of him and throw her onto the bed. Kinni realized her error and tried to scoot away from him but his powerful hand held tightly to her arm and he squeezed until she howled in pain. All was lost now.

"You think you're gonna' hit me and get away with it?" he yelled while single-handedly sliding his belt off with one hand.

Kinni knew that the buckle was coming next. Claudia grinned, now pleased with this sudden turn of events and began yelping as if she were cheer-leading Matar from the sidelines of Kinni's bed. Meanwhile, Binta steadily tried to stand back up. Matar swung the buckle down and struck Kinni's knee. Binta could hear the metal cracking Kinni's bone and ripping the flesh. She desperately tried maneuvering herself over toward Matar.

"Matar! Matar! Stop! Please," she pleaded with him but her screams seemed to spur him on.

He was determined to kill Kinni once and for all this time. After several more strikes, he swung the buckle away from her knees and up to her head. Kinni was very familiar with this torturous routine but the hurt and shame of it nearly crippled her this time. The strokes this time were much more spirited and severe. Kinni bled all about her face and neck as he continued whipping her and tearing brutally into her skin. The blood gushing out of Kinni's mouth didn't stop his insistent blows. However, Binta's terrifying shriek finally did force him to cease.

"Ouch!!!!" Binta squealed.

All three of them turned to find Binta standing in a pool of water and blood. All this commotion had induced labor.

"Mom! Mom!" Kinni cried while jumping off the bed and catching hold of Binta as Binta slammed down onto the floor.

"Call a doctor! Call somebody! Help! Heellllpppp!" Kinni yelled at both Claudia and Matar until they awakened from their trance. Both Claudia and especially Matar each took their sweet time walking over to the nearest phone. Kinni made a mental note of their indifference and reminded herself that her mom and she were definitely going to be getting as far away from that house as possible. It was just a matter of time.

Chapter Twenty-One

Matar waited despondently as Binta and Kinni got into an ambulance and went off to Mount Sinai Hospital. He and Claudia stood by the door with their faces wrinkled up pouting that their little fun time of beating up Kinni had ended so abruptly. Matar wanted her to be the one leaving his house in an ambulance or preferably in a body bag that evening and not Binta. He was most annoyed with Binta for choosing that precise moment to have yet another bastard child. Though he lay with her to produce this baby, he would once again take no credit for it and was resolved to be only meagerly financially responsible for it. As far as he was concerned, Binta was once again all on her own with this one, the same as the rest. Matar's desire was to have a child with his new love, his new wife, Claudia. For she was the one he was supposed to be with all this time that he was fulfilling his mother's wishes and family obligations. He felt as if he had earned the right to now live his life free from the Gambian tradition and instead act a little like Americans who did whatever they damned well pleased. He never wanted to spend the rest of his life with the likes of Binta anyway. He hoped a long time ago that she would just die. He found himself wishing that she would while giving birth and that her womb would spew out a dead baby as well. He was seething so much with anger that it hurt him to stand at that doorway and feign concern. Yet he knew that he had to at least if for no other reason than to show Claudia that despite his hatred of his miserable family, he could be the bigger person. He wanted to make sure that she had it firmly fixed in her mind, that he was in fact the victim here.

"I just can't believe that daughter of yours," Claudia said

while closing the front door before the ambulance had made its way down the block.

Matar walked over to the couch intent on sitting and concentrating on what to do with Kinni next. Instead of plopping down on the cushions, he found the blankets and pillows that Binta had been using still strewn all over it.

"Look at this utter mess. I don't know how you stand it," Claudia told Matar while taking everything off the couch so he could sit.

"Thank you," said Matar tenderly.

"It's just horrible the way they treat you around here. I can't even believe it. If we were back home they would have been severely beaten and then thrown out by now. America hasn't any values," Claudia told him, "It's just a disgrace."

"You see for your own eyes now, right?" Matar confirmed with Claudia.

Claudia shook her head from side to side while tidying up the entire living room. She moved quickly and efficiently. She was extremely skilled at house keeping. She had been trained at doing so since she was a mere three years old. Matar loved that about her. She was the perfect wife. He felt that he had finally been blessed by Allah to have a wife who knew her place. After Claudia folded and wiped, she walked over to Matar and lifted his feet onto the ottoman. Then she proceeded to remove his shoes and rub his feet. He leaned over and kissed her forehead. Claudia had accomplished something that Binta would never in a million years understand. Matar needed all the attention and empathy. Claudia was a master at delivering such a gift to a man.

"I…" Claudia started then hesitated.

"What?" Matar gently asked, "What would you like?"

"Well…" she said turning to face Matar, "I'm not trying to

make things difficult for you, Matar. I'm your wife and I would do anything for you."

"I know that, Claudia," said Matar, "What is it you would like? Tell me."

"Well...I do not believe that we can live with...that girl..." Claudia told him frankly.

Matar stood up.

"That girl must go! You are absolutely right!" he shouted then quieted down as not to wake the house.

Then suddenly Matar jumped up and raced right back into Kinni's room and continued what he had started earlier before he was so rudely interrupted.

"I know that that girl is up to no good," Matar told Claudia, who scurried alone behind him.

Matar immediately found what he was looking for, Kinni's backpack lying right in the middle of the floor. With all the goings on, it had fallen and Kinni had forgotten about it completely. Unfortunately, Matar was now free to do his little investigation.

"Let's just see where she's been and who with?" he queried happy that he would finally have an honest answer to that question.

He unzipped the main compartment and reached inside. Claudia stood leaning over his shoulder respectfully. He pulled out a plastic bag that smelled of fish. They both lifted their head in shock when they discovered its contents.

Kinni stepped into the house in the wee hours that following morning. She was exhausted and wearily opened the door to find that thankfully all was quiet. The entire family's sleep had been sporadic that particular evening and she knew that she wouldn't see a soul until the sun was firmly high in the sky. She went straight into her room and collapsed upon her bed. She prayed that her father had gotten over his anger at least long enough for her to catch her second wind. She needed some strength if there was going to be a second round. Her thoughts were on a great many things but mostly they were on being able to be there for her mom. She had rationalized her father's absence at the hospital by telling herself that at least he wasn't a hypocrite. As she escorted her mom down the hospital corridors that's what she wanted to say to Binta to stop her from feeling sorrowful, but somehow the words wouldn't come out. She knew that if she had, it would have crushed Binta even more than she already was. However, unbeknownst to Kinni, Binta was completely used to Matar never being around. With all her other pregnancies he barely wanted to take her to the hospital at all. Once he even told her that she could take the bus and then call him when it was all over flinging quarters at her while she packed her overnight bag.

Kinni slept rather soundly despite it all with lovely thoughts of her new little sister, Bina, on her mind. She couldn't get over how wonderful it was to actually be a witness to such a miracle. She stood by the hospital nursery glass and marveled at how tiny Baby Bina was and how helpless. She found herself making baby sounds along with everyone else who was there. Binta had been so brave. Kinni didn't hear her cry out once, even though all the other mothers were hollering at the top of their lungs throughout the ward, but not Binta. When the nurses finally told Kinni to go home, her first instinct was to convince them that her mom needed her to stay the night. Before Kinni could make a solid argument, Binta ordered her to go.

"It's all right," she told Kinni, "I've done this before, remember?"

Kinni smiled and painstakingly released Binta's hand and left.

It was noon and Kinni was still fast asleep. How could she possibly know what her father had in store for her, what he had been scheming for since she returned from Gambia? Matar had gotten up early being the light sleeper that he was and began implementing a plan. He had been waiting for just the right opportunity to come along so that he could once and for all rid himself of pesky Kinni. By 12:10 there was a mysterious pounding on the door. The kids were all seated at the kitchen table eating. Claudia had prepared pancakes of all things, which gave Matar great pride. Binta would only occasionally feed the kids American food, but Claudia insisted on it and even got up early to shop for what she called the essentials, pancake mix, whole milk, miniature candy bars, potato chips and anything else she could find that was fattening, sweet and most importantly required little to no preparation. Claudia loved everything American especially the food. She actually got zero complaints from anyone in Matar's household. Matar leapt up from the table to open the front door. He had the most mischievous look upon his face.

"Right this way," he told the men who came barging in.

Then he led them grinning all the way down the hall to Kinni's room. Once again Kinni would be abruptly awakened. This time by three uniformed police officers who swarmed in and stood around her bed like a S.W.A.T. team demanding that she get up.

"Ah, wake up, Miss!" barked the tall Black one.

While the skinny White one poked Kinni with his nightstick. Kinni was so tired that though she was now only half asleep, she was too lethargic to move. That didn't stop them from grabbing hold of her arm and forcing her into a seated position. Kinni was startled when she finally fully opened her eyes and could see a bunch of strange men in her room. Then she was frightened. 'What now?' she thought. Matar just stood beside the bed grinning and gloating the whole time.

"Is this your backpack, Miss?" asked the Black officer.

Kinni froze. That got her attention.

"Yeah..." Kinni hesitantly answered.

"You're gonna' need to come with us, Miss," the Black one ordered.

"Www..hat?" Kinni asked him while wiping gook from the corners of her eyes.

She wasn't quite putting any of this together and couldn't stop herself from yawning throughout the entire interrogation or whatever it was. Again she looked over to find some answer from her dear old father, who only returned her bewildered gaze with a big fat sneer. She had her wits about her enough to know that having a wad of money was not a crime in and of itself. 'Why all the fuss,' she wondered.

"Kinni, get up! Can't you see people are tryin' to talk to you," Matar yelled.

At that, Kinni finally came to her senses enough to realize that whatever was going on, her father was at the center of it. She was alert now and although terrified knew that she had to play it cool. She looked at the backpack and again recalled what was in it, just money. Right? Then she whipped her head around and eyed her father, thinking now the unthinkable. 'Had he changed something somehow?' she wondered.

"Get dressed, Miss. You're coming down town with us," the White one said.

"Sir, we have to bring her in for questioning," the Black one said to Matar.

To that Matar shrugged indifferently. Kinni stood up. She

was already dressed in the same clothes from yesterday. She knew that she had to, so she went quietly not because she hadn't anything to say but because she was still very much in thought about her treacherous father. He had everything to do with this early wake up call and Kinni was determined to get to the bottom of it once she was released.

"You bastard," she called him under her breath.

"What you call me?" Matar asked knowing what Kinni said but wanting her to repeat it in front of the police officers.

"She called you a bastard," Claudia offered from the doorway.

Kinni pushed one of the officers aside and reached out to grab Claudia by the throat. It took all four men in the room to pull Kinni off of her.

Twenty minutes later Kinni was seated across a large old plastic table from a woman who looked not that much older than Kinni. She told Kinni that she was Detective Litton but that Kinni could call her Detective. They were in a small partially empty room with flickering fluorescent light bulbs and no air to speak of. The one and only tiny window was sealed, painted over in semi-gloss gray and apparently nailed shut. The detective was looking through a manila folder that had in it among other things, Kinni's freshly pressed fingerprints.

"Do you know why you're here, Miss…Miss Kinni Bragia?" Detective Litton asked her.

Kinni nodded no but didn't make a sound; she was too busy wondering how she got there in the first place. How could she, a relatively smart girl, have been so careless? She kept thinking that she should have known that her father wouldn't ease up on his curiosity. He just couldn't let anything go. She kept thinking that she should've known somehow. He was looking inside that bag and trying to find something incriminating while she was at the damn hospital. Then she recalled him trying to follow her to Devon's one evening a few weeks earlier. She couldn't be totally sure that he hadn't finally seen her going into Devon's place. She had let her guard down. She had been duped by her father once again and that just made her feel amongst other things - ill. He didn't seem that clever and yet there she was sitting across from some detective, having been read her rights, disrobed, patted down, deloused and generally humiliated. She also couldn't help thinking about dirty, rotten Claudia who actually told the police officers that they were welcome over any time as if she were hosting a dinner party instead of an arrest. Then there was her father who looked as if he was actually paying them off. He even offered them brunch, some soggy leftover pancakes and burnt coffee. Kinni couldn't believe any of it. She just couldn't believe that she was in the middle of such an obvious set-up. She thought that she had smartened up but it was clear to her now that she hadn't, not nearly enough.

"Miss Bragia...?" the Detective started.

"Yeah...Yeah..." Kinni started to tell her something then decided that maybe she should hear what they had to say first before she gave them anything else to use against her.

She kept wondering what they could actually charge her with. It wasn't as if she had stolen the money and besides she didn't have any drugs in the bag just cash, right?

"...No. No, I don't know why I'm here except that my crazy father may have lied on me. That's what I think. It wouldn't be the first time he did something like that," Kinni told her confidently.

"Well, the charge is not lying. It's possession," Detective Litton told her.

"Possession?" asked Kinni sitting upright within the hard

folding chair.

"Yes, possession," replied the detective matter-of-factly.

"I wasn't carrying!" Kinni shouted at her with a mix of hysteria and confusion.

"Well, Miss Bragia, there was at least a pound of methyl amphetamines in your backpack," the Detective said thumbing through her folder and handing Kinni a picture, "This is your backpack, isn't it?"

"Well, yeah, but…but…" Kinni could not believe what she was hearing.

'Black people don't do meth,' Devon would say. Kinni almost wanted to tell her that but knew that that wasn't really an argument that would make her case. She now knew beyond a shadow of a doubt who put it there, her father. He had to have planted it there himself.

"But, what, Miss Bragia? Is it yours or not?" the Detective asked again and this time as if Kinni was the liar.

"I wasn't carrying! I didn't even have anything in the bag except books and stuff. And besides I don't even know what metha…lam.. whatever is," Kinni shouted out her response.

The Detective stood up at that point and stared down at Kinni, trying to intimidate her. It was working. Kinni was off-balance and nervous.

"Then answer me this, Miss Bragia, how did it get there?" the Detective leaned in and asked Kinni.

"I don't know! Ask my lying, low down father and his b-tich of a wife! How the hell do I know how it got there? I was at the hospital. I wasn't even at home. They woke me up…They woke me!" Kinni went on and on with her explanation and denial.

Detective Litton just watched her as if Kinni were some kind of lunatic ranting and raving. She didn't seem particularly interested in Kinni's details of how her own father was trying to frame her.

"Oh my God!" Kinni yelled in exasperation recognizing that Detective Litton wasn't even really listening.

"Listen, we believe you. We believe you," the Detective said sarcastically and then calmly sat back down.

Kinni calmed down too now that she thought she was finally being heard.

"But..." Detective Litton went on, "...do you know a guy named Devon Hunter?"

When Detective Litton mentioned Devon's name, Kinni felt a deep lump in her throat the kind that went down into the esophagus. She panicked realizing suddenly that her father had in deed found a way to follow her without her even knowing. She knew now that she had been painfully foolish to assume that he wasn't a bigger threat. There were no lengths to how far he would go to strangle the life out of her and she began to feel that there was no hope for her leaving there without doing at least some jail time, the thought of which scared her to death.

"Yeah...yeah, sure, I know him. So, what?" Kinni answered now on the defense.

"Well, he sells doesn't he?" the detective asked her.

Kinni shrugged her shoulders not willing to volunteer a single word to incriminate Devon. It was bad enough that somehow the money was never mentioned. She wouldn't be at all surprised if Claudia used some of it on the shopping she did that morning. Kinni's stomach was it knots.

"So, you don't know him very well then? Is that what you're saying, Miss Bragia?" Detective Litton asked while searching through her folder once more and pulling out a photograph.

Kinni didn't quite know where to look. Finally she managed to look down at the picture recognizing it as their first date at Houlihan's. Her heart was melting as she came to know that the cops were watching Devon the whole time while her father was doing the same to her. Kinni got really scared thinking that there was a strong possibility that they followed them when they went to Queens to see Rex. Her only question now was how much time were they planning on giving her. She didn't have a clue, ten years, twenty? She struggled to remember something she heard on television about doing time for possession. More than anything else she recognized that her father had finally won. All her life he had been trying to kill her one way or the other. Now, Kinni thought, he had finally succeeded. He had planted evidence and with all of Kinni's so-called criminal element friends, all of her hanging out and erratic behavior, these detectives were going to make a very convincing case against her. It was all going to be woven together by mere coincidences. The innocent circumstantialities of which didn't seem to matter to anyone save Kinni.

Chapter Twenty-Two

After ten grueling hours of questioning, Kinni was arrested. She was charged with possession of an illegal substance and allowed one lousy phone call.

"Dev, it's me, Kinni," she said in a whisper.

"Queen Kinni, how you doin'? Haven't heard from you in two days, girl. What's goin' on?" Devon cheerfully asked.

"Dev, I...I have some bad news," she said.

"What's wrong, baby. Let Dev take care of it. You know I'm good with my hands," he said with a giggle.

"It's real bad, Dev," she told him trying to find the words.

She was stressed and out of her mind with worry but mostly she was ashamed. Then the operator interrupted the call.

"Ten cents please for the next five minutes," an electronic voice told them.

"Kinni, where are you?" Devon asked now concerned.

"Dev, I'm in jail," Kinni told him trying her hardest to sound like she wasn't completely terrified.

"Ba-by, no..." Devon sighed.

"Yeah, I got busted," Kinni said.

Silence.

"Babe, you didn't have anything on you, right? Did you?" Devon asked trying to understand.

"Dev, it was my father. He planted something..." Kinni said but the phone went dead.

Devon's voice was like an angel echoing brightly in the darkness. The phone click represented for Kinni the last shred of the life she once had. Her heart sank thinking that she would never hear that voice again. She didn't even get a chance to really tell him anything, not even that she loved him. She also wanted to warn him that he was being watched. Once again Kinni felt abandoned. And before she could recover from that realization, she was walked back over to the Police Station's dreary holding cell. She hadn't heard from anyone, not even her mom, no one. She remembered this feeling well from her days in Gambia, that isolation. One would think she was used to it, but how much can one take without choking from the loneliness. She walked into the cold, dirty cell and sat down on the wooden bench. The clank of the metal door vibrated loudly and actually hurt her ears as it closed with a clank. The female guard didn't even look at her the whole time. Kinni was just another nameless, faceless, no-body local criminal with a long disturbing number assigned to her now. She thought that her entire body had been emptied out and that there was nothing left but polluted air. She couldn't do anything else but wallow in fear. It was coming out of every pore. She reeked of it. And she was so exhausted from it that she knew she would not sleep well ever again. For one, the plastic bench wouldn't allow for comfort, it was too small and rigid. And secondly, she was scared out of her wits. When she thought even slightly about the possibility of being in prison, actual prison, not the dank holding cell, she couldn't stop the tears from flowing. She was to go before the judge the very next day. And things didn't look good for her. They had eye-witnesses, Detective Litton told her, who alleged that they saw her carry the backpack into her house. Kinni's anger brewed to overflowing knowing that by eye-witnesses they meant Claudia and her father who no doubt volunteered that little piece of information without having been asked for it. She kept wondering how her father got a hold of crystal meth in the first place. It wasn't as if he traveled in those kinds of circles but who knows. There was a possibility that he got it from someone who frequented his restaurant. She wanted all of the details of this audacious, fraudulent act so that when she finally got out of jail, she'd have a good enough reason to kill him dead. With a criminal record there wouldn't be anything stopping her from gunning him down the next time she saw him. This time, she told herself, it wouldn't be some fantasy or dream, this time it would be for real.

Everything after that first night in the holding cell for Kinni was a blur. She went straight to court that very next day as promised. Judge Margaret White presided over her case. She was an elderly Caucasian woman with gray hair and tiny square glasses that sat unsteadily atop her angular nose. She looked like a witch in the dimmed courtroom as unusual shadows cast off her wrinkled face, darkening it in the most unflattering ways. Yet when she spoke, she paced herself and sounded pleasant and for the most part friendly. Kinni thought for a moment that she might have a chance at one point because Judge Margaret White mentioned that no one actually saw Kinni with the drugs and that simply because it was in her bag didn't actually substantiate the prosecutor's case. However. The 'however' filled the courtroom like stink in a public restroom. However, because Kinni had a certain reputation, which included the hospital's incident report which stated that she tried to kill herself and the fight she had with Claudia whom she just met, the Judge was inclined to believe that the drugs were indeed hers. Kinni felt as if she was standing on some rare variety of quick sand. Her entire body was sinking under the stench of it and as she drowned there wasn't a single soul who was willing to send her a life raft or toss her a rope. To add insult to injury, her father and Claudia were there at the sentencing smiling and feigning concern for Kinni. Kinni couldn't look in their direction without wanting to leap over the wooden courtroom partition and deck them both. Instead she looked in the Judge's mouth as she handed down the verdict.

"Two years..." Judge White declared.

Both Matar and Claudia looked elated and outwardly ecstatic.

"Miss Kinni Bragia, because you are only fourteen, and still a minor and by law still under the juvenile penal code, you are hereby sentenced to the Spofford Correctional Facility for youth. Your sentence shall begin immediately following this court session."

With that statement, Judge Margaret White banged her gavel down and Kinni was scooted out of the courtroom without so much as an opportunity to tell her side of the story. Her free attorney was some trainee that the State sent over that morning whose legal strategy was to listen dutifully to her elders. Kinni kept looking over at her wondering why she wasn't defending her at all. It was only while being taken out of the courtroom that Kinni came to the conclusion that everybody including her legal aid thought she was guilty. She really didn't have a chance. The odds were stacked in favor of her father's lie. There was nothing she could do but pretend to look as if she wasn't phased by it all as she walked right pass her all too pleased with himself father and his side kick, Claudia. She looked for her apparently absent mom but realized that she was probably still recovering after having Baby Bina.

Kinni was placed in the back of an empty yellow school bus equipped with bars on the windows and a bullet proof glass parition separating her from two armed guards, her escorts to her new home. She watched from the tiny mesh bar openings as everything familiar to her passed by in an instant. All the while, seething with hatred at recalling over and over again, and now with greater detail, everything that had transpired in her house that fatal night. More than anything else, she longed to rewind the events and go back to find what she could have done differently to have avoided all this. She had been up against Big Mike, mutt and jeff and horrifying Rex and now to have her idiot of a father bring her down was totally unacceptable. She never thought that he could ever get to her again. She figured that after her stay in Gambia that that would have been the last thing her father would be able to pull on her. And where was Devon? She wondered if he knew where she was. She longed to see him and to tell him how much she missed him, how much she wanted to kiss his handsome face. She needed someone on her side, someone who knew the whole truth, someone who could see that she'd been ambushed. Then before she knew it and all too soon, they were in the Bronx, even though, it was congested with midday traffic and the bus crawled uptown at a turtle's pace. Kinni, at this point, just wanted to get there and get the whole nightmare over with. If she could have she would have blinked and been back to her normal life. However, the ride there was a premonition of what her sentence would ultimately be like for her, painstakingly slow and dreadfully abnormal. And that reality began the very first day she arrived.

After the obscenely personal physical examination, Kinni was given a change of clothes, drab green fatigues and what appeared to be a half chewed up toothbrush. Then three male-looking, female guards walked her to her cell. As they took her down the hallway, inmate girls began banging their fists upon the bars of their cell in an attempt to get Kinni's attention.

"Hey, girl, what you doing here, Prin-cess?" one rather overweight girl yelled at her.

Another started laughing hysterically when she saw that

Kinni was drowning in the clothes she had on. Kinni took no particular notice to any of it. She had been so numb to everything that past few days, that she couldn't even speak at all by the time she entered her own dingy cell. As she walked in she saw bunk beds with a girl already occupying the bottom bunk. The girl was passed out, draped across it with her underwear exposed and drool coming out from her half opened mouth.

"Get up, Tasmania," the bigger of the three guards said to the sleeping girl.

"Name's Tashamani! Tas," the girl corrected the guard and then immediately popped up and stood at semi-attention.

"You have a smart mouth, don't you," the guard said poking her on the chin with a nightstick.

The other two guards stood completely still at the entrance without saying a solitary word. They looked cold and uncaring, but mostly bored, same as Kinni.

"Yeah, well... whatever. I call you whatever I like. You got that," the guard said poking Tas a little harder.

Tas felt the pain but pretended like it didn't mean anything to her. Then she clamed up completely while the guards allowed Kinni farther into the cell. Kinni didn't know where to stand or what to do with herself. The big guard took the spare prison clothes that Kinni had in her hand and placed them on the top bunk. Kinni just looked at everyone around her and truly just wanted to pass out. She honestly didn't think she could take any more disappointment. She just didn't think she had it in her. Hadn't she been through enough? When would it all end? Why her? Why here? Why now? She had just come back to the place where she felt like her old self again and that took some doing still living under her father's roof. It wasn't that long ago when she was tricked into a marriage with Mandinka husband and forced into slavery within his household. Didn't she deserve better? Hadn't she finally escaped from the tyranny of her Gambian father and his ways?

"Hey, you? You hear me talking to you?" the big guard yelled and Kinni awoke from her self pity.

"Yeah," Kinni answered though she hadn't heard a word she said.

"I'm Ms. Bing. You will call me Miss Bing and nothing else. You understand me?" Ms. Bing asked Kinni.

"Yes…Ms….Bing," Kinni answered.

Ms. Bing laughed in her face.

"You two are going to get along just fine," Ms. Bing told them both, "Both of you are weirder than a cold French fry."

All three of the guards howled in laughter then left, latching the cell door behind them and walking back down the hall. Kinni could hear all the other girls clamoring to get their attention as they trotted away. They were apparently asking for things like outside privileges and cigarettes and such. Kinni stood frozen in the middle of the cell for several minutes. She hoped her new roommate wasn't a talker because that was the last thing on her mind. Tas rolled back onto her bunk and tried to fall back asleep, leaving Kinni still dead center looking lost and confused.

"It'll take a few days," Tas told her before covering her feet with a blanket.

Kinni looked around. She thought it ironic how much it reminded her of a great many places she had been before, her room, Gambia, the mission. Life was painfully repeating itself for her. Once again, there wasn't anything really to see. She had an open toilet, a cot and a sink. That was the sum total décor. She thought about Devon's apartment, with it's large windows facing the Harlem streets and the wide planked shiny wooden floors. Devon had an old-fashioned claw tub and a pedestal sink. Kinni couldn't help but feel remorseful for neglecting to savor his place just a little bit more. She wondered where he was at that precise moment. Though she hadn't a clue as to what time it was, she figured it was early afternoon and that he was most probably in the park hanging with his associates. She longed to be sitting right there with them, laughing and joking around until the sun set. She wanted him to nibble on her neck and kiss her cheeks until she couldn't take it anymore without having to make love to him.

"You're in my light," Tas barked.

Kinni suddenly snapped out of her daydream and once again had to face her stark, cold reality. She couldn't move without wanting to weep amid every step. She wondered if there was anyone who could relate to all that she was going through. As she looked down at Tas and at the other inmates across the hall from her with their faces squeezed through the bars looking forlorn, somehow she figured that the answer to that question was a definitive, resounding yes, though that revelation didn't comfort her. Kinni moved out of Tas' light by leaping up onto the upper bunk. It took all the strength she had to do so. Once there she collapsed wearily as if she had led in her belly.

An hour later a bell rang so loudly that Kinni swore that it was tearing a hole into her eardrum. Tas rolled out of bed casually and stood by the door to the cell. Kinni could barely hear Tas though she repeatedly uttered, 'Take's a few days,' because Kinni's hands were covering her ears until the gongs stopped. Then the cell door slid open with a grating rusty squeal.

"You comin'?" Tas asked Kinni while exiting swiftly out of the cell.

Kinni jumped down to the floor nearly wrenching her ankles.

She couldn't wait to get out of there only to find thirty or so other girls waiting patiently just outside of their cell doors, including Tas. It was only one step beyond the cell threshold but it was like Mecca to Kinni. Then the same three guards marched all of them single file down the long corridor until they reached a large room with tables set up in cafeteria style. Unlike her Gambian mission experience, no one served them in an orderly fashion, complete with harmonious rhythms, and definitely not with a song in their heart and the loving tempo of life surging through their veins. Instead everyone queued up and took an ashy beige tray from one table and shuffled down a long counter to receive something the guards referred to as dinner, soggy potatoes, dirty, lumpy gravy and something that looked like meatloaf but tasted more like stale month old cereal. Kinni choked as she bit into it. The girls at her table sniggered out a muffled laugh.

"It takes a few days," Tas grinned and patted Kinni on the back forcing what she had just eaten down her throat.

For Kinni there wasn't anything funny about the place. She couldn't even return their joking for the absolute despair she felt at her current state of affairs.

"Moody, huh?" someone asked Tas as if she knew her new roommate well enough to agree.

Tas shrugged her shoulders and continued eating her dinner. Surprisingly, she was nearly done yet they had just sat down. There wasn't any blessing given, no speech, nor sum up's of the day's events. There was just this pitiful display of some meager, unsatisfying nourishment. Kinni pushed all of it around on her plate with her fork until Tas started picking at it with her before eating it. Kinni allowed her to do so because she didn't think she could stomach any of it anyway.

"You better eat something, girl. W'ain't got no dessert,"

some practically toothless girl informed Kinni, "Don't let dat 'lil greedy monster take it'll."

Toothless was referring to, of course, Tas, who had eaten half of what was on Kinni's plate in one giant gulp. Kinni thought for a moment that she was back in Gambia with the reigning champion of wolfing down a meal.

Chapter Twenty-Three

Days stretched into weeks, weeks lengthened into months, hour by hour life dragged on and on wretchedly creeping, virtually at a standstill. Kinni didn't notice the Autumn leaves changing from green to orange and red, or the outside air shifting from cool and warm to cool and wintry cold. She hadn't looked up at the clear blue sky to see the geese migrating south nor the City being transformed into chill with festive holiday cheer blossoming from it bringing a spirit of friendliness and goodwill. She barely raised her chin off her chest for the past three long months that she had been at Spofford. Everyone thought she was mute and therefore crazy, of course, which became her nickname. Though forced to speak at their group therapy sessions, she'd answer direct questions in short grunts and groans.

"Tell us about your father, Kinni," Mrs. Gonzales would implore.

"...f'i...ne," Kinni would respond voice cracking from lack of use, looking to the girl next in line pressuring her to go and spill her guts to a bunch of strangers.

No one would receive another peep out of Kinni regarding that particular subject, but she might offer a similar response to another question if asked. She wouldn't have spoken at all had it not been for Ms. Bing stating that cooperation meant privileges, "privileges" that included food and water among other things. Kinni wasn't trying to die at Spofford, though she believed herself already dead, a walking dead of sorts. So, she knew that she had to give them something even if it was curt replies to, in her mind, ridiculous questions.

No one visited her as yet, no one called or wrote, not even her mom. Why communicate with the dead? Instead Kinni observed all the goings on in the cave, as Spofford was known. Kinni thought the word didn't aptly describe it. A cave meant an oasis to her from the elements, a place where one could hide and find refuse should they luck upon such a dwelling made by God when there was nowhere else to run. She refuted the sheer notion of the dank, over heated, filthy toilet smelling combined with heavy ammonia reeking cover-up place as being referred to as anything other than a tomb. And as such she knew that she was there rotting away same as everybody else like they had been shoveled over by a mountain of dirt. The whole vibe of the place made her think of a homeless hooker trying to avert attention away from her stench with way too much cheap impostor perfume. Unfortunately, there wasn't anything that could clean up the place though each girl had a full day of chores in which to try. Truthfully, the place needed to be demolished, then after the soil was tested for bacteria contaminates, concrete pulled for foundation and then a city park erected instead of a prison, maybe then it would be passing fare but just barely. Everything about the place had someone needs to make a living written all over it rather than the rehabilitation that Mrs. Gonzales spoke of nauseatingly. Kinni knew that Mrs. Gonzales was probably a nice lady beneath the psycho babble notwithstanding. Everyone knew that she got her psychology degree from the University of Mexico, which was to them the equivalent of a Cracker Jack box. Everyone believed that she wasn't good enough to get into an American college. She never pushed Kinni or anyone else for that matter to greater heights in the self exploration. The least amount of resistance and she would back up to the door of the session room and call it a day.

"Well," she would say, "moving right along."

Kinni would just look at her and wonder if she even knew how to ask a question that would compel a real response. Everyone lied to her to get some of those so-called privileges that Ms. Bing constantly spoke of. Toothless was in the prison clinic every other day. She complained to Mrs. Gonzales that her poor self image was getting the better of her. So, Mrs. Gonzales prescribed Wellbutrin Xl, an antidepressant medication. Then Toothless said that she was upset because people kept laughing at her because of her poor oral hygiene condition. And although, no one cared to injure her in that way, Mrs. Gonzales recommended that the nurse give her Lithium. Between the highs and the lows of the drugs, Toothless was rarely lucid at any given time. Kinni would watch her in amazement as she sloughed with her chin leaning slack against the cell bar and her head stuck between. She'd be fast asleep while standing up. Kinni thought she looked a lot like a jack-o-lantern and would laugh whenever she saw her in this particular state. Kinni would catch herself at those times smiling and wonder where that surge of energy came from. She'd try to suppress it wanting to think only of the glorious day when she'd be released. Toothless' roommate caught her grinning one day and Kinni threatened her life with something as simple as a penetrating ugly stare. Then Kinni would return to her thoroughly disgusted gaze as if she hadn't been observed as a real human being at all. She flat out refused to be seen as anything other than buried alive. She started the day in complete silence and went throughout the day saying as little as humanly possible. She didn't want to be referred to at all. She wanted to appear as a ghost. In fact, Tas began to speak on her behalf as if she didn't exist.

"Yes. Yes. She did have a problem with her father. Yo, why don't you prescribe her some marijuana to calm her down, ya' know?" Tas would say when Kinni didn't answer Mrs. Gonzales for the third or fourth time.

The whole room would burst out into raucous laughter. Kinni had to hand it to Tas, she had a way with people. Everyone respected her though she didn't really do anything to deserve it. She was the laziest person Kinni had ever met in life. She was so lazy that when showering she'd actually sit down on the shower floor with the soap atop her head.

"See, when the water comes down and hits the soap you get suds. And I'm clean," she'd say.

Tas was that way with everything and everyone. She wouldn't lift a finger if any of the girls was in trouble unless there was something directly in it for her. Kinni trusted her completely for that fact alone. One always knew where they were with Tas. She never claimed to have anyone's back or to be anything other than a girl after her own needs and no one else's. Kinni liked the frankness and clarity of her resolve. She was comparing her, of course, to almost everyone else she ever met. Kinni was tired of the hypocrites, who showed a clean upright person of integrity when confronting the public but meanwhile in private, behind closed doors any and every disgusting trait could be witnessed. Kinni was referring, of course, to her father. Tas' bluntness was an absolute breath of fresh air.

"Uh, I'm not in here to be nobody's friend. Who do they think I am," Tas would say if someone asked her for anything that took her more than a minute out of her usual routine, a routine that invariably led her to or in the vicinity of food.

Like Tas, Kinni spent her days at Spofford looking around showing vague to no interest at all to anything or anyone. Kinni didn't give a damn about anything at Spofford including herself.

She overheard Tas say to Toothless one day that no one wanted her, that is, for any type of romantic entanglement. Kinni had seen a few of the girls getting overly friendly with one another on several occasions. Even that didn't daunt her in the least. She had seen and heard enough to know what went on in places like this to be shocked. Besides she was too preoccupied with being utterly despondent with life to really consider how everyone else was coping. She had become once again the Gambian orphan child with one dress and hair undone, unwashed, un-kept and definitely uncaring. Her mood was always a puke yellow shade of sullen. Loathing everything was her general state of being and her cynicism was so acute that when she did speak it came out harsh, caustic and bitter. Toothless inquired one night at dinner as to whether Kinni was going to finish her partially, eaten, messed over corn bread.

"What are you gonna' chew with?" Kinni answered Toothless back with a smirk.

Toothless stared at Kinni peculiarly for several minutes never fully gasping the subtlety of the insult. Everyone else within earshot, however, waited for the victim of Kinni's vitriol to react. Toothless merely leaned back wondering if Kinni meant yes or no. Ms. Bing could overhear Kinni's embittered repartee' from time to time and suggested, as a warning to the other girls, that Kinni was looking for a fight. Kinni knew deep down that she was right. She wanted more than anything else to rip someone's head off. She would have preferred her father or Claudia but at this point beggars couldn't be choosers. She would gladly kill anyone else in their stead. As it were, many of the girls had issues of their own and for the most part at Spofford, Kinni went relatively unnoticed. Sadly, Kinni was one of many angry, disillusioned young ladies. Everyone had a grudge or something to prove or was depressed to the point of chronic pain. Having a chip on one's shoulder was as common place as flies in an outhouse. Kinni was not by any stretch of the imagination unique in a place like Spofford.

One typically boring day, Kinni actually received to her surprise a letter. What wasn't a surprise, however, was the postmark dated a whole twenty days prior to her receiving it. She figured that someone had already read its contents. Ms. Bing pushed it to her through the bars and she slowly picked it up and nonchalantly jumped atop her bunk to examine it. She thoroughly explored the outside envelope. Oddly, it was from someone who knew her but she couldn't figure who that was because the delivery address was a post office box and the name illegibly printed above it was Randolph Jackson.

Randolph Jackson?
Randolph Jackson?
Ran-dolph Jack-son?

"Aren't you gonna' open it?" insisted Tas being casually nosey and alittle impatient.

This, after Kinni had stared at the unopened envelope for nearly an hour and a half. Kinni recognized that Tas was right. All she had to do was pull the letter out. As delayed in delivery as it was she wondered why they didn't have the decency of at least resealing it so that it looked as if it hadn't been tampered with. She slowly slid her finger beneath the lip and ran it across the loose flap. Then she removed the folded piece of paper within, all the while not recognizing who sent it. She discovered that the actual letter had more of the same scribbled writing. So much so that Kinni couldn't make out its garble. 'Dere, Cani,' it started, 'Big Mike here and I hav sum ding ta ell yu. it bout deb, he ded.' Kinni sat up on the bunk nearly slamming her head into the ceiling with force. 'What?' she wanted to scream. It didn't make sense. She kept trying to understand what ded meant. For that matter she wanted to know who deb was. It went on, 'he kot chot. Dey wontd dey monie he oh dem. Ah dank Ozman did it,' it continued. Kinni was so confused, that she read it all again. 'Dere Canni…it bout deb, he ded.' Then she read it again hoping that what she was beginning to decipher wasn't what Big Mike actually meant. 'It bout deb, he ded,' she read again and again. And before she knew it, her cheeks were wet with tears and her breathing had completely stopped. 'Does he mean Dev,' she thought. 'If it's Dev, what is going on with him?' she asked herself still trying desperately to understand Big Mike's poor spelling not to mention his equally poor penmanship. He was no scholar, that was evident, but Kinni was happy that he thought to sit down and actually write to her, but what on earth was he trying to say? 'What does 'ded' mean, for goodness sake? And Ozman must be Ousman,' she thought and once again read the letter but this time out loud. Tas was on the toilet singing because she didn't want anyone to hear her doing her business. Kinni seized that moment to possibly say more than she had said in the past three months. She remembered from English class that bringing a voice to letters often allows for total coherency. Suddenly, 'deb' sounded clearly like Dev and 'ded' was definitely dead. 'Dev, he dead,' Kinni realized was exactly what Big Mike was trying in his own lack of an education way to say. 'Ah dank Ozman…' was I think Ousman did it. Somewhere in her soul she actually knew that that's what it was from the very start. Once she fully grasped that fact, she fainted. Her head slipped from the side of the bunk and the weight of it carried her all the way down to the concrete floor. Tas watched in horror as she saw Kinni plummeting like a brick. Toothless screamed at the sight of it too and immediately called for help.

"'elp! 'elp! 'Omebod e…'elp 'er!" Toothless yelled.

Ms. Bing came charging down the hallway to see Toothless pointing into Kinni's cell. Kinni's head was surrounded by a pool of blood with her legs twisted beneath her body like a rag doll.

"We need you down in cell block seventeen, now," Ms. Bing radioed immediately to the nurse's quarters.

Chapter Twenty-Four

Claudia climbed out of the tub feeling pretty pleased with her self. She had never been lavished in such luxury. She ran the bath as soon as everyone had left the house and had sat in bubbles for more than an hour, small television on, watching the weekly morning shows, Good Morning America, then Maury Polvich, which she just loved. Her mouth lay agape as one young woman told of her exploits as a teenage hooker. Never in a million years would a Gambian woman put on such a display in front of total strangers. Polvich tried to be respectful and not get into all of the dirty details however everyone there in the studio audience wanted to know all about it and came right out and told him so. The frightened girl told them all to go to hell and stormed off the stage. That's when Polvich with a cameraman trailing in toe walked off after her and gently persuaded her into coming back onto the set. Claudia couldn't believe the sordid tale the girl told once she returned. It was a story of hundreds of men from one state to another. The most horrible thing was that her mother knew all about it and even encouraged her. Claudia's mother would have killed her stone dead, for that was the Gambian way. Female virtue and virginity define a family's reputation in the Gambian culture, so it was the women who were punished if that reputation was even perceived as sullied. There was no way that she would have befallen to such a state of affairs. Claudia was born to be married and married well. In other words, she was supposed to become rich by marrying. That was her complete and utter mission in life and here she was in America living such a miraculous destiny. She had been smart. She had been an obedient daughter. She did exactly as her mother had told her whatever the request. And she learned all there was to learn about becoming a good, and honorable wife. Then she just waited patiently and dutifully until a marriage was arranged for her. All along she and her family hoped and prayed that it would be Matar Bragia. She had known him ever since they were children. His family lived in her village and she saw him practically everyday playing with his friends, or at market or at the village's various celebrations and ceremonies. She adored him and he her but when Matar was of marrying age his family simply wouldn't hear of him taking her as a wife. She couldn't understand why and longed many times to just ask but that was not the Gambian way. Women were not supposed to ask such questions, leaving all the important decision making to the elders of the household mainly her father and her mother. The truth came out one day while she was drawing water and she over heard her mother say that his family was foolish to believe that money was everything. Claudia's family wasn't by any stretch of the imagination poor but compared to Binta's family they only had meager possessions. Binta's family was into every kind of trade; Claudia's was just into livestock. Binta's family won. Claudia remembered being devastated at the time but she was too well bred to let her feelings show. Instead she'd go off for long walks around the village so that she could cry in peace.

As she stepped out of the tub and admired herself in the hanging full-length mirror, she had to admit that the way it finally happened was even better than she had expected. When Matar moved to America with Binta, Claudia reasoned that all was lost. He was one of the most eligible men her age and with him leaving, there was little to no chance of her finding someone else who could take his place. Though her mother tried to introduce her around even to other villages there wasn't really anyone who even came close to being what her family wanted for her. There was one man named Abdelahi Bellamy, whose family hailed from Somalia, who had asked for Claudia's hand in marriage. He was a gentle and sensitive man, himself coming from a war-torn country, he could eventually tell that Claudia's heart just wasn't in it and called off the engagement at once. Her mother tried to get her to understand the importance of going on with her life but Claudia had a difficult time letting go of what she lost in Matar. She had already fallen in love with Matar and mourned his exit from Africa as if he had died. No one was more shocked than she when Matar finally asked her father if he could have her as his wife. She couldn't believe her good fortune. For too many years since his departure, she had begun resolving in her mind that she would grow old as an unwed woman. It would bring shame on her family and would cause her mother a great deal of sorrow but she just couldn't let go of the dream of someday being the rich wife of Matar Bragia. And while that was the furthest thing from reality, she just couldn't bring herself to be with anyone else in the meantime. Who could have known that this love she had for Matar was vastly becoming more like an obsession. She had secretly gained his address from one of his good friends who was also from their Gambian village and with it had written to him often. Binta never knew what was going on right under her nose. She was too busy just trying to survive in a household with a man who didn't love her or her kids. Then to add insult to injury, Matar had married three other women besides Binta. Forbidden to marry Claudia, he would marry all those who reminded him of her. Both Matar and Claudia had one thing in common, they each longed for what they couldn't have. Fourteen years had gone by and Claudia and Matar finally got what they both desired. Matar's mother died leaving him free and clear to do what he had only hoped for – to marry Claudia. And ever since Matar informed her parents that he would be sending airfare for her to travel to the States, Claudia's excitement and joy was bursting to overflowing. Marrying Matar was the fulfillment of all she had ever imagined for her entire life. Part of that dream had never included being an American citizen and yet there she was living the American dream equipped with citizenship. All her life she had only seen Gambia and Senegal and not much of either country. She was a product of her environment and only had a limited view of the world beyond. The most she ever really expected for her life was to lay eyes on Matar again if for no other reason than to say that she still loved him and yet there she was, married to him.

She wrapped the soft giant cotton towel around her firm naked body and swore that she looked like one of the women from the many soap operas she now watched daily who seemed to have all the time in the world to just pamper themselves and look gorgeous for their husbands. She liked the sound of that word, husband. She would show Matar what he'd been missing while married to the likes of Binta. She had known Binta also since they were all kids and never thought that Binta could hold a candle to her. Binta wasn't what anyone would call beautiful though she did have pleasing features. Binta was more of what Claudia would call a handsome woman. She wouldn't have thought that Binta would be the one to take Matar away from her and then to move all the way to America. It just wasn't thinkable but that's exactly what happened. Claudia was shrewd. After Binta and Matar married, Claudia, though scarily jealous, always treated Binta kindly. She never wanted Matar to view her as anything other than benevolent. Though a struggle,

Claudia even managed to bring a gift to their wedding ceremony and to smile along with everyone else during the festivities. The only one who noticed a change in Claudia's behavior was her mother. She would often ask if everything was all right. To which Claudia would respond warmly, "Yes, of course." Meanwhile, Claudia was planning her strategy, her next course of action to win Matar. She was a desperate woman. She saw her entire life flashing before her eyes. Matar was her future. Though it took a decade of convincing Matar that he couldn't live without her, coupled with his mother's death, Claudia had finally won. She looked out of the window at New York City and smiled at all that had transpired in what seemed like to her such a small span on time. She was the queen of Matar's castle. Before she came into Matar's home, she thought that Binta would be the bane of her existence. She envisioned arguments, full out brawls for Matar's attention, only to come to find that Binta rarely had any contact with Matar at all other than to receive funds for food shopping, clothes and such. Then she thought that perhaps Binta's pregnancy would have been an issue, but Matar wanted nothing to do with the baby and told Claudia that he had been drunk and lonely when that unfortunate seed was planted. Whenever Binta even looked as if she would be a problem for Claudia, Matar would scream, "That's my wife!" He'd say that referring of course to Claudia as if there were no others. Then Matar threw all of Binta's clothes out of her drawers onto the living room floor and put Claudia's in them instead. Binta had instantly gone from being the lady of the house to the maid of the house. It was either that or be thrown out on the street, a sentiment that Matar also repeatedly shouted at her. Now that his mother was dead, Matar felt no obligation what-so-ever to the promises he had once made.

Claudia had been in the house a whole week before she even saw Kinni. However, Matar had told Claudia all about her prior to that rude introduction. He said that Kinni was what he liked to call a bad seed and that his wayward daughter preferred to stay out at one of her many boyfriends' houses instead of the lovely home he had provided for her. He also told Claudia that she hadn't any respect for the family that she was a wicked child worthy of being stoned. He also told Claudia that he doubted if he could do anything to fix her except to kill her with his bare hands. He told her many, many times that he had tried. Before Claudia even met Kinni, she knew that unlike Matar's other extremely well behaved children, Kinni would definitely be the troublemaker. Looking out again at the sunshine sparkling against the stoop's railing, Claudia couldn't believe how lucky they were to have gotten rid of her too. 'Kinni was now firmly tucked away in a jail cell hopefully never to return,' Claudia thought with a smile. Yes, Claudia was very, very pleased with the results of all her waiting, wishing and hoping. Yes indeed, life was sweet. She sat down upon the bed thinking of her many blessings while also wondering, merely wondering about that which she and Matar had found hidden in Kinni's backpack. It was just a fuzzy inkling in her brain, nothing hard and solid, she was just thinking about it. She had only seen a glimpse of it when Matar opened it, flashed the treasure in her direction and then quickly closed the bag. Claudia hadn't the time to fully register what was even in the bag. All she knew was that it was a lot of money. She couldn't tell whether they were hundreds or tens or singles. She hopped off the bed and began ever so gently opening Matar's top drawer. It began innocently enough. She was just going to peep inside and see if any of it was in there. She stood there staring at the neatly folded shirts, thanks to Binta, then she slid her hands beneath to see if anything was underneath - nothing. She put everything back in place, closed that drawer only to open another, and then another. After half an hour of searching and not finding anything, she stopped thinking that the whole notion of a treasure hunt was utterly ridiculous, wasn't it? She thought instead about what she should put on. Then suddenly she realized that anything Matar had hid wouldn't be in a place where Binta could easily discover. With that in mind, Claudia started moving furniture around. She pushed with all of her strength and moved the chest away from the wall – nothing. Then she went into the closet and rummaged through shoeboxes, underneath Matar's many hats, baseball caps and tams, and even through his coat pockets – nothing. She sat back upon the bed and laughed at herself. She didn't really need anything and everything she ever wanted would be granted by Matar but for some unknown reason she just wanted to feel it in her hands. At least that's what she told herself. It didn't have any real significance she told herself. It was merely to fulfill yet another dream of seeing that much cash so up close and personal was all. She hadn't yet put on any clothes and thought that if she found Matar's hiding place, that she might just roll around it too for that matter. She'd put it right back for Matar to do with it what he willed, she told herself. He had loved her all these years, hadn't he? He'd probably lavish it all on her anyway, wouldn't he? If it weren't for his mettlesome mother, he wouldn't have married Binta, he'd have married her first, right? After all, she was his true love, wasn't she? She thought for a moment about that. She didn't like the way her delicate mouth began a frown at the corners thinking on how long it took for him after his mother died to send for her. It wasn't as immediate as she believed it should have been. 'A day or two maybe but not three long months,' she thought. Then she tried to push those thoughts out of her restless mind. She was now his number one wife and wasn't that all that mattered, wasn't it? As she scooted up on the bed she felt something beneath the covers. She reached down spreading her hand gently over the sheets. They were tucked and smooth. Yet when she bounced upon the bed there was something there, something definitely below, possibly just her towel curled and wrinkled but she could see its edges and knew that there was something more. She jumped down off the bed again and stood staring at the mattress. 'Yes, yes,' she thought, '…something is stuck between.' Hurriedly she yanked the blankets from the bed and hoisted up the mattress. She froze. It startled her. She was shocked and exhilarated. There lying upon the box spring was yet another miracle, something that could actually warm her heart, she was afraid to say, in a way that no man not even Matar could – money, loads and loads of money, all hundreds.

Chapter Twenty-Five

Kinni groggily awoke in the medical wing of Spofford.

"Ah, back from the dead. Ah, how you doing today, young lady?" the Nurse Rhonda Polk asked her.

Kinni couldn't clearly see her and couldn't really answer her if she tried. Her throat felt as if it were welded shut by a hot poker.

"Not talking anymore I see," Polk joked.

"…hut?" Kinni asked wanting this nurse to just go away and leave her be.

"What's that you say? You do know that you speak a lot in your sleep? Well, you have a concussion and you tore a few tendons. Jill had a big fall," Polk mused while checking Kinni's vitals.

Kinni did know for sure that she hated this nurse with her sing-songy humorous bedside manner. The high pitch of her voice scratched against Kinni's eardrums.

"This is a first at Spofford. Normally, someone gets pushed but not you, Jill. Jill had a big fall," again the nurse amused herself at Kinni's expense.

"Hey, you," Tas shouted from a few beds down greeting Kinni, happy to see her awake.

Kinni wearily looked over and could have sworn she saw Tas mopping the floor. She wasn't fully conscious but she could see something that looked like a mop handle in Tas' hand. Plus she could smell the ammonia assaulting any semblance of clean air. She began to choke and the nurse quickly reached for some water and started forcing it down Kinni's throat.

"'..ait a dam min..ute!" shouted Kinni with whatever strength she had left, which wasn't very much.

Kinni ached all over. Even the tips of her fingers hurt. Nurse Rhonda Polk pulled away immediately when she saw Kinni trying to curl her hands into fists.

"Jill doesn't want to fetch a pail of water, does she?" Polk continued with her nursery rhyme.

Kinni loathed her and darted her eyes in annoyance. Nurse Rhonda Polk seemed not to even notice and went merrily along to her next patient.

"I see you're among the living again. No, the sky isn't falling, Miss Penny," she told the next girl.

Tas plopped down onto the corner of Kinni's bed.

"She's nuts," Tas said very matter-of-factly about Nurse Rhonda Polk.

Then Tas tried unconvincingly to act as if she wasn't really staring hard at Kinni. Tas had traded a girl food for her infirmary mopping duty because she wanted to see for herself the damage that Kinni's fall had rendered. It was all anyone could talk about at Spofford. Tas had never seen anyone take a spill like that in all her days. Kinni went from sitting upright on the bed to soaring down head first as if someone clasped a heavy weight around her neck. And the worst part was when she saw Kinni's back buckle once it made contact with the hard cement floor. Tas sat on the toilet in a state of shock not knowing quite what to do and not being able to move a muscle. She had seen her share of horrors certainly but this was one of the most peculiar. Kinni looked so broken and fragile like a smashed egg. Good thing Toothless was coherent enough that particular day to call for help. Tas was too bewildered and hadn't the wind in her lungs to yell at that precise moment.

"You alright, girl?" Tas asked her, trying to sound as casual as possible.

Tas really and truly believed that Kinni was dead that fatal day lying there seemingly lifeless, and in her hands was a single sheet of paper that she was clutching.

"Here," Tas motioned towards Kinni and handed her the letter.

It was crumbled in deed from being passed around no doubt and read repeatedly. Kinni's face filled with tears as she realized what it was there placed between her fingers. She turned her head at the shame of it knowing that Tas also knew the reason for her accident.

"They thought I did something to you. Imagine?" Tas told her.

Kinni heard her but didn't respond, so lost was she in her own thoughts.

"I told them to get a clue," Tas continued.

Kinni's mind went straight to Devon with a dreamlike vision as if she was with him the day he died and could see everything that had occurred. It was so unfair. It was so heart wrenching. She wished he would have called her or written to her so she could have at least told him where the money was or more accurately who had it. She longed to rewind the racing clock of life, the very hand of time and dive into the past making changes to all that had occurred. She longed to be by his side more than anything else. She yearned to hear his voice and to have him touch her in the way that only he knew how. She pressed her face strongly against the pillow willing it to swallow her whole. If only she could just evaporate into the atmosphere. She wished she could. She cried out in agony at the thought of him leaving her behind, only to find Tas and Nurse Rhonda Polk glaring at her as she riled unashamedly in pain. The bruises were all on the inside away from prying eyes and yet there was no way of burying them from the whole world. She would inwardly bleed forever in remembrance of him, Devon, her love. He would eternally be the one that left her heart hollow, the one she knew for whom she could not fully live without.

She was now fatally living beneath the world in the middle of the earth where supposedly fires burn ceaselessly. Nothing and no one mattered anymore to Kinni. She might have once avoided certain people and slightly dangerous situations at Spofford but now she mingled with and edged around them as if she couldn't be harmed by anything any further. The darkness that was her heart swelled and collapsed in breathing but by all other accounts, she was a corpse. She continually refused food and had to be fed intravenously weekly. Tas feared for her life but that didn't stop her from stealing food off her plate. Kinni was oblivious to it all. She walked the halls as if she were on one of the many mind numbing drugs that Toothless routinely took. No one and nothing could get through to her, could penetrate the fortress she had constructed around herself.

"Girl, do you want this or not?" Ms. Bing asked her angrily while literally forcing a new freshly washed blanket into her hands.

Finally Ms. Bing tossed it onto the bottom bunk, which was now Kinni's, as she was no longer able, nor willing to climb to the top one. Before the switch, Tas would find Kinni leaning against the wall of the cell in the middle of the night, eyes open and weary from lack of sleep. Tas confided in Toothless that Kinni scared her at times with her eerie catatonic stare. Kinni would be resting with her eyes bulged wide. Tas would poke her with a finger and Kinni wouldn't budge. Tas accidentally scratched Kinni once drawing blood and once again nothing, no response what so ever from Kinni. Tas thought it creepy and was rumored to have asked for a cellmate change. She was denied because Ms. Bing believed that no one else could handle Kinni in this particular state. She needed someone like Tas who enjoyed being alone and she was definitely alone in Kinni's company. And still the days and night labored on with a stiffness and lack of agility. Kinni had stopped her daily crying for hours at a time and instead whimpered like a wounded puppy underneath her breath, with visible tremors and shakes. It was safe to say that she was indeed going crazy and some often said it repeatedly regarding her and often out loud straight to her face.

Then on yet another typically ordinary, uneventful day, Kinni received at long last a visitor, her first not counting her incompetent legal aid. She was escorted down the long cellblock corridor to a drafty room towards the front of the prison. In it were small desks with two chairs besides each one and not much else. The only difference with this room as opposed to all the others was the overdose of pine wood polish. The old desks were lathered in it layer after grimy layer. So much so, that one could etch their name in its thickness and several had accomplished such a feat.

"Keep your hands on the table at all times," the guard barked.

Kinni remained perfectly still at the entrance unwilling to move without authorized assistance.

"Seat, *crazy*," the guard snapped at Kinni then exited slamming the door behind.

Kinni could feel the guard's sour spit against her face from the force of expelled venom in her speech. No one liked it in this place, not even the guards. Kinni was used to it, this hostility of everyone she encountered at Spofford. She tried to turn her much impaired ability to focus to the present. There was no excitement at all in anticipation of who it might be coming to see her. It had been nearly a year, someone had mentioned regarding the length of her stay so far. For Kinni it was much, much, much, much longer. By her calculations, it was a lifetime that had no purpose save torture. She refused to sit, refused to contemplate who would arrive, refused to care, and refused to give who so ever entered that claustrophobic room the time of day. Then the door at the back of the room opened and someone vaguely familiar to Kinni walked in. It was as if she were seeing a vision. A light flooded the room and temporarily blinded her. She just saw a figure coming in her direction whose features she didn't immediately recognize. As this stranger slowly sat, this guest of Kinni's, another guard stuck her head into the room.

"Fith 'teen men'nuts," he mumbled and closed the door.

Kinni struggled discretely and unnoticeably to see who it was and yet at the same time told herself that deep down she really didn't care. It had been ages and not a word from anyone except Big Mike. Ah, Big Mike. At that thought she wanted to cry once more for Devon and knew that she couldn't, not now, not in this setting, not with this stranger.

"You don't know me, huh?" the dark figure spoke sitting upright at one of the tables cloaked in the shade of sunlight.

Kinni knew the voice instantly. It was one she had heard her entire life and yet she still didn't have any desire to move in its direction.

"I guess I deserve that," the stranger said to Kinni sloughing back down in the chair.

The stranger's head hung down in shame and Kinni simply stood still, motionless staring at this figure as if it were dust. Then the figure rose to its feet and motioned toward Kinni. Kinni quickly took a few steps back as it approached.

"You don't want to hug your momma no more, huh?" Binta told her and reached out to embrace her daughter.

Binta placed Kinni right at her breast and wrapped her arms

around her with the strength and purposeful grip that only a mother has, loving and safe and warm. Kinni stood rigid but only for a few moments before the comfort and familiarity sank into the marrow of her bones. She couldn't resist even if she wanted to. She found herself sinking into that space that was specifically designed just for her. It was as if she were back at home safe and sound without any memory of Spofford. After several long moments, Binta released her and reached right up to wipe the tears from Kinni's eyes. Her kind hands against Kinni's bare skin sent a surprisingly comforting spark down Kinni's back. Standing there before her, Kinni blinked out a small hint of astonishment. She didn't recognize her at first realizing that the last time she saw her was in the hospital having her baby sister. Kinni felt guilty realizing that she wasn't quite sure whether she was happy to see her mom or not. She really couldn't determine what she was feeling at that moment with this sudden reappearance. The only thing she did know was that it didn't bring her peace. Binta pulled Kinni over to the table and they both sat down. Kinni sniffled the whole time but she didn't speak.

"Are they feeding you well?" Binta asked somewhat nervously.

Kinni sat still looking elsewhere never directly at Binta.

"Your friends…" Binta started but when she saw Kinni jerk away at the mentioning of friends, she paused.

Kinni couldn't think about any of her former life without riffing in excruciating inner heartache. She just couldn't bring herself to even wonder what anyone she loved was doing on the outside of this place she found herself merely existing in.

"Well…enough of that…I miss you," Binta said pulling something out of her handbag.

Then she placed a Snicker's chocolate bar on the table. At

that moment the guard peeked through the viewing window on the door and Kinni hesitated before picking it up.

"I thought you might have wanted some yogurt but Matar said…" Binta couldn't finish.

Kinni put the candy bar back down on the table and stood up. She never wanted to hear her father's nor Claudia's name ever again.

"Sorry, baby. I'm so sorry about everything," Binta tried to apologize.

Kinni stood by the window and looked out as if Binta wasn't even in the room anymore. Abruptly, the visitor's door swung open.

"Time," the guard said titling her head towards the main entrance.

Binta stood adjusting her clothes and walking slowly and obediently toward the door. She desperately wanted Kinni to turn and face her, to say good-bye or just to acknowledge that she was there with her in the room. She had traveled by train from Harlem to the Bronx and knew that her heart would break if she had to ride back knowing that her daughter refused to talk to her. She believed that this meeting would have gone differently. She hoped that they would even be the way they had been at home, above all, kind to one another and knowing that they were each other's support for life. She wanted Kinni to know that more than anything else she was there for her, that she could be a shoulder to lean on. Kinni didn't know that Binta had to be medicated and that the hospital finally had to induce labor. Kinni didn't know that Binta had some internal bleeding and that her baby sister had some distress coming out of the birth canal. Binta dragged her feet while exiting believing in her heart that Kinni would eventually reach out to her to say something that would lead them to reconcile. She longed for it but as she approached the doorway and a very exasperated guard, she knew that it wouldn't happen that day. She turned one last time before leaving willing Kinni to come to her. Kinni continued to stand motionless at the window and waited for the door to close firmly shut. She hadn't a shed of emotion in her body save loathing and unfortunately it spilled out onto her mom. However, once Kinni heard Binta's footsteps against the hallway tiles and knew now that Binta was indeed leaving her alone behind in this place, she turned and ran to the door. Once there she pounded upon it.

"Mom! Mom!" Kinni shouted.

Hearing this, Binta broke stride with the guard and ran back to the door. The other door opened behind Kinni and the guard stood waiting for Kinni to come out of the room.

"Come on, *crazy*, let's go," she said bored with it all.

Kinni pressed her hand against the visitor's door while Binta did the same on the other side.

"Mom!" Kinni cried, "Don't leave me, please! Don't leave me!"

"I'll be back, baby. Don't worry. I'll be…" Binta cried.

Kinni was pulled away from the door and shoved with pokes from a nightstick by the now impatient guard. Kinni didn't even notice the blows as she was being shuffled to the prison side door. She couldn't believe the avalanche of tears that gushed from her eyes. She missed her mom and as much as she would have loved to deny it, there wasn't anything she could do except wait patiently for her return.

Chapter Twenty-Six

What now? Kinni could not argue that this freshly new acquired feeling was toward something that she could only loosely describe as life. It was bubbling up inside her and sprouted like a weed into the most darkened areas of her psyche. A veil had been lifted at its corners and she was able to peek and see something that resembled sun and blue sky though her surroundings were still in fact gray and corroded with a film of dust covered over. Now, suddenly there seemed to be, albeit remote, nonetheless a kind of sort of reason if not for true living at least for waking and moving forward. Though it was just for a minute and somewhat shallow, she caught a glimpse of it irrefutably. She walked a little bit straighter and actually paid a little more attention to the goings on around her including those at session. Mrs. Gonzales still didn't pry but she was happy that Kinni had more than just murmured responses. They were now a full two to three actual, audible words, small, yes, but for Mrs. Gonzales, resounding progress. She would be sure to pad her curriculum vitae and say that this particular small step forward in the psychotherapy process occurred largely due to her expertise in dealing with troubled youth. In truth, the change in Kinni was brought on by the fact that she had made peace with herself and with her mom. She realized that they were still close and that if she had taken this long to come and see her, that it was largely due to the horrible circumstances at home. It was relatively easy to forgive her mom and to place all of her hatred instead on her father. He deserved all of her bitterness and all of her anger, not to mention her disgust. Every hell for her had its origins with her father and now with his new wife as well.

As time passed at Spofford, Kinni would linger over the conversations she had with her mom, savoring every last word that was spoken. They'd make very good use of their fifteen minute sessions. Binta brought a one million piece puzzle for them to try and although they'd have to start each time afresh, it didn't seem to bother either one of them. They just loved being together and Kinni slowly learned to accept her current circumstance with much more courage then she ever thought possible. She ate most of her dinner those early nights of visits for the first time since receiving that tragic letter from Big Mike, to Tas' dismay. Though she would never find anything to replace the hole in her heart left by Devon's demise, she was able to push aside her sullenness for longer intervals of time and focus somewhat more precisely on the present. Though the present held for her a cloudy, rather distorted reality, she was straining to see it with newer more pristine eyes. She knew that she would never love so deeply and completely again and that she would always look for him in every man with skin as dark and as beautiful as the midnight sky. This phase called acceptance was a tremendous struggle for her but she was trying her hardest to survive it now that she could see a small glimmer of life on her horizon. Binta promised to visit often and to bring treats for Kinni whenever she came. This promise was wonderfully and religiously kept. As a consequence, at Spofford, Kinni became the go-to girl for sweets. She had Chips Ahoy chocolate chip cookies, Snickers bars and rolls of red and black licorice Twisters, family-size bags of Smarties and an assortment of delicious sucking candy. Everyone, thanks to Kinni, had a goody stash tucked beneath their pillow or wedged between their bunk bed and the wall or any other hiding space they could find in order to keep prying eyes and thieving fingers at bay. Ms. Bing was not at all happy with this new found happiness of the girls and grew increasingly tired of confronting the girls who possessed a thick wade of something on the surface of or still being masticated within their mouths, especially Toothless. Toothless looked too scary whilst eating anything but especially that which she loved. She'd slobber brown chocolate as if it were grimy sludge slipping through her gums and between broken teeth routinely when she spoke, leaving virtually everyone running from her at even the remotest hint of her making a sound. Ms. Bing would slowly turn toward Kinni and squint first in horror and second in recognition that she was the cause of all of this. Ms. Bing also knew that the girls were allowed treats and as long as Binta's treasured gifts to her child were thoroughly inspected, there was little she could do about it. So instead, Ms. Bing had to actually set a time limit for chewing.

"From now on, I don't wanna' see no mouths movin' after sev'n o'clock, ya'll hear mey?" she shouted not at all like a question but more like a firm proclamation.

She knew that she couldn't really enforce this rule but at least in her mind she wouldn't from then on have to catch them in the act, which was just fine with her. Yes, for a long while at Spofford, things were pretty sweet for everyone thanks to Binta and Kinni. Suddenly, Kinni was the name on everybody's lips for something other than to call her crazy. She went from that nickname to any other name indicating pleasure, well-being, generosity and kindness. Momentarily, she was the star of that entire dreary place. Everyone respected her and would cater to her every need should one arise.

The love that began to flow through Spofford though directed towards sweets, self satisfaction and pleasure was nonetheless infectious. Kinni had an overwhelming sense of well-being that took her completely by surprise. As in Gambia, she began to see that one could survive under the worst possible conditions and actually begin to strive as if one's problems were shrinking and one's coping skills could not only shine through but, in fact, take their place. She'd awake somewhat good natured and that proved to be enough to sooth her soul and sustain her throughout her long, endlessly routine days at Spofford. She had even received time off of her sentence for something the Warden called "good behavior." Kinni had to laugh at that description of her low estimation of the place and therefore her silence. She marveled that she received such a reward for merely keeping her mouth shut, but she took her rewards where she could find them. It was doubtful that anyone really cared why she preferred silence all those many months besides, of course, Ms. Gonzales.

Before Kinni knew it, on yet another typically ordinary day, she was released from Spofford. She had not arrived there carrying any of her personal possessions thanks to her father therefore none were given upon leaving. She merely had the clothes on her back. There was no fanfare or ceremony either. No one even came to pick her up. The Warden shook her hand and told her to keep her nose clean. Other than that, the whole thing was fairly unremarkable. She had eaten dinner for the last time at Spofford the night before, showered and then went straight to bed. To her surprise, even she wasn't as excited as she thought she might be with the prospect of parting and refused to entertain questions about her sudden departure with anyone. Not that she wanted to stay, she just felt apprehensive about the whole thing. The entire night prior she thought it best to remain silent as it had worked in her favor so many times before. As promised, at ten in the morning that following day, the large, heavy metal prison front door closed shut behind her and the relief that she felt at its impressively loud clunking sound was so palatable that it could be seen slicing through the wintry air. She would miss no one, and nothing about the place she told herself. Same as with Gambia, she never wanted to step foot there again. She even swore that she would never willingly chose to visit the Bronx for any reason whatsoever other than to pass through. As the cold engulfed her, she would forever wish to freeze her tedious months at Spofford and hurl them through space to float into a black hole of void. At nine-fifty she had walked the long corridor waving mindlessly at faces that she realized she had barely really looked at during her long stay there. She shook hands with some of them and had even kissed a few good-byes, like Tas and Toothless. In return some had patted her on the back and wished her well. While others smirked and jeered at her willing that somehow there would be an overturn of her unexpected exodus and that she would have to stay after all. One could grow very cynical in a place like Spofford. Kinni knew this and just kept walking. She knew that those were the ones who didn't stand a chance of having their sentences reduced. Those were the ones who had decided to mouth off at the guards and to resist every instruction or correction. Kinni paid little or no attention to them. In fact, she was jaded to it all.

And once again she was free. She knew this sensation well. She had felt it many times before and with wisdom also knew how elusive and fleeting it really was. She couldn't get but so thrilled at all until Spofford was a mere speck out of the smudged back window of her taxi cab. Though even then, she would not allow herself the luxury of truly relaxing. She was uneasy, unwilling to trust what was right there before her very eyes. It was difficult for her to believe in anything. Everything that ever mattered to her seemed to be too slippery for her fingers to hold onto. She didn't think that she was being overly dramatic in her thinking either. She had proof to substantiate this claim. She had trusted in Devon and in his love for her only to have him disappear while her back was turned. He had died as if to say to her that true happiness wasn't something to be counted on in this life. She had trusted her mom and she too had deserted her leaving her abandoned in Gambia and then at Spofford without a word. Alas, she had even trusted her father once believing that flesh and blood meant that there could be also security or at the very least something called family responsibility. She had been wrong on all accounts. There was no more innocence left in her. She turned around again in the back seat of her taxi and saw only houses and cars and broken road. There wasn't even a trace of Spofford to wave at. So instead she faced forward and looked out the front window immediately realizing the symbolism of having also to face her future ahead. Alas, she had no idea what that all entailed. Binta had told her many, many times during their visits to come back home and stay. Kinni had no desire to do so, though she longed to see her brothers and sisters. She so wanted them to remember her as she once was even before Gambia when she was big sister protector. She knew that she had aged beyond recognition even though she was just sixteen. Her life had been accelerated somehow. She had been through incest rape, brutal betrayal, forced marriage, beatings, degrading servitude, courageous escape, blissful, heart-wrenching love, a life of crime including murder, more betrayal, death and imprisonment. What would her brothers and sisters think of her now? What could she, the eldest, teach them anymore? Would it be anything useful? Heck, she might begin by saying to them, 'Thank Allah, you're not me.' She would never, ever wish such a fate on anyone, not even an enemy. They, by their youth, had been spared the true nature of her father. His brutally was never fully experienced by any of them. They had only seen the after effects, mere glimpses really. She, however, had been swallowed up by it as if it were the under-toe of the mighty ocean. She had not seen the wave approaching and coming forward, not even a warning before being dragged under. She had tasted the saltiness of it and been hit upon the rocks below. It dawned on her that by Gambian law she was actually still married to Mandinka husband, that brutal beast who was a carbon copy of her father. She thought long and hard about how her mom managed with a man such as him for oh so many long years. She couldn't have been happy with such a man but at least her upbringing in Gambia had prepared her for a life of longing. Kinni's childhood however, there in Harlem, hadn't given her that kind of preparation. She had by five already begun believing in the American ways, and had stumbled into the Gambian alternative literally kicking and screaming. Had she known that by this stage in her life she would have experienced a lifetime of hurt and pain, she might have killed herself at age five. She knew that somehow she would have been better off had she done just that. Yet, she stood up, she stepped out of the taxi and breathed in the delicious Harlem morning air feeling the familiarity of it and welcoming it into her system. She was still very much alive, still young and still capable of accomplishing a great deal in her life. Sixteen was not fatal. Now she just had to make it through the day, while everything inside of her was telling her to run away. The thought of facing her family seemed daunting and perplexing. On the one hand, she missed them but on the other, she was ashamed of where she had just been and didn't want a slew of endless questions to mar their reunion. Yet, her love for them pushed her forward allowing her to continue on. Technically, she was legally mandated by the courts to go back home and live under the watchful eye of her parents. Tas told her that she only really had to stay for a week or so, until the parole officer forgot her name and replaced it with the next nameless ex-convict. Kinni figured that a week's time was about all she could reasonably take of her father and hoped she'd have secured alternate lodging by then.

She was at her front door and suddenly at a lost. She wasn't afraid or anything, just knew that the inquiry would choke and bind. She wasn't sure if she was ready for that. She was already sore with the many abysmal facts of her life and would rather not rehash or repeat any of them with her family. She reluctantly knocked twice and someone she barely recognized opened the door. It was her youngest brother, Jumu, now as tall as his father with a similar sounding voice.

"Who?" Jumu asked, obviously not recognizing Kinni either.

"It's me," Kinni said playfully forcing her way into the house.

He stepped aside puzzled and allowed her entry, though the entire time not really knowing what to say or do.

"Ma!" he yawned like a privileged rich boy, Kinni thought, 'Maaaa.'

Binta walked into the living room, and dropped the freshly washed clothes she'd been carrying in order to stretch her eager arms around Kinni. They hugged and danced for several minutes while the rest of the family gathered round to see what all the commotion was about.

"It's your sister! It's your sister," Binta joyfully shouted to Deebal, Jumu and Sara.

They each one by one hugged her but it was a cool reception. Unlike Binta's warm, engulfing, loving embrace, theirs was barely there, stingy. Kinni wanted to believe that it was merely her imagination and that they were just tired or preoccupied as young people tended to be. However, as the day wore on, there was little to no more contact from them towards her. She supposed that maybe they wanted her to reach out to them. So, she'd enter a room or two and sit on the bed making small talk. Only to find out that that's exactly what she received in return, very little talk. She mentioned this matter ever so delicately to Binta.

"Nah, girl. They're just in their own worlds half the time. Pay them no mind. They'll come around after dinner when the house quiets down. You'll see," she told her.

Kinni wanted to believe it though later on no change in their behavior surfaced. It was particularly interesting when Matar finally came home. Kinni thanked Allah that it was too late for them to get into an argument. What little he said to her was in a whisper. In fact, she got the distinct impression he was actively avoiding her altogether. She thanked God that she couldn't hear him but ever so faintly detected that his mannerisms seemed almost cordial. Binta was one of the only two people in the entire house who had anything pleasant to say to Kinni. The only other person was Kinni's littlest sister, Baby Bina, who was only nineteen months old. As a result, Kinni found herself conversing with the nearly two year old at great length.

"And how are you ta-day? And how are you ta-day? Yes, you are. Yes, you are. Yes, yes, you are," Kinni went on pressing Baby Bina's little stomach as if it were a button. The kid loved it and squealed with laughter. Kinni needed that. She needed to feel needed by her family. She realized that unlike before prison, now the love she so desperately needed, wasn't going to come easily.

"I guess you want your room back," Deebal asked her curtly over dinner while Binta was preoccupied feeding the baby.

"No," Kinni simply told him, "I may start looking for my own place," she muffled under her breath.

Binta did, however, manage to hear that part of the conversation.

"Kinni, you're gonna' continue with your school werk," Binta told her flatly, "...and I don't want to hear 'nother werd about it."

"But..." Kinni started.

"No argument. School comes first," and Binta wouldn't entertain a single word to the contrary.

Then Binta turned abruptly and exited the kitchen with Baby Bina in her arms. Kinni didn't bother following after as she might have done in the past trying to reason with her. She knew this wasn't the time or the place for such a discussion, particularly in light of her present situation. She didn't really have a solid leg to stand on. She was in the custody of her parents as if they were Spofford guards. Any wrong move, word, gesture and she could find herself back in a cell. She sat silently and ate as if she sort of agreed with Binta, as not to appear to have any opposing view in front of her siblings. Though secretly, she knew that it was only a matter of time before she'd be out on her own again enjoying life outside of the confines of her parents' roof. By the end of dinner, she was emotionally spent. She felt as if she was a guest in her own home and not a very welcome one at that. She couldn't even wash the dishes because her siblings didn't want her on the rotation.

"That's okay," Jumu said when she offered, "It's gonna' throw us off. Then I'll get the weekend."

"Yeah, Kinni, go and watch TV," Deebal told her.

Watching television would lead her into the living room with her father. Kinni decided against that and turned tail into the baby's room where she would be sleeping until other arrangements were made, so she was told.

She found Binta putting the baby to sleep when she entered the large closet turned baby room. Binta put Baby Bina on a pink all over flannel pajama suit complete with the feet attached. Baby Bina stretched and yawned and didn't seem to notice Kinni as she came in and sat on the only available chair, Baby Bina's little pink stool.

"I'll make something for you in a second," Binta told Kinni.

"Mom, you don't have to make a fuss on my account," Kinni informed her.

"A fuss, huh? For my oldest? I can make a fuss if I want to, okay," Binta notified Kinni with one hand on her hip.

As soon as Baby Bina's head touched her little pillow, she was fast asleep.

"Wow," Kinni said noticing Baby Bina's tiny snore.

"It's the breast milk, you know," Binta said with a wink, "Now, for my other baby."

Binta turned and held Kinni's face between her hands and kissed her forehead gently.

"I'm so happy right now. I've got my whole family under one roof again," Binta told Kinni.

Then she reached over and started making a pallet for Kinni.

"It's not much but we'll get things together later," Binta told her meaning that she would have to convince Kinni's brother to give up Kinni's old room. Both Kinni and Binta knew that that would take some doing.

"Mom, what ever happened to…" Kinni broke her question off with a few shoulder shrugs.

"Claudia?" Binta asked her knowing that that was the issue.

"Well, yeah. I thought that that would be a problem, you know, seeing as that's what got me…" Kinni broke off again not wanting to labor too long on the past.

"Well, one day…" Binta leaned on the chest of drawers, "…one day she just left. No, good-byes, no nothing."

Kinni was eyeing Binta strangely.

"Just like that?" Kinni asked.

"Just like that," Binta continued, "I know for a fact that Matar doesn't even know where she is."

Kinni stared at Binta curiously regarding the 'I know for a fact' part.

"Maybe she just wanted her citizen papers," Kinni suggested.

"Perhaps," Binta said with a wink and a smile.

Kinni thought that Binta was just trying to be brave for her sake. They both knew that the whole thing was a nightmare for her. Matar did unspeakable things to Binta and that was the way things were in their household even before the likes of Claudia. Kinni stood up and hugged her mom. She really didn't want to let go but they both could hear Matar's voice calling for Binta to get him something. It would have been a small miracle if he actually got off his privileged butt and got whatever he wanted for himself.

That first night home for Kinni was emotionally and physically hard. She slept on the floor between the baby's crib and the pink decorative flowered chest of drawers. Binta had laid down three old, worn blankets for her to sleep upon but the wooden floor was a solid force which relentlessly penetrated through the thin over washed down comforters and poked and prodded her back and shoulders. The protruding wooden floor nails and the baby's cries of discomfort for the wet diapers not to mention her morning colic, had rendered Kinni wide awake most of the night. So much so that she had a rough time seeing straight the next day. She tried to take it all in stride though believing that a prison cell with Tas was not exactly a picnic. Binta straight away noticed the changes in her. Kinni was much more subdued. One could say that she was much more accommodating and adaptable than her days prior to prison. She hated to think about it but ever since Kinni came back from Gambia there was this impenetrable sorrow that hovered over her wherever she went. Prison wasn't the type of place that would remove it, but Binta hoped that just possibly coming back home would. Kinni had always been helpful around the house, practically running it single-handedly from a young age but now she was exceptionably more so. Though it was only her first day back, it wasn't long before Binta viewed this behavior as a sign of avoidance of the real world. She enjoyed having her daughter around the house but knew that this was not healthy for her.

"Kinni, don't you want to visit your friends and see how they're doing?" Binta asked her one day, "Surely, you don't want to sit up 'neath you old momma all day, do you?"

Binta was being as gentle as she knew how.

"I'm all right, really," Kinni told her.

"No. No, you're not. You need to have a life. I appreciate your help and all but… Honey, go. Go out and enjoy yourself, 'kay," Binta pushed Kinni towards the door.

It had been three weeks since Kinni's return home and she had not so much as called Michelle, Saundra or Trese. She did think about them, though and wondered what they were up to but her curiosity hadn't led her to reach for the phone. Plus they hadn't bothered to reach out to her either. She had been at Spofford for an entire year and nine months and not once during that entire time had they bothered to call, write or even send word through Binta. Kinni really didn't know how she felt about her friends anymore. She wasn't quite sure if she indeed still had any. All she knew was that she couldn't express any of that to Binta.

"They're probably in school, you know. It's the middle of the day," Kinni enlightened Binta baiting that she stop this implore.

"Kinni, I want you to put some clothes on and go outside right now. You hear me, young lady?" Binta spoke gently and kindly but firmly.

Kinni couldn't deny her mom anything and this was such a simple request. She knew that her mom just wanted her to be happy. So, with that, she showered and put on some jeans and a t-shirt and ventured out. She was swimming in everything she owned and looked as if she was anorexic, but prison life was hard on her stomach and she refused to ask her father for a dime in order to buy new clothes. She'd have to wait until she got a job before she'd hopefully look like her old self again.

She opened the front door and sauntered down the steps and then paused there on the last one. 'Now where to first?' she thought. She hadn't a clue. Normally, she'd have been in class same as everyone else underage and penniless. If not there, then with Devon, but neither option was available to her now. She turned retreating back into the house, but that wasn't really and truly where she wanted to be either. As much as she loved being with her mom, there was always something around the house that needed fixing, cleaning, mending or with a new born anything and everything else. If there wasn't one thing there was another that pulled Binta in a million different directions and unlike Binta, Kinni didn't thrive on the busyness. Kinni was a typical teenager who loved just laying around the house with her feet up and listening to music or watching television. She turned back around and faced the street again. There she was once more, having to confront her future head on without the faintest idea of what to do or where to go. She was hungry suddenly, realizing that in some ways she was still on the prison clock. Spofford served lunch at twelve on the nose every day, according to her calculations, she was an hour late and her stomach was going into a kind of shock. Kinni leapt off the stoop and headed two blocks over to 125th Street. At first she felt as if she was in a strange land. She was definitely the foreigner, the alien and at times thought that everyone was staring at her. She tried not to feel out of place, after all, this was her home, her Harlem. Yet, it was a different home, a different Harlem than what she had remembered. For one, her low down father had a bustling restaurant right there on the main strip for all the world to see. She didn't think that a man like him deserved to have a profitable business. 'Life is so unfair,' she thought. Then she turned to walk in the opposite direction. At least she didn't have to see it or him or any of the foolish people who obviously didn't know where his hands might have been before serving them food. There were more clothing stores around than she remembered, mostly fashion. She walked into K & G Clothes and started looking through two racks towards the very front of the store, then remembered that she didn't have any money and therefore turned back around and left. 'I have to get a job,' she thought. Everything she saw she wanted, but asking either of her parents for money was a slim to none option. Besides, she never wanted to see her father again let alone ask him for money. She walked away from the clothing and music stores feeling terribly disappointed. Then she thought about possibly going over to the school and asking one of her friends to cut a class or two so they could hang out but somehow she just couldn't find the courage. She didn't want to be pitied or to be looked on as an ex-con. She glanced up the block in the direction of her school. It seemed like such a long time ago that she'd walked these same streets to its doors. She was thankful that Binta graciously told her she deserved this week off. As she stared and thought about the past, she noticed a Barnes & Noble bookstore at the corner. She couldn't remember if she ever saw it there before. It might have been there the whole time but she'd been busy going further uptown to notice. She walked over and went inside. There were books by Black authors everywhere and patrons were actually allowed to take one from the shelves and sit in the back and read for hours, which was exactly what she did. It didn't much matter what she chose, from Zane to Dr. Miles Munroe. She loved to read anything and everything. She swore one day that she would even pen her own tragic story. Though she couldn't imagine where she'd begin. As she read, she let her thoughts drift elsewhere. It was too painful to dwell on things gone by. Besides, she preferred being caught up in someone's fictional life rather than her own. While reading, it took her mind off of everything including her hunger.

CHAPTER TWENTY-SEVEN

As she stepped out onto the street two hours later, she noticed a sidewalk book stand just a few yards away from Barnes & Noble's. It too had some of the same books that Barnes & Noble was carrying prominently displayed as if that was the very definition of free market. Out of curiosity Kinni ventured over. She decided to price compare just in case she suddenly hit the Lottery or fell into some money somehow, someway. When she got a little closer, she had to laugh. The arrangement was almost exactly the same as the Barnes & Noble window. Although her head was down admiring the many covers and descriptions, Kinni could feel the vendor's eyes upon her. She glanced up ever so nonchalantly. A young man, possibly early twenties, thin as a nail but handsome in his own way smiled at her.

"You like to read, huh?" he asked and Kinni detected some kind of accent, African perhaps.

She wasn't impressed. She had been there and done that.

"Yeah," she mumbled unsure whether he was flirting or not and not really caring.

"Me too," he grinned.

"Hum," she shrugged in a vague acknowledgement that he was speaking to her.

Then she picked up a book entitled, <u>Black Slave-owners: Free Black Slave Masters in South Carolina, 1790-1860</u>, by Larry Koger.

"Most people don't know that, you know," he told her referring to the subject matter of the book.

"Well, it's not like they teach it in school," she offered

wondering if he even knew what he was talking about.

The vendor merely eyed her almost as if he were impressed.

"Speaking of which, why aren't you in school?" he pointedly asked.

Kinni wanted to tell him to mind his own business at that point but something deep inside of her was telling her to be civil.

"I'm getting my G.E.D.," she lied.

She didn't know why she lied to this complete stranger other than the fact that she knew that it sounded better than saying she was an ex-convict out of work, out of school, just plain out. Though when she was running for Devon, engaging in conversations about prison life was like talking about one's Alma-Mata. Some would actually say, "Yeah, man, I learned how to really kick ass in Rikers," or "State taught me how to hide my piece." Kinni had heard it all. She didn't think that she had learned anything, however, from Spofford, except how to feel like she was in an alternate universe. She had to say that Spofford took her totally by surprise. Before Spofford, she remembered being happy for the first time in her entire life other than those fleeting moments with Binta, playing tag around the house. She loved Devon. She loved the freedom of what having a few dollars in her pockets meant. She loved going to the store and being able to purchase whatever she wanted or better yet having her man insist on buying those things for her. She loved being taken care of and the simple pleasure of being treated like a lady. It had all begun so quickly and had ended even quicker. Who could have predicted that it would have been so short lived? It wasn't even a complete year and then just like that, poof, it was gone.

"Would you like to read that? It's an awfully big book for such a little girl," he flirted, definitely a flirt.

"I'm…" 'broke,' she started to tell him but felt ashamed in

admitting that.

"On the house," he said as if reading her mind.

She put the book underneath her arm and thanked him.

"You're welcome. Do come again," he smiled.

Kinni nodded and trotted down the street waving a tightfisted good-bye at her benefactor. Once she was a block or so away from him, she shook her head in annoyance. She decided that he was not as charming as Devon. No one could be. She practically felt insulted that he would even try.

Back home, Kinni, unfortunately, walked straight into the middle of another one of her parent's arguments. Though, this one was tantamount to a mild hail storm, Matar was slinging insults and accusations at Binta with piss and vinegar and bitter squall as usual. While Binta sounded polite and steady and calm. It was the most Kinni had heard from her father in all the time she had been back. Though curious at his previous silences, she was never concerned enough to inquire. She had just enjoyed the peace and quiet of the house, that was up until this day.

"What are you talking about, Matar?" Binta asked him bluntly.

"Nothing! Nothing!" he responded in a blinding rage because Binta wasn't following his train of thought, "This is my house. My house!" he shouted.

"Of course, this is your house, but..." she tried.

"I say and do what I like to do! You don't tell me how to act in my house," Matar barked.

"Of course, Matar. Of course. But what did I say?" Binta asked innocently as not to make him even more upset than he already was.

Matar stomped around the kitchen huffing like a wild boar.

Kinni thought he was insane and just wanted him to go back to his mute state.

"Don't talk that way to me! Don't you dare," he snapped and drew back his fist as if he would hit her in the face.

"Ma-tar," Binta spoke, calmly, "Now, Ma-tar, what is this all about?" she asked.

Matar continued to stomp and yell and taunt her with every gesture.

"I don't like that! I don't like the way you're talking to me like that in my own house! This is my house, dammit! My house! My gotdammit house!" he hollered again and again, "My house!"

Kinni wanted desperately to laugh when she saw Binta exiting the kitchen with a peculiar strained look upon her face. It was as if there was a huge question mark atop her head. Kinni could tell that Binta honestly and sincerely had no idea what he was ranting and raving about. Kinni tip-toed pass the kitchen and disappeared into Baby Bina's room. She didn't want to be the next one Matar attacked for no apparent reason. 'Out of sight, out of mind,' she thought. Unfortunately for Binta, Matar was not quite through with her or his tirade. He followed her out into the living room and continued his, for lack of a better word, speech.

"Who do you think you are talking to? I know you're not talking to me like that? This is my house! My house!" he kept yelling.

Kinni held back a laugh. Matar really sounded more and more like an overgrown child to her. She wondered why she hadn't noticed that before but there he was throwing a tantrum like a two-year-old. She swore Baby Bina had more common sense than him. 'Why did he constantly insist on telling Binta that this was his house?' Kinni wondered, 'Wasn't that a given?'

Not one soul in the house had a penny to their name. That was the Gambian way. The man shall provide. It was extremely doubtful whether Binta knew what the house note was or how much the utilities bills were or anything concerning the upkeep of the house besides the cooking and cleaning. Matar preferred to have everyone come to him for their provisions. Then he'd sit there and make them wait while he decided whether their requests were valid or not. It always sickened Kinni to have to ask him for anything. She knew that she had to get a job and to get out of that house as soon as humanly possible.

"This is mine! You hear me? Everything that comes to this house is mine! Mine!" he continued.

Kinni could see her father pushing something into Binta's face. She couldn't really make out what it was but whatever it was he had gone ballistic over her touching it.

"Matar, I didn't touch anything of yours," Binta tried.

Then Matar swung at Binta with the back of his hand. Next thing, Kinni could hear Binta tumbling down onto the floor. Kinni sprung into action, sprinting out of Baby Bina's room like lightening but before she could put her hands around Matar's shoulders to yank him down, he was already exiting through the front door. Kinni's arms were still in mid air reaching for his back at the slamming of it.

"Are you all right? Are you all right?" Kinni turned immediately asking Binta and panicking as she knelt down to pick her back up.

There was something different in the way Binta reached out for the couch behind her Kinni noticed. She was older now and riffing in pain. She put practically all of her weight on Kinni's arm in order to hoist herself up. Kinni saw the change in her instantly. She was no longer able to recover so quickly from Matar's malice. It had taken its toll on her body which seemed to be run down to a perceptible halt.

"Mom?" Kinni asked Binta trying to get her attention.

Binta was lost somewhere, staring around the room in anguish.

"Mom?" Kinni repeated placing her hand upon Binta's hand, gently stroking it.

Binta didn't turn to face her. She was in too much pain both physically and mentally and didn't want Kinni to worry.

"Mom, you're scaring me," Kinni confessed.

"I'm…I'm….all right…" Binta told her, head bowed and eyes filled with tears of remorse.

Kinni didn't believe her and held on tightly to her hand to make sure that Binta wouldn't tilt right off the sofa. Binta looked so frail to Kinni, not like her usually strong self.

"What was it about this time, mom?" Kinni ever so gently probed.

Binta leaned back on the chair easily and comfortably. Kinni could see that the wheels were churning in her brain and that she was steadily trying to discover the truth about it herself.

"He just came in yelling at you just like that?" Kinni asked bewilderedly.

"No," Binta finally spoke, "No."

"I just don't understand him," Kinni shook her head in disgust.

Binta just sat on the sofa nodding her head as if she agreed with Kinni. She was still trying to put the pieces together herself.

"What happened? Did anything happen?" Kinni continued.

Binta just shook her head now seeming too confused about the whole thing to respond. Matar hit with the full weight of his body. Now that they both were getting older, Matar's hand across her face didn't sting like it used to. Now it was more like a freight train slamming into her scull. Binta realized that she was actually dizzy when her knees buckled and her legs gave way beneath her body. He had whacked her with his knuckles right at the temple, near her eye.

"Oh, my God!" Kinni shrieked staring at her mom.

"What?" Binta asked standing and looking in the mirror above the couch following the direction of Kinni's blanched stare.

"You're turning blue, mom. That doesn't look good," Kinni told her.

Binta was horrified when she saw the damage that Matar had done. Kinni was right. There was a thick blackest discoloration pressing across the entire right side of Binta's cheek. Binta swayed as she looked at the enormity of it.

"You all right, mom?" Kinni caught her on the way back down to the couch.

Binta fell onto it with a crash.

"Maybe we should go to the hospital. You don't look all right, mom. You're scaring me," Kinni confessed practically in tears.

"Get me some ice, will you, baby?" Binta managed to ask Kinni.

Kinni obeyed without question but she watched Binta the whole time as if she might collapse at any moment. Kinni wasn't sure what was happening to her and didn't want to leave her alone for even a second. She went into the kitchen and threw ice cubes into a dry dish rag then raced back into the living room. When she walked back in, Binta was stretched out, feet atop the arm rest, reposed, trying to relax.

"I just need some time to think is all," Binta said trying to reassure Kinni that everything was fine.

Kinni knew better than that though. It was merely her

mother's way of denying herself and thinking only of others. Kinni was determined to make sure that Binta recovered from this latest episode of horror caused by none other than her father. It was so typical of him to inflict grief on others and then run away like a scared little rabbit.

"Kinni, baby. I just need to close my eyes for a second. Just for a second," she said reaching out for the ice pack and placing it on the side of her face.

She winced when the cold remedy touched her sore skin.

"Mom, you are not all right. Why don't we just go to the hospital and let someone take a look at that. God!" Kinni begged.

It was to no avail. Binta closed her eyes and began drifting off to sleep. Kinni would watch over her all night if she had to in order to make sure she was still breathing. She had never seen her mother suffer so. This was the first time she had ever imagined that there might one day be a life without her. 'I'll kill him,' Kinni thought, 'I'll kill him dead,' Kinni wished that she had entered the living room just as her father was swinging at her mom. She would have taken a knife from the kitchen and simply stabbed him to death. Her life didn't matter anymore, all that mattered was that she couldn't live without Binta.

Meanwhile, Matar had stormed back to his restaurant, stomped into his office and shut the door tight behind him. Then he roared to everyone within earshot that he did not wish to be disturbed. He wouldn't get an argument from anyone there. His entire floor staff of three people tried not to stare. They knew him as well as Binta and Kinni and never, ever confronted him with anything that wasn't absolutely necessary. They would never think to ask him if he needed help of any kind, especially now as he practically pushed them all out of his way in a huff.

Then he latched his office door. As he sat at his desk fuming, he thought, 'She's my wife! My wife! She can't just do this to me! To me!' he inwardly screamed, hands shaky and sweaty. Then he reached down deep into his pocket and pulled out a single sheet of paper, a letter. 'Who does she think she is?' he pondered but all of his anger was not about poor, simple Binta, but rather, about Claudia.

Chapter Twenty-Eight

Kinni beat the salespeople there that morning. She had managed to get up early despite all of the tossing and turning that night. She wanted to make a good impression and had asked her mom if she could borrow some of her clothes. Binta couldn't deny her daughter anything and even ironed them for her that morning. She gave her a brown pleated skirt and a white cotton blouse. Though they were two sizes too big for Kinni and made her look like she was a third grader, they looked better than anything else she owned. Binta thought she was finally going to school. Kinni stood patiently though she had been waiting for over an hour already. She refused to leave until she put in her request. She would sweep the floors, clean the toilets, arrange any and every bit of inventory in the store so long as they paid her whatsoever they decided was fair. 'Something was better than nothing,' she thought. She just had to get a job. She had to get out of her father's house. Either she'd work for them or McDonalds or whosoever was hiring young people. She just couldn't live in her father's house another minute, not with him flying off the handle like a madman whenever the mood struck him. The unpredictability of his tirades was beginning to unnerve her. She had stayed awake all night only closing her eyes and nodding off in short intervals while every ten to fifteen minutes checking on Binta to make sure that she was all right. She continually had this nightmare where she saw Binta's black and blue rapidly spreading over her entire face and then hardening and turning into stone. She'd awake sticky from perspiration and panicked at the mere thought of it. Even when she went to check on her, still lying on the couch where she'd left her, Binta looked as if she were dead. Kinni would tip-toe in a hurried rush over to her and literally place her shaking hand over Binta's nose until she felt the warmth of an exhale. She really didn't think it possible to hate her father even more than she already had but alas she did. She loathed him so much that even the thought of him caused her angst. The bacon and eggs that she had for breakfast was churning in her stomach when Khadyjah Jones, Trainee Day Manager, walked over and unlocked and rolled up the security gate. Kinni had frequented the store so much that they had become like old friends by now.

"Hey, KJ," Kinni greeted her.

"Hey, KB. What are you doing here so early?" Khadyjah asked with a smile, "No one loves reading that much."

"Well...well...I needed to talk to you," Kinni told her.

"Yeah, what 'bout?" Khadyjah asked while bringing in the morning paper that was lying on the ground and turning on all the store lights.

"Well, I know that I'm young and all and that I don't have any experience and all and that I didn't finish high school yet and all and that..." Kinni rambled while instantly realizing the obvious flaws in her implore.

"Yes?" Khadyjah politely interrupted.

"Well..." Kinni hesitantly continued.

Kinni thought this would have gone a little more smoothly than it was going.

"Well, KJ, I mean Miss Khadyjah..." she decided to be a bit more formal in order to make up for her stumbling attempts.

"You wanna job, right?" Khadyjah jumped right in and asked thinking she might spare Kinni any further embarrassment.

"Well...yes," Kinni answered sheepishly.

"How old are you anyway?" Khadyjah asked while putting a

pot of coffee on.

"Sixteen, be seventeen in August," Kinni answered hoping the 'seventeen' would make her look a little older than her outfit, which was hopeless she realized.

"Let me ask you something?" Khadyjah queried indicating that a question of a personal nature was coming next.

"Yes," Kinni answered giving her permission though she hoped it was something that wouldn't cause her further awkwardness.

"Why aren't you in school? I mean, not that I mind, but you're always hanging around here and I just think that maybe you might want to be at school instead of this dreary place. I mean, I have to be here. I need books, tuition money, and rent, but you…" she asked, "Why are you here?"

"Well, I'm not in school right now but one of these days I'm gonna' go back, you know, get my degree and do something with my life," Kinni told her wanting so desperately to believe it herself.

"Well, I figured there was more to you than just hanging out at a book store," Khadyjah said with a gentle smile not wanting to offend her.

Then she poured them both a cup of coffee and started fixing hers up with at least six packets of pure sugar. Kinni followed suit really just to see how it would taste. Then she thought about what she had just told Khadyjah. She realized what little thought she had given her own future. Every single person who'd ask her that question would receive a different answer. In truth, she was a weed blowing in the wind, running away from her father's wrath and her mom's sorrow, not to mention her own.

"You know, Kinni, you have to start thinking about these things, if not right now, sometime. You can't let the world define you. I'm just saying," Khadyjah spoke but could see that Kinni was only partially listening. She wasn't sure if she was merely contemplating her words of wisdom or if she was bored by them. At any rate she said what she felt was her responsibility as the elder although she was no more than five years Kinni's senior. Kinni put her head down very much mulling over Khadyjah's sentiments. If only she knew what to do with them though? Her entire life had been simply about survival and not much about what comes after. As far as she was concerned, nothing comes after.

"Where do you go to school?" Kinni asked.

"I'm at Hunter…mathematics. I know. I know. Dull, right?" Khadyjah laughed.

Yet it didn't sound funny to Kinni. At least Khadyjah was doing something with her life.

"So, you wanna work here, huh?"

"If there's…yes…Yes, I do," Kinni finally answered firmly.

Khadyjah pulled two muffins from the cake display and dropped them onto an empty plastic plate. She slid the plate towards Kinni down the long counter.

"You can have the chocolate or the banana. I like them both," she told her.

Kinni wasn't really hungry but started in on the banana to be polite.

"Well, I guess I could use some help around here. Junior doesn't clean worth a damn. You know, the way I'm used to anyhow."

She was referring to the night janitor, Junior Allen. He was a decent enough fellow but all he wanted to do was chat with the patrons, especially those of a female persuasion. Kinni often heard him boasting about his many Jamaican exploits. Apparently, he was a big shot there and everybody just loved him and worshipped the ground he walked on. Though here in

America, Kinni couldn't see to look at him, why so many women were enamored by him. Kinni just saw a short, round portly man with an ego that seemed to fit around him like an oversized cape. She was not impressed.

"Yeah, I know what you mean," Kinni agreed.

She liked things clean too. Though, she wasn't always happy about being the one doing the cleaning. She figured that at least at Barnes & Noble, she would get paid for doing it.

"Well?" Kinni asked.

"Well. Yes. Yes, but I have to get it cleared with my boss, you know. No one's the big boss around here. We all have someone to answer to, you know," said Khadyjah with a chuckle.

Then they both sat silently for a moment looking out of the store front window as people hurried by to their several destinations. Kinni would have loved to just sit there all day. She didn't look forward to going back home having to explain to her mom that she wasn't actually going back to school just yet but that she got a job instead. She knew that that was not going to go over well. Even her father would have something to say about that. Not that he sincerely cared. He was simply anti Kinni. She, on the other hand, was elated and couldn't wait. She would finally have her own money again. It would be a far cry from the thousands per day that she had grown fairly accustomed to but she couldn't bring herself to be a runner again without Devon. In truth, Devon was the appeal to that type of lifestyle not the money. At the thought of Devon she felt the tears welling up in her eyes before she could stop them.

"You're not gonna' start crying about working here, are you?"

"No. No. It's nothing like that," Kinni wiped her face and tried to recover quickly.

She hated the fact that everything she felt caused her eyes to moisten up.

"Look, I promise you that I will do everything I can to help you out. I know we don't know each other that well but my word is solid. You hear me?" Khadyjah said smiling warmly while sipping coffee and chewing the rich chocolate muffin.

Kinni exited out of Barnes & Noble with her head held high, whilst feeling a little disappointed. She would have preferred to have left with a job firmly in her grasp. She didn't like the whole idea of waiting for this one to call that one in order to give her a yes or no answer. 'And how long was all of that going to take?' she asked herself. She wanted to be able to tell her mom that although she wasn't in school she could at least contribute something to the household. Money was always needed. She raised her head from her thoughts and could see the Black book's vendor setting up at the corner again. She admired the fact that he was an early riser too but side stepped around a mailbox to go unnoticed. She had already thanked him for the book and didn't want to strike up a conversation about it. Especially since she had tossed it onto Baby Bina's little two foot tall desk and hadn't thought about it since. Plus, she was tired and wanted to see if she could catch up on some much needed sleep.

"Hey, you!" he shouted out to her.

Too late, Kinni reluctantly turned to see the vendor grinning, arms filled with a stack of books. She really hoped that all he wanted was a quick hello, how are you and then he would send her on her way.

"How's it going?" he asked luring her over to him with a head nod.

Kinni felt a little obligated to at least go over and be courteous. She berated herself for taking gifts from strangers, a momentary action, a lifetime of debt. Now, she had to spend a minimum of ten minutes with him each time she passed by.

"Hey," she managed all the while wanting to keep things brief.

"Hey, what do you think of my display, seeing how you're always up in B&N. Is theirs better than mine?" he asked somewhat smugly.

Kinni wanted to run away. She could tell that he wanted a lengthy chat.

"It's fine. I guess," she answered barely audible.

He reached around and pulled some more books out of the back of his van.

"I'm just asking because you seem like you would know," he continued.

Kinni felt a headache coming on not to mention a yawn.

"Most of these people just throw everything they have on the table without even thinking about what's hot and what's selling. That's why I'm asking because my customers know better than I do what they like. Know what I'm sayin'?" he shrugged.

Kinni nodded in agreement with what little strength she had left. She was patiently waiting for the part in the conversation when his lips would stop moving and she could gracefully move on. By the looks of things that seemed to be no time soon.

"Could you lay those over there for me?" he asked indicating that he needed her help while he retreated back into his van and returned with some more books.

Kinni, though languidly, placed the books onto the cloth table. She instinctively placed the children's book in a circle and the adult books flat one partially atop another.

"Wow!" he shouted turning and seeing what she had done, "I like that!"

Kinni hadn't a clue as to what he was referring to. He walked around the table and looked at her arrangements from the customer side.

"You have some skills. I should hire you to help me!" he shouted joyfully.

Kinni's ears perked up slightly at the word 'hire.'

"I'm telling you I never would have thought to place them this way but that's exactly how they should be, you know?" he shrugged.

Kinni again nodded and wondered if he was serious about the whole hire thing or was he just saying that.

"So how 'bout it?" he asked her trying to place the remaining books on the table the way Kinni had fashioned the others.

He wasn't quite doing it as nicely as she and Kinni politely reached over him and fixed his semi-circle of children's books. They looked more like a square when he was done.

"See, it needs a woman's touch. How 'bout it?" he asked Kinni again.

Kinni still wasn't quite sure if he was making her a sound offer.

"You gonna dis me like dat, huh?" he asked with a little smile at the corner of his mouth.

"Huh?" Kinni asked squinting at him as if he had two heads.

"Do you want a job? I'm real easy to work with and I will pay you in cash," he said.

"Cash," she repeated.

"Cold cash."

Kinni couldn't deny that she liked those words, 'cold cash.' Even he was looking better and better to her now that he had mentioned money. As she looked into his dark brown eyes she had to admit that he had something going for him. She could see the outline of a muscular toned body beneath his partially opened shirt. There was definitely some definition of a well sculpted torso, flex of hair sprouting up and a slight sheen from perspiration. She thought she would die when he caught her staring.

"So, what do you think?" he asked.

She hoped that he meant about the job and not about his physique.

"How much?" Kinni asked being shrewd about this offer although knowing she didn't have much of a choice.

She knew that she couldn't depend on Barnes & Noble because she didn't really have any experience and she hadn't even completed her education. Khadyjah liked her and all but could she count on her, probably by the book, supervisor? She knew that it wasn't something she could bank on coming through. However, this job offer was guaranteed. Heck, it was practically being handed to her. Plus, she figured she could make her own hours this way too. She thought about those rainy days when she wouldn't even have to get out of bed. All in all, it seemed like the right thing to do.

"Okay, so you're interested, huh?" he asked.

Again, she hoped he meant about the job.

"May-be. How much?"

"Let's say...every book you sell, I'll give you a commission on it," he bargained.

"How much?"

"What's fair?"

"I don't know. You're the book expert, not me."

"I'm not an expert but okay...how about twenty-five percent of my commission. I mean, I've got to make some money too," he said with a wink.

Kinni thought about this for a moment.

"Hey, why do you need me anyway? Wouldn't you want to make all the commission?" she asked with a serious concern.

She wanted to make sure that he wasn't trying to get a

girlfriend out of the deal. She wanted their business relationship to be just that – business.

"Look, I'm here everyday all by myself and it's hard. Man, can't even go do his business, you know what I'm sayin'? Sometime even I need a break," he said.

"Yeah, I guess," Kinni agreed.

She had wondered about how street vendors spent all day everyday out on the street without the use of a toilet and running water. 'Well,' she thought, 'I'm about to find out, aren't I?' She looked forward to it too. She was tired of hanging around her father's house and feeling helpless. She was about to embark on some honest to goodness independence.

CHAPTER TWENTY-NINE

He had eaten breakfast in absolute silence and had walked out of the house without making the slightest sound that would draw attention. The soles of his shoes didn't squeak and the friction of one pant leg rubbing against the other barely swooshed. He was by all accounts completely mute - again. He just couldn't stop thinking about it. All day, moment by moment it practically overshadowed his normally transparent thinking. It was definitely a dark cloud, a black hole and an endless void all at the same time. In fact, his mind had been in utter turmoil ever since. If only he could turn back the tides of time and rearrange everything that had transpired that particular day. Now that he had time nothing but painstaking time to ponder it. It had been an absolutely fretful day. Had he known it was going to be the last time that he would lay eyes on his unfortunately unforgettable wife, he would have approached things much more differently. Maybe he wouldn't have said some of the things that now looking back on them were words filled with fire. Evidently, he had lit a veritable flame underneath her. He had pushed her to the brink. He had inadvertently touched some dormant part of her that, once awakened, threatened to unleash an avalanche of longings. He had, unbeknownst to him at the time, of course, forced her hand in some awful way that was now apparently unalterable. He regrettably didn't know anything about it. He now sincerely wished he had. He hadn't a clue that one such as she could learn a whole new way of thinking and behaving so quickly and efficiently. Yes, he had underestimated American television, newspaper and the like. It had taken Binta a long time before she even began to show signs of standing up for herself. Yet even she wouldn't have dared to answer back to him nor second-guess any of his decisions even to this day. When they were first married, he was assured of her submission and loyalty through thick or thin. It was the Gambian way. Sure, she had witnessed American woman twisting and bending their husband's words around to favor themselves but Binta hadn't succumbed to this manipulative mistress. She was docile while he beat her and quiet when he forced himself upon her. Of course with the latter, he counted those unfortunate times as moments of weakness. He considered it his right as a man and his duty as a Gambian to have heirs. Though he never ever wanted to have any with Binta, he justified the first mistake, Kinni, and the last one, Bina, thusly. Kinni occurred soon after they arrived in this strange land called America and with Bina he was filled with his love for another and couldn't possibly be responsible for his actions.

There he was literally bursting at the seams and wantonly ready for his wife, the real one, the right one. He had come home early that afternoon knowing that she would be waiting for him. They hadn't been together for some sixteen years. He just assumed this was obvious. They were like kids again except this time he could act on all the pent up feelings he had as a young boy. He opened the door to their room and there she was sitting atop the bed beautiful and naked, freshly showered and lusciously inviting. He could barely control himself. He had only been thinking of her all day in all the intimate ways that they had been just that night prior. There was nothing she wouldn't do for or to him and that excited him beyond strength and vision. He didn't even bother to take anything off before jumping on top of her warm body and going at it with great gusto. It was funny now looking back he hadn't noticed anything different in her demeanor. In fact, she moaned louder than she had at other times but he just thought that the early evening surprise was as tantalizing for her as it was for him. Her kisses were smooth but passionate as ever. Her tender nibbles against his hot skin, just as cool and as soft as a baby's bottom. Yes, he enjoyed himself so much that afternoon that he went there twice. She rolled underneath him and panted for air like a woman immersed in happiness, satiated and comforted by her man. She kept repeating his name over and over again and this, of course, drove him on like a wild teenager.

"Ma-tar. Ma-tar. Ma-tar! Ma-tar! Ma-tar! Ma-tar! Ma-tar!"

As he came the second time, her words rattled out like a machine gun firing and her breath quickened, sweat glistening off her belly gluing him and her together. He loved her. It was simple. It was the intrinsic thing that had actually defined him for years. He and Claudia would wed and they would live happily ever after.

"The divorce rate in this country is disgusting," she uttered as if preoccupied in thought.

At the time, this statement didn't faze Matar in the least.

"Yeah," he grunted.

He was preoccupied in thought as well, perfectly contented with his very existence. He rested completely on the soft Downy fresh pillows, thanks to Binta, holding onto himself with his right hand allowing the sensation of their lovemaking to precipitate slowly out. It was tantamount to a balloon deflating. He could still hear in his minds eye his name being chanted and cheered, 'Ma-tar. Ma-tar! Ma-tar! Ma-tar! Ma-tar! Ma-tar!' Yes, he was a pig in slop, unaware of the wheels that were churning within his lady love's head.

"I heard it on Good Morning America and I just couldn't

believe it."

Matar wasn't really paying attention. He knew that he had it good, a woman to wash and clean and raise children and a woman to do what was necessary for a man to be a man. He pulled Claudia towards him and placed her head gently on his other arm. He liked the feel of her breast poking at his side and her smooth thigh rubbing up against his. He was a blessed man who didn't have to worry about such things as divorce rates and the like.

"Poor bastards!" he told her with a sloppy grin.

He was not referring, of course, to himself. He was talking about the mindless array of losers who couldn't keep their households together for any respectable length of time. He hadn't much respect for Americans anyhow after all they'd come to his restaurant, asking a bunch of inane questions about Gambian cuisine, culture and customs. To which he'd answer in his best mannered way, because after all they paid for their meals in cash. As always, the gentleman, he never let on that he believed his culture superior to theirs. Instead he'd play up the whole history of Black people being descendants of kings and queens. He wasn't referring to them, naturally. They were descendants of slaves and therefore possessed the slave mentality. The fact that most of his own family still lived in mud huts equipped with cisterns out back, where women were castrated after toddler hood and men could marry as many women as they could reasonably afford was never mentioned. He would always neglect to tell them that much information in case their larger than life image of him should then be diminished in any way, of course. Besides he was the owner of his establishment. They had to come to him and not the other way around. He had the real power in this equation. They were mere clientele who now on top of quibbling over his entrée prices had the nerve to ask him for favors. Some would approach him seeking the use of his restaurant as a nightclub. "You won't have to worry about a thing," they'd tell him, "We'll supply the liquor and the women." The women! He'd grin in their faces all the while thinking that they were lazy and shiftless just desiring to use his good name and prominence for their own lustful cavorting and greed. He'd tell them that he would think about it and then never get back to them. This way he always appeared somewhat approachable, like the caring neighborhood businessman who sincerely thought about the needs of his community. He thought about them all right. He thought they were dirty rotten leaches and wished they would get off their assets and open up their own businesses just like he had. He'd neglect to tell them that he came to America with a small fortune that was handed to him during his wedding. Years ago when he came to America, he possessed over fifty thousand dollars, to which he immediately put into a brownstone in Harlem. His down payment in 1987 was only twenty thousand dollars. He rented the first floor apartment for $450 per month, which was a lot of money then, to an elderly man named, Otis Rosenberg. Everyone thought he was Jewish including Matar until the day of the lease signing when a six foot two, seventy-year-old Floridian man showed up. He quietly told Matar that there was a lot of interracial marrying in his family. This was said in order to get Matar to close his mouth, ajar and shocked at seeing what looked like a Black man standing before him but he still wasn't quite sure. Otis, himself, was fair enough to pass for Caucasian or at the very least a light-skinned Hispanic. He preferred not to talk about any of it and when asked his nationality, aggravated he'd respond, "Black," as if he had resolutely chosen that side of the racial divide. He was an old man with an intriguing past and that made any further discussion with strangers impossible.

Mr. Otis Rosenberg paid his rent every month in cash and that was all Matar really cared to know about the old man. During that time, he also rented two rooms upstairs to college students. He informed their parents that he would be like a father to them, to which their worried minds believed. In truth, Matar exclusively leased to medical and law students thinking that they wouldn't have much time for anything else besides studying. He was right and rarely saw or heard a peep out of any of them. He charged their parents, who were lease guarantors, a whopping $200 per week per room. That price was four times the market value at the time. Matar had his mortgage paid each month and his accountant wasn't quite sure how he was doing it. Matar never made a full disclosure. It hadn't occurred to Matar not once that his money came from Americans whether they were renters or diners or even the owner who sold him his property.

"Baby, what do you think?" Claudia asked Matar referring to the issue of divorce.

"It's plain and simple women don't know how to treat their man. They act like the man's the wife," Matar responded bluntly.

Then he looked down at Claudia's radiant body and swelled with pride. 'This was the life,' he thought. There wasn't anything that he wouldn't do for this woman. He couldn't express how hard it had been for him when he was forced to do the once upon a time unthinkable – marrying another woman, Binta. He secretly wished that he would have died before the wedding ever took place. He had to go to America. He had to escape. It was always entirely his decision. Claudia never found out about that. He told her that his mother had encouraged him but it was the other way around. He couldn't wait to leave

Gambia. He just couldn't face Claudia each day knowing that he was someone else's husband knowing that she wasn't his wife. Knowing that he could never marry her, although he had the money, his mother never believed her a suitable match. It was simple, Claudia's family was of poor stock. He would never mention that little fact to Claudia. He did, however, promise himself that one day he would eventually send for her. Then each year there was some other reason why he didn't or couldn't. The first year it was the new marriage to Binta and the new house, the pride of his life, his Harlem brownstone. The next year it was Binta and her damn pregnancy. Then came his business interests. That lie lasted a good seven years. Claudia didn't need to know that he wasn't actually building anything or that he had the money and was simply waiting for the right opportunity. He told her countless times how he was sacrificing for her. He explained the hell that was his life with the likes of Binta and her demon child, Kinni. The other children were merely gifts to his sickly mother, nothing more, seeing as they were all from different women. He had to have some decent heirs to all that he had diligently worked. The other marriages were explained away also as family obligations. Matar's excuse was that he was making alliances with other Gambian tribes. He didn't need to say much more than that. Claudia, a Gambian woman, would understand what that meant without question. He knew that their bond was strong. Besides, polygamy was a way of life. Ironically, it was Matar's mother who would eventually be the actual catalyst to their marriage. She died. Matar never would have been able to have Claudia as his wife had it not been for that one fact. As they lay in bed together that afternoon with the hum of The Oprah Show in the background, things couldn't be sweeter. Thank goodness they were still young enough to enjoy each other. He rationalized all of his decisions by saying to himself that he had done it all for Claudia. Surely she could see that too and adore him for it forever. Yes, he loved her and knew that now that they were married she'd spend a lifetime showing her gratitude. Those were his thoughts then. Yes, that day he was positive she believed in him, that he had in some way saved her life. He was going to make all of her dreams come true in this incredible land of opportunity called America. That's what he thought. It had never occurred to him that when she asked him about divorce that he had basically blamed the entire female population for it.

However, now holding onto the only thing that was left of Claudia, a thin, crumbled note, he was forced to think about that day, that woman and that statement. The letter was short but certainly not sweet. It read:

Matar,
To hell with men!
Love, Claudia

"Love Claudia," he mumbled in a high-pitched squeak.

This particular sentiment cut him to the quick. Obviously she decided that if she'd been waiting for a man all her life in order to have the things she wanted, why not do away with the man entirely, and just have the things. He thought he was going to be sick. Somehow he had decided in his head that she left because of Kinni or Binta and the whole blending in with the new family dilemma. He had no clue that he sparked this betrayal. He came to this conclusion when she first left town with yet another affront to his kindness, another poison pen stating only, "Matar, Bye. Claudia." The cursed letter was left underneath his pillow. After three days of wondering and worrying where she was, he stumbled upon it while rolling over and hearing a crumbling of paper. He cried himself to sleep for weeks after that, refusing food, where daylight actually hurt his eyes once he finally decided to leave the house. Back then he mourned for her, moaned for her, wept like a grown man should never be seen doing for her. Binta hadn't an inkling, so she told everyone, what was going on. Meanwhile, Matar felt every emotion as if Claudia had just died. Until a bit later on when he began to think that maybe just maybe she should have. This way he wouldn't have to endure such pain. From that day forward he still thought of her, however, his brand new thoughts of her were more of the brutal killing kind. He just couldn't get this image out of his head of her gallivanting around spending his money. Okay, it wasn't exactly his money but the treasure of his bastard daughter, but still he acquired it and hid it where only he knew its whereabouts, so he thought. Now, in retrospect, there were a great many things he wished he could change. After all, he brought Claudia into his home, married her, lay with her, fed her, gave her everything she ever wanted and this is how she repaid him. 'Ungrateful bitch,' he thought. This brought about a feeling within him that he had never experienced before, shame. Then came yet another repulsive emotion trailing in its wake like a slithering snake, embarrassment. He was not a weak man. Even in his wrong choices he always managed to come across as if he meant to make them. He had that skill. It was deafening to realize that Claudia had reduced him to a simpering, whimpering little boy. He hated her for that. In fact, if he could find her, he would wrap his hands around her pretty little neck and wring the life right out of her. This thought was not an exaggeration either. He felt that it was his right as her husband to do so. For the sake of his honor, he would make sure she breathed her last breath. He was so besieged with rage that the only thing he could do to regain his footing within his own household was to beat Binta. In his mind it was the sanest thing he had done in the year and a half that Claudia had been for lack of a better word, gone. That single act of putting his fists in about Binta's head made him feel right with the world, like his old self again even. Suddenly the earth was on its axis again where it belonged. It sort of gave him back some of his dignity. He knew that Binta hadn't tampered with his mail. He picked that fight on purpose. It was simple. He needed to feel alive again. He was angry enough to hit something or else burn down the house. Binta was a good little wife. She could take it. Heck, she'd even understand. It was the Gambian way.

Chapter Thirty

She felt cold air coming from someplace. Suddenly, it was so drafty. Her feet were actually shivering and her teeth were chattering. Her eyes reluctantly opened and all she could see was a lone streetlight popping on and off undecidedly. She observed it flickering madly before it finally shined brightly. She couldn't remember what side of the bed she fell asleep on to put her in view of the street lamps. She quickly thought about the layout of Baby Bina's room. It didn't even have any windows. She squinted and tried to wake the heck up, suddenly recalling with faint clarity where she was and that she definitely wanted to be elsewhere in a hurry.

"What's your name, girl?" he had the nerve to ask her rolling over cocooned within the sheets.

This made her want to crush his skull in with a blunt object. It was bad enough that she was in his bed and that he had taken all the covering off of her leaving her naked, cold and uneasy. She glanced down and saw ashy ankles and knees, which instinctively prompted her to immediately reach for her clothing flung at the foot of the bed. Her feet leapt onto the floor. Then when she glanced over and saw also four used condoms, it was by far her fastest time ever getting dressed.

"What's the hurry? Stay. How 'bout some dinner?" he asked.

She couldn't even think about eating and certainly not about eating with the likes of him. 'Him,' she thought, 'Who is this guy?' She hadn't the faintest idea how she ended up there in the first cotton-picking place. She was selling books for goodness sake last she remembered, now this. Where was she anyway and what time was it? Had she been there all night? How long had she been asleep? 'Asleep,' she thought panic stricken. She could smell his sweat from where she was standing and it acted as a catalyst to send her sailing back to him in a warm embrace. She flashed on his hands roaming all over her body and his tongue exploring the far reaches of her mouth. She felt a chill down her spine and spun out of his room as fast as light travels. She was sure there were skid marks on his floor.

'Tano? T...a? What in the world is that boy's name?' she thought. She couldn't believe what she had just done with him. It was practically indecent. She didn't even like sex or rather she didn't think that she liked it at all. She had never done anything like that in her life. The only time romantic things meant anything to her was when she was with Devon. Yet there she was with this complete stranger doing things with her body that she wouldn't mention to a soul. She just met him. He meant nothing to her whatsoever. She didn't know where he was from, or what his mother's name was or father's for that matter, really she knew absolutely nothing about him. She barely knew where he lived and she had just been there. She wasn't paying attention when he took her. She just knew that she wanted him in the worst way in a sudden blind desire that seemed to overtake her. She turned down Fifth Avenue and 124th Street then remembered somewhat hazily treading that same path several hours earlier. That was another thing, what time was it? She hadn't the vaguest idea. It wasn't as if he were so suave or good-looking or a fabulous dresser. In fact, she didn't think that he was amazing in any way. Heck, he wasn't even good enough to be average. Yet there she was in his arms apparently for hours because it was now pitch dark outside and she knew that she saw daylight when they arrived at his place. She walked and wondered, wondered and walked. It was as if her body needed it. She could mentally care less one way or the other but her flesh apparently had a mind of its own. Her skin yearned to be touched. Her lips begged to be kissed. In truth it probably didn't matter much who she ended up with that night. She had been feeling utterly trapped in her father's house for the past six months with no money, no friends, her whiny brothers subtly trying to force her out of the house, and a depressed mom.

To her dismay, with each step she recalled the sensation of her new lover inside her, on top of her, caressing her and placing his lips all about her. Sure, he meant absolutely nothing but there was something undeniably irresistible about his touch. It seemed to enchant her. Her legs tingled with exhilaration from being twisted and intertwined with his. Her back recalled the sensation of his hand roaming freely up and down barely coming in contact with the surface, driving her wild with desire. His fingers were cold and left a sparkling ripple that she could still feel upon her flesh. His thighs were strong though slight and his arms forceful and eager. She tried desperately to rationalize her strange behavior. She had been lonely even though her house was always full of people. She had just recently gotten out of prison where she was surrounded by a bunch of desperate girls. She could easily have explained her bizarre conduct with that fact alone. Obviously, there was a hidden part of her that was crying out for some attention. It took this mystery man to come into her life in order to bring those feelings out. She couldn't even begin to think about what she would do the next time she saw him. She'd be awkward. He'd be awaiting another go around. She'd decline, wanting desperately to forget the whole thing ever occurred. Unfortunately, she only had until that next morning in which to formulate some explanation that would be acceptable. She would tell him that it was just a once in a lifetime event. She'd say that she was lonely after the death of her lover. She'd say she simply didn't really see him in that way but just as a friend. She kept walking mulling over the plausible possibilities for ending her affair while acknowledging that there was something about him that wasn't altogether repugnant.

Kinni heard the laughter of a group of girls coming towards her. Before she could make out their faces, one of them was right next to her, grabbing at her and hugging tightly.

"Girl," the stranger yelled and the others squealed loudly beside her.

A very surprised Kinni looked up to see Michelle, Saundra and Trese, and some unknown person gawking at her.

"You got some s'plaining to do. Girl, where you been?" Trese asked playfully shoving Kinni with her shoulder.

Michelle shoved Trese to be quiet. Kinni shrugged as each of them took turns saying hello and wrapping her in big long bear hugs. Kinni wasn't sure if she was actually happy to see them yet. She didn't think she had it in her to explain anything. It was awkward running into her friends this way, on the street in the middle of the night. She already felt like the world was watching as she tip-toed out of a strange man's bed now this.

"You look good, girl," Saundra told her.

"How was Spoffo...?" Trese asked and Michelle actually kicked her.

"Why'd you do that?" Trese yelled.

"You need to shut that trap of yours more often is all I'm sayin'", Michelle told her.

"I just want to know what it was like," Trese said to everyone as if she wanted approval.

"Yeah...well..." Kinni told all of them.

"You don't have to say anything about…" unknown said out of the blue.

Kinni looked to Michelle for an explanation.

"Oh, this is Bonnie…from school," Michelle said.

"Hi," Kinni offered.

"Hi," Bonnie offered right back.

Kinni wasn't going to say a single word in front of her replacement especially since she seemed to be wondering about her business right alone with everyone else.

"It's nothing really," Kinni said playing it all off.

She hoped that she looked tougher now that she had been on the *inside*.

"Your mom used to tell us how you were doing whenever she visited," Saundra blurted out.

That statement didn't give Kinni comfort. It made her remember that Binta took a long time in coming to see her.

"You coming back to Good-Marshall's?" Trese asked.

"Yeah, girl, the place ain't the same without chu," Michelle told her.

"You ain't missing a whole lot," Bonnie slipped in as if she were one of the crew.

Kinni decided that she didn't like her and just didn't pay any mind to her or her comments.

"You lost some weight, girl," Saundra noted looking at Kinni's baggy clothes.

"How's that guy..a…a.. Dee…Dev… You know?" Trese asked.

Kinni put her head down when she heard Devon's name mentioned. That was still a really sore subject. This was hard for her, this little reunion.

"He…he…died," Kinni finally uttered realizing that that was the first time she had ever said it aloud.

Michelle pushed Trese out of the way cutting her eyes at her meanly.

"What I say? What I say?" Trese baulked.

"Sorry to hear about that," Saundra told Kinni while patting her shoulders.

Then all of them looked awkward for several silent moments.

"You are really missed, Miss Kinni," Michelle said grinning from ear to ear.

"I know. I know. I miss you guys too," Kinni said as truthfully as she could.

"Why don't you come with us?" Saundra asked.

"Where you going?" Kinni asked not really interested but continually trying to be polite.

Bonnie pulled a flier out of her pocket and waved it in front of Kinni's face. Kinni definitely didn't like her one bit.

"It's *the* only house party, girl," Bonnie sang loudly for the entire neighborhood to hear.

"It's this guy named Sam Tuba that throws these parties. They're fun. You always have a good time," Michelle stated as fact.

"Why don't you come? I want to catch up on things. It's been too long," Saundra pleaded.

"Yeah, there's always some free drinks," Bonnie added in.

"There's always some fine looking fellas," Trese added.

Kinni would have loved this little get together if it wasn't for the fact that it was with her friends who knew her. It would have been easier with strangers. She missed them too but just couldn't bring herself to sit around for hours combing over her past. She especially didn't want to labor over them with the new girlfriend Bonnie listening in on all the sordid details making first impression judgments.

"Uh..." started Kinni with a shrug then shook her head "no."

"Come on," they all chimed into Kinni's ear.

She felt a little pressured by their requests and sincerely wished she had it in her to go with them. After all it wouldn't have been so bad for a few hours to simply forget about everything in her life and drink and dance. Yet, it seemed uncomfortable to walk back into a life that she barely remembered.

"Turkey," Trese said jokingly.

"You really don't want to go? It'll be like old times," Michelle pushed Kinni's shoulder and hugged her again.

Michelle was right and it was tempting but Kinni fought against her desires to just sink back into the past. In truth, she didn't even know why. It would have been nice to go with them and have some fun for a change. That was probably the reason she ended up in a stranger's bed that night. She missed being young and carefree. She missed not having to baby-sit or comfort and nurse her mom. She knew that she needed a day off indeed.

"Not tonight, okay, but call me," Kinni told them all including Bonnie.

"Are you going to another school, working?" Saundra asked Kinni as an after thought.

"She's not coming. We can talk about it later," Michelle said scooting everybody forward.

"It was nice meeting you," Bonnie said nodding at Kinni.

Kinni nodded back at her out of politeness happy to see her moving on down the street. Michelle smiled at Kinni recognizing that Kinni didn't like Bonnie.

"She kind of grows on you," Michelle said to her with a smile.

"She gets us into parties and stuff like that," said Saundra.

"Good. Good," Kinni told them knowing full well that she

didn't have any right to complain in any way about the changes to their little click.

"You're still my home girl, woman," Trese joked.

Kinni had to laugh at Trese. She had forgotten how funny Trese could be. Trese kissed her on the cheek and started walking away too.

"Call me if you want to get together sometime, okay?" said Michelle.

"Yeah, any day, any time," Saundra told her with another hug.

"See ya'll," Kinni said waving good-bye.

Her friends skipped down the street in one direction while she went in the other. All the while she wondered what had just happened. She kept thinking that there was no real reason why she just didn't simply join them. She hadn't a real job, or school or any other obligation that kids her age had. What she did have however was a life that aged her beyond her years. She did have the weight of the Gambian world traditions pressing down upon her shoulders. She did have a father that among other things had her sent to prison. She just didn't think she had much to talk about with her friends anymore. What she really felt like was a freak of nature now. They were laughing and giggling about a party and meanwhile she was wondering and worrying about her future. Their futures seemed set and perfect and hers was uncertain, unsure, and undecided. She crossed 125th Street kicking the curb with her toe, wanting to sink into the asphalt. It wasn't a shining moment for her to have to suffer through an introduction of someone who obviously was her replacement. Heck, Bonnie was even her height and coloring. Kinni didn't like that one iota. Then, the whole idea about hanging out without a care in the world made for some interesting nausea. Every day was a different adventure for her and not in a good way. She didn't know what she'd be walking into this night. It was only two nights ago that her father slammed her mom into the floor. No, she was not in the mood for a party.

Two seconds later, only two feet into the house and it was already obvious that something was amiss. The house was too quiet for starters. That was never a good sign and secondly Kinni wasn't in the right frame of mind to deal with anything or anybody. She hated the fact that she immediately wondered who fought with whom, where were they now and why would it all somehow become her problem? There was no such thing as privacy in her house. Matar had made sure of that. Kinni quickly dashed into the bathroom trying to avoid it all, and slipped out of her oversized everything. Then she hopped into the shower and literally scrubbed each inch of herself until every piece of skin was red and raw. Even after lathering up three times, she could still smell the scent of that man she allowed to touch all over her just mere hours ago. There was something about him that lingered within her. She could still hear him whispering into her ear and kissing her neck. It was down right intrusive and irritating. She let those thoughts go and rinsed again and again, that is until someone flushed the toilet. A rush of frigid cold water suddenly engulfed her.

"Ouch," she shrieked.

Then she ripped the shower curtain open and was surprised at who she saw.

"Mom?" she said recognizing Binta now seated on the toilet.

Binta was doubled over waving Kinni to go on and continue whatever she was doing. Kinni was already stepping out of the tub and toweling herself off.

"You don't look good, mom," Kinni just flat out told her knowing already that Binta would deny that claim.

Kinni then tried to reach out to her and comfort her.

"Baby, I'm okay. I never need nothing. You know that," Binta said proudly.

Kinni could now see the full black and blue which was now definitely all black.

"That doesn't look right though. Should it be that…hard?" Kinni tentatively asked her.

She knew that once Binta said she was all right there wasn't much she could do short of forcing her into a taxi. However, she wondered if perhaps she might convince her by scaring her into going to see a doctor. It seemed impossible because Binta always tended to see everybody's pain except her own.

"Where've you been?" Binta asked Kinni clearly changing the subject.

"Out," Kinni said glibly.

"I'm still your mother, you know? Even though you think you take care of me," Binta spoke with authority.

"Yes, mom," Kinni answered head down in obedience.

She didn't like the fact that Binta always, always brushed her off on any topic involving her health. Kinni was not a child anymore who needed to be shielded from life's horrors. She was living with and surrounded by them in this family, some of the worst of what the human race had to offer was present.

"Remember when we used to talk about Mecca, mom?" Kinni started.

Binta shook her head smiling wearily.

"I still want to take you there, you know," Kinni told her longing to just hoist her up, pack and run off.

Binta looked so tired, so run down. Kinni didn't like the sorrowful glances that her mom was giving her. She seemed so lack luster. She wasn't even using the toilet anymore, she was just sitting on the open lid as if she was taking a long desired break from something.

"That would be nice, Kinni," Binta said dreamily with a heady mix of fatigue and depression.

"Why didn't you ever leave him?" Kinni said in a shuttered whisper.

She knew from the shocked expression on Binta's face that she had gone too far with this question. Neither one of them had to guess or explain who Kinni meant by 'him.' Binta took it well, though. She assumed that if her daughter was old enough to ask such a question about Matar then she would at the very least consider a real response. However, what could she say?

"Well...he is my husband, Kinni," she began knowing that that answer was what she would even give to a stranger, "...We Gambian women...we...we don't believe in leaving..." Binta couldn't even finish without tearing up.

Every other woman in Matar's life had left including his so-called love, Claudia. Who was Binta kidding? She was in America now. She could have left him a long, long time ago. What had kept her there?

"Mom...go on...I really want to know," Kinni knelt down and sat on the bathtub edge facing Binta.

She wasn't going anywhere until she got an answer, any answer, so long as it was true.

"I don't know really," Binta said quietly as not to have anyone else in the house hear her.

She shrugged and looked around the room as the showerhead dripped the last few drops of water into the drain.

"I was very young, so very, very, young you know. Children often have a small view of the world. You're so innocent then. You think that everything is going to be fine once you have this or that. Then you have this or that and somehow realize that it's not what you thought it would be like at all. Gambia is different than America. We were raised to get married. That's all we had to look forward to. Who you married was the most important decision that one's family had to make. According to my family, the Bragias were the richest family in the village and the most influential. Then...then... Well, then it's hard to change things when there's only one thing you really know," Binta offered her curious child, now evidently, a woman.

It was the closest thing that Kinni had ever heard Binta say as to some kind of admission that there was something wicked about her father. Binta never so much as threw her hands up in anger of Matar behind his back. Kinni had never seen her mother curse anyone but she thought that her father deserved at the very least some foul language thrown his way. And yet, she wouldn't get any from Binta. Binta was completely silent on the subject. If she suffered at all, she suffered all by herself. Kinni looked at her now, hunched over and broken. She seemed to be shrinking into the paisley wallpaper design. The curve of her spine had taken the shape of a snail. Kinni wrapped her arms around her and lifted her up off the porcelain.

"Mom, go to bed," Kinni ordered warmly.

"Yes, my daughter, my love. I do what you say," Binta responded with a grin.

Chapter Thirty-One

"They let you wear that to school?" Binta asked Kinni who was clad in a baggy jeans and a cut off t-shirt. Kinni had already forgotten that she hadn't mentioned her change in career plans. It hadn't occurred to her in the months that she had been selling books on the street.

"How about this?" Kinni asked throwing a denim jacket over her shoulders.

Binta was getting dressed also about to take Deebal, Jumu and Sara out shopping for new shoes. Kinni, of course, was not invited. She hadn't been along shopping with her family since she was age nine. That's when she had asked her father for a pair of Converse sneakers. He yelled about the price of his heating bill, water and sewer and anything else he could think of in order to justify him not buying her anything. She could have any other type on the market but not a pair that cost sixty dollars. Then he took off his belt and beat her with it. That was the very last time she had ever asked him for one a red cent. Anything she acquired clothing wise was bought by Binta. Binta would get three hundred from him and bargain shop for the miscellaneous items on her list, i.e., t-shirts and such, making sure that she had a few extra dollars left to get Kinni something. Her thirty finds made for a good enough wardrobe but nothing was durable and would fall apart after five or six washings. That's when Binta started buying her clothes two sizes too big so that if and when they shrank there would still be some wear left in them. This system worked when Kinni was a normal weight and size but now after Spofford's cuisine she was too thin for any of it.

"Eat something," Binta ordered.

She pulled out a chair and forced Kinni into it. Kinni didn't feel much like food.

"It's okay. I'll be late for school, remember?" she winked at her mom.

"Yes. Yes. I'm so forgetful these days. Go on then," Binta continued with the hot cereal she had on.

Kinni slipped out of the front door and hurried down to the street.

"Where's Kinni going?" Deebal asked yawning and sliding on his slippers into the kitchen.

"School. Your memory is getting as bad as your momma's, huh?" Binta joked.

Deebal put his head down on the table and tried to get a few more minutes of sleep.

"What?" he mumbled.

"We going shopping today?" he asked a little more enthusiastically.

"Yes. Yes," Binta said stirring the mixture on the stove.

"After school, huh," Binta told him.

"Ma, we don't have school today. It's Saturday," he said.

"What?" Binta asked surprised and perplexed.

"Thank Allah for Saturday," shouted Jumu as he entered the kitchen.

"She thought Kinni was going to school," laughed Deebal to his brother.

Then they both howled loudly at the table ignoring Binta's shocked look.

"She thought it was a school day," Deebal kept on.

He and his brother began poking each other on the shoulders and continued to snicker with abandon. Meanwhile, Binta glanced over at the calendar and started counting days in her head.

"Thought we had to go to school," Deebal drooled through his laughter.

It was no longer funny to Binta. She was already wondering how she was going to approach this subject with Kinni.

Then Matar walked into the kitchen.

"Okay, that's enough now," Binta told Deebal.

"What's enough?" Matar asked.

"Nothing," Binta declared just as Deebal was about to tell his father the joke.

He lowered his head when Binta nodded in his direction.

"It's not nothing. I could hear Deebal's laughing from down the hall," Matar stated.

"Matar, have some breakfast. You must be hungry," Binta placed a plate on the table motioning him to sit down.

He never took orders from Binta or any other woman for that matter.

"I want to know what's going on right now," Matar ordered.

Then he looked from Binta to Deebal and back to Binta again. Binta left the spoon in the pot and the fire on and simply walked out of the kitchen.

"The food is done," she said while exiting.

She just didn't want to get into it that morning with Matar. She didn't want to be struck by him or to have him laugh in her face about Kinni's lies or anything else for that matter. She hadn't been feeling well since she acquired the Subdural Hematoma on her face thanks to his swift backhand. She received that diagnosis from Mr. Chin when she went to wash the heavy blankets at his Laundromat. She had been experiencing dizziness and severe headaches every other day since and just didn't have the energy or the patience to endure any further aggravation at his hands. Kinni was the only one who had even bothered to notice it and to express some concern. Matar pretended that the huge black mass upon her face was nothing more than a blemish. No, she was decidedly not in the mood for her husband that day. So, she escaped into Baby Bina's room and literally woke the child up so she could have something to do besides talking to her husband. Baby Bina awoke with a start and cried at the intrusion.

"Hush now. Hush," Binta told her softly.

Baby Bina quieted down and faded in and out of sleep for a few more minutes. Binta had her resting in her arms when Matar stormed into the room.

"Where is she, Binta?" Matar yelled.

Then Baby Bina yelled too and cried at the sound of Matar's harsh voice.

"I don't know," Binta tried to say calmly but she knew the words stuttered out of her mouth.

They could both hear Deebal and Jumu laughing hysterically in the kitchen still. At times, they both reminded Binta so much of their father. Matar lifted Binta up from the little baby chair and started to slap her face even with Baby Bina in her arms but he stopped as the light of the sun illuminated Binta's cheek. Matar stared at the black mark in horror then he pushed her back down into the seat. Binta nearly fell and dropped the baby as her buttocks descended awkwardly on the back of the small chair.

"Matar!" she yelled extending her arm on the crib in order to catch herself.

Matar exited the room muttering something offensive about Kinni. While Binta now held onto her head and the now howling baby.

"Hush now...hush...hush," she tried but to no avail.

She'd have to go into the kitchen and get her something to eat now. It was her fault she thought. She shouldn't have awakened her. She shouldn't have come into her room. And maybe she should have left with Kinni wherever she was going. Maybe the two of them should never look back.

Kinni was actually wandering aimlessly through the streets of Harlem that early morning with no place in particular to go. She was scheduled to sell books that morning but that wouldn't be until eleven or so. She had approximately three hours all to herself. So she strolled, and thought. She wasn't really upset at the idea of her entire family going shopping without her. At least that's what she kept telling herself. She was offended that no one even bothered to ask if she might like to join them. And as much as she loved her baby sister, she didn't want to be the one stuck babysitting her again. She had been the good daughter lately. She was on her best behavior. Each time her mom asked her to do something, she obeyed without a fuss. She merely needed some alone time. She had a little money in her pocket and with that came a unique sense of freedom. She wanted it. She needed it. She had been mulling over her mom's comments about her father for days and the realization of her mom's inherit weakness had placed her in the strangest disposition. This new information about her heritage was difficult for her to swallow. She could understand her father being the monster that he was and that he was made that way, raised that way and wouldn't change ever. However, it was her mother's state of being that caused her anxiety and self-reflection this time. She didn't like the fact that her mom had lived a life that literally was the sum total of the needs of such a man. What kind of a life was that anyway? Kinni wanted more for her even if she didn't want more for herself. It pained her to think that her mom's very existence had been for her loathsome father. That just couldn't be right. There was something so perverse in that paradigm that she actually shuttered. She didn't like the whole idea of it. It unnerved her. As she walked in front of K & H Clothing, she wished it were after ten so she could shop for some new clothes that fit for a change. She didn't need her father's money or a shopping spree with the family in order to do that now, thank goodness. She thought about her mom and how in all of her life, she was never able to do something as simple as just walk into a store and buy whatever she wanted with her own money. In fact, her mom would never ever be able to do something as carefree as that. Her mom was in an alternate universe, where women didn't exist except to please their immature, babyish men. 'That wasn't a life at all,' Kinni thought. She had to get her finances in order. She had to find a way to get her mom out from underneath his thumb once and for all. Surely she could do something about it. She was practically grown. She could get an apartment, move out and then set aside a room for her mom and Baby Bina. The rest of his kids could stay where they were for awhile. She hated to admit it but they were already spoiled by her father's meanness, especially Deebal and Jumu. They didn't think about anyone in the family except themselves. They were the ones who were always making fun of her and sitting around while she and Binta cooked and cleaned. They would never think to lift a finger to help out. It was scary. Kinni was beginning to compare them with Mandinka Husband's kids. The similarities were uncanny. She couldn't believe that her very own brothers were included in that horrible group known to her as men. Unfortunately, that was yet another thing she'd worry about, her brothers growing up to be just like their father. It was bad enough that he ruled their lives as if he were God. Now, her brothers were showing signs of becoming him. She just couldn't let that happen either. So long as there was breath in her body, she was going to make sure that they saw at the very least that they had other options. She didn't know how she would do it, but with all she had in her, she would work something out. She realized that if she wasn't intending to go back to school that she would have to do something to get some money. It was the only way. She had to be in a position to eventually move everyone out of that house. She knew that if she could get her mom out then everyone else would soon follow, but she had to work quickly because the boys were getting older. Right now they were still listening to Binta but sooner or later they would tower over her and eventually start treating her like Gambian men treated all women. She already catered to their every need, same as with her father and asked nothing of them except that they grow up to be princes. Kinni loved them but sometimes she resented them too. They were boys and that was their only requirement for being the "royalty" of the family. Kinni knew better and would always want more for them. It appeared to be destined for her to make things right. It was fate that she would be the one who'd witness the extent of her father's wickedness. That she would be the oldest trying to alter the family's lifestyle that needn't even have existed in America. It occurred to her that each of her parents could have made their collective lives anything they wanted it to be but in her mind they had chickened out and decided to keep to the old ways, adhering to the well-worn paths. Then, as providence would have it, they had forced those same ancient systems upon their children. Maybe everything that happened to her was leading her to one inalienable truth, that she'd discover the error of their ways. She was the only one who thought that it might possibly be wrong to live in the past. She came to that conclusion regarding her very own life. Why would she want to remember Mandinka Husband or his horrible children? Why would Spofford be on the list of fond memories or the rape or the death of Devon? She had one lousy regret after another. As far as she was concerned 'past' was an offensive four-letter word. It was becoming apparent to her that if her family was to be saved that she was the one to do it. She had to rescue all of them from their past but not just her generation but the one that started a long time ago on the other side of the world. She had to do something to get her family away, away from a legacy of hurt, of damaging sorrow. It was the only way. It was her father who wasn't allowing any of them to be anything except slaves to his history, his precedent, his culture. The Gambian ways only served him. It was plain to see that no one in her family had the strength or knowledge to get away from him on their own. She'd move everyone out and leave him, her loathsome father, all by his lone-self. That's what he deserved, to be sitting around scratching himself and ordering take-out, completely miserable like he made everyone else.

"How'd you do it?" she asked him before the door swung completely open.

She stepped pass him into his apartment and placed a winter green pine into his sink and ran some water over it.

"What? What? Oh, hey. Good morning to you too," he replied wiping sleep from his eyes and yawning.

"Put your clothes on. Don't we have work to do today," she asked him whilst turning on the television.

It came on with a harsh gravely sound and Kinni quickly changed the channel to something a little less irritating.

"Make your self at home," he told her none too politely.

Then he walked over to the bathroom and urinated with the door wide open, his bare bottom facing her. He reached his hand behind and scratched it.

"That's not right," she said shielding her eyes.

"That's what you get for barging into my place

unannounced," he said sharply.

"You don't have to be so mean all the time," Kinni informed him.

"Who's mean? I just like a little warning is all," he said leaning over and kissing her cheek.

His breath smelled rank. Kinni waved in front of her nose because the odor remained in the air long after he closed his mouth.

"Did you even wash your hands?" she asked.

He had a lot of good qualities but cleanliness was not one of them.

"Like I said, that's what you get. I never said I was an angel," he laughed and headed for the kitchen.

He pulled two beers out of the refrigerator and flipped the tops of both of them.

"This helps to settle the stomach," he said handing her one.

Kinni took the bottle but placed it down on the end table. She had no desire to start drinking at 10:30 in the morning and wondered what on earth he was talking about.

"Why do you need your stomach settled? Were you doing something you weren't supposed to be doing last night?" she smiled.

"Probably," he burped.

"'Cuse you," Kinni said.

"See, that's what you get for coming over here un-nounced," he waved and went into the bathroom again.

This time he stayed in there a long time. Kinni could hear the shower going. She didn't like the way he said that she should have called first before coming over. She hoped he was joking but somehow each time he said it, it sounded more and more like a threat. She got up and walked around his apartment. Sparse was really not the word for it. Like many studio apartments there was one room delineated into three or four areas or zones. However, his room was used "as is" for three or four different purposes. His end table was the only table in the place. It was used for breakfast and dinner as well as a footrest. It was a cube on wheels that he got from Ikea and put together. His couch was a pull-out, a Jennifer convertible special. Kinni had seen this one in their sales advertisement for $199. It was plaid, brown with white and beige. It had cigarette holes all over it and a blue blanket throw rested upon its back. The kitchenette had a small refrigerator, a sink and stove in an area that was less than two yards wide. There was a window overlooking the back of the building's industrial sized garbage bins and a street lamp on the corner. This view equipped with flies from the trash was the best feature of the apartment. Still Kinni saw its possibilities. She had been staying there off and on for several weeks now, that is, whenever either of them were in the mood. She stared at his black and white television and wondered what else she could buy in order to spruce up the place. The pine was not enough. She scanned her eyes over to the bare window again and figured that a curtain would be nice. She'd have preferred to get some cable but she couldn't afford the monthly payments. She couldn't believe he didn't have it already. She was certain that even homeless people watched cable television. The Saturday morning cartoons looked grainy and discolored on his pitiful thirteen inch.

"Didn't you ask me something when you walked in?" he asked walking naked from the bathroom to the one closet.

It took him exactly one minute to get fully dressed, oversized denims and two oversized shirts one atop the other. From a distance he was any black American young male in those clothes, which was the whole point.

"I want my own table," Kinni said more as a question than

anything else.

"What's this?" he asked reaching into the sink fondling the pine.

"It's a plant, man. Don't you know what a plant is?" Kinni asked shoving him away from the sink and grabbing it from his poking and prodding.

"You act like that's your child or something," he joked.

"Or something, huh?" Kinni joked right back.

"What you trying to tell me?" he asked leaning against the counter and pulling her towards him, plant and all.

"I was just trying to make this place look a little more livable that's all," Kinni stated emphatically.

"More livable for who?" he nibbled her neck.

"Men," was all Kinni could offer.

Then she pushed him aside and placed the pine on the empty window sill.

"I sit there," he told her.

"Tse, please. It's just a freekin' plant. There needs to be some life in this place. It's empty," she told him.

"We're here! It's not empty now," Tse said loudly with a little comedic flair.

"Rrrriiiiggghhhht."

Tse sat on the sofa and pulled Kinni onto his lap.

"So, you don't like working with me no more, huh?" he asked pointedly.

"No. No, it's nothing like that. It's not like that at all," she said kissing his cheek.

"What's it like then?" he asked sitting her next to him so he could look directly into her eyes.

His face was no longer playful but serious. His forehead wrinkled in a knot.

"Baby, I'm just trying to make a way for me and my family.

That's all," Kinni said.

"You and your family...why not keep working for me and I'll pay you a little more then?" Tse asked her as an alternative to her request.

"Why can't I just try this all on my own?" she asked in a controlled scream.

"Calm down. I'm just trying to understand what you're talking about," he confessed.

Kinni stood up. She didn't mean to get so angry but she felt as if he wasn't really listening to her.

"You talking about your father?" he asked.

"Who else?" Kinni sat on the end table, "It's just too much, you know?"

Tse shook his head in agreement.

"You should see my mother's face right now," Kinni mentioned perfectly ashamed.

"That's one thing I'd never do..." Tse said scooting next to Kinni, "...hit a woman."

Tse put his bony but strong arm around Kinni's shoulders. Some of the tension that had been building up within her began to dissipate. Tse had his moments like this one that made it easy for Kinni to be around him.

"Has he ever put his hands on you?" Tse asked her while staring directly into her eyes.

Kinni didn't have to say a word. Her face turned to stone as she lowered her head and fixed her eyes onto the floor. Tse pulled her even closer. Yes, Tse had his moments, those moments where Kinni could see them raising children together and buying a summer home outside of the City. He kissed her lips and she felt them tingle from the peppermint in the toothpaste he had just used. She didn't want to get this close to him, a fellow African, a man without the means of really supporting her, yet there was something that she just couldn't resist about him. She was deafly afraid of getting hurt again. She felt as if her heart just couldn't take another disappointment. She pulled away.

"Let's hit the street," Kinni told him.

"What's the rush? Let's get some breakfast," he suggested.

"Something to go with our beer?" she joked.

"Why not? We're grown. We can make our own schedule. We can do whatever we want," he informed her with a twinkle in his eye.

Kinni wanted to hate all of this getting to know you stuff. She wanted to walk out of his apartment and do everything she had it in her mind to do all by herself. At least that's what she kept telling herself.

"Listen, if you really want to go at it on your own…I know…well…I could help you," he mentioned while stepping over to the stove and placing a frying pan onto one of the eyes.

Kinni watched him prepare to make Western omelets, his favorite meal. She would have made them for him but she got such a kick out of watching him shake his butt as he flipped the eggs.

CHAPTER THIRTY-TWO

It was just a feeling really. Sort of like a prick or pinch within her soul. Kinni awoke with an uncontrollable urge to urinate. That's how it all began. She rolled over on her floor pallet restlessly deciding whether or not to run into the bathroom or to put it off for another fifteen to twenty minutes for some more much needed snooze time. One minute later she couldn't take the pressure on her bladder and went racing to the toilet. It was free. She was ecstatic that she didn't have to compete with anyone else. The release was almost spiritual until she sat there and began thinking. She wondered exactly when it was the last time that she saw her period. By her calculations it was nearly two months ago. She reached over and opened the cabinet beneath the sink. There was almost a full box of Pathmark brand sanitary napkins. 'That can't be right,' she thought, 'Can it?' As she counted and then recounted the days and weeks, she tried her hardest not to go to pieces. This was all she needed right now, Tse's baby. He was just a baby himself, for that matter, so was she. She wasn't ready, able or willing to support another living thing. Plus, she wasn't sure if Tse really liked her. And the jury was definitely still out on her feelings towards him. 'Was he father material?' she speculated. 'Would he have a fit if she told him she was pregnant?' she thought. She just couldn't be pregnant. All that time when she was with Mandinka Husband, and then Devon without protection and now with Tse only a few weeks, she conceives. It just wasn't fair. 'Yeah,' she thought, 'I'm pregnant all right. Just my luck! What else could it be?' Her menstrual cycle was like clock work. It came every month on the fifteenth or there about without fail.

Kinni was surprised that Binta hadn't mentioned anything about it because both theirs came around the same time. Binta used to say that when two women were around each other a lot their cycles tended to run together. 'Oh my God! Oh my God!' Kinni thought in quiet disbelief. She felt pale. It was as if things went from treading water to sinking. She couldn't be pregnant. It was not the right time to have a child. She had things to do. Things were finally picking up for her. Tse had already arranged for her to meet his book selling people. She had filled out the necessary paperwork for a New York City vendor license. She was on her way to getting her own business, which was going to bring her that much closer to helping her family, her mother, herself. She just couldn't be pregnant. She just couldn't be. Then she leaned over and vomited into the sink.

"Kinni, you all right?" Binta asked from the other side of the closed door.

'Uh oh,' Kinni thought. She was categorically not in the mood to discuss this new little development with anyone, especially not her mom. That's all a dysfunctional family needs, an illegitimate baby by their high school dropout.

"Fine," she managed, barely, and slumped over the faucet.

She was holding her stomach suppressing a repeat hurl into the bowl, which already possessed chomped up chicken and rice from last night's dinner. She kept telling herself that this just couldn't be happening. Then she reminded herself that she wasn't a doctor and that she could be entirely wrong. Then she heaved again.

"Kinni, you sure you're all right?" her mom asked.

Kinni gripped the edge of the tub, held her nose and began running water into the bowl. She had to erase the evidence. The smell alone was assaulting her equilibrium.

"I'm fine," she stuttered thinking that it was simply

impossible to do anything in her house without the whole world knowing about it.

"Good, because I need to talk to you about something," Binta told her.

Now was not the time for a little chat. Kinni was all smelly and sweaty and hyperventilating with worry. The last thing she wanted was to have a heart to heart with mom. She just wanted to lie back down and sleep this whole nightmare off. She had long since gotten used to the floor and at times found it surprisingly comfortable. The baby's cries were no longer a bother either. Kinni felt that Bina and she had come to an understanding. Kinni would burp her and change her at eight, bath her and then off to bed she'd go, happy and contented. Baby Bina would then sleep until six or seven o'clock. She had accepted the fact that her brothers took her room. The sum total of her possessions could and did fit into a single drawer of Baby Bina's tiny dresser. Kinni had two pairs of shoes, All Star sneakers and a pair of dress shoes that somehow managed to survive Deebal's redecorating. Apparently, Deebal emptied out all the contents of Kinni's old room into a single trash can. When Binta caught wind of his clearing out technique it was already too late to retrieve any of Kinni's stuff.

"Why'd you throw out your sister's things, Deebal?" Binta asked him after the fact.

"Daddy told me to clean up," Deebal answered defensively.

Both Binta and Deebal knew that by 'clean up' Matar meant 'throw out' and that Deebal was more than happy to oblige his wishes. Binta looked in every direction except directly into Kinni's face when she told her the news. Kinni took it well, though. She didn't have a tantrum or harbor any ill feelings towards Deebal or her father for that matter. Her father was already dead to her and Deebal was just doing what any young boy would do under the circumstances. Besides, Kinni had long since detached herself from all things material thanks to Mandinka Husband and his horrible, destructive children. Even when she was with Devon who practically bought her a brand spanking new wardrobe, she was less interested in the things and more in the person giving her those things. With him it was the best she had ever felt in her life. Without him she was just limping along trying hard to get through each day. Tse with all of his flaws was actually helping her to that end, so was her mom and little Baby Bina. Tse had helped, that is, up until the day he got her pregnant.

"Kinni!" Binta called to her again.

She hadn't the energy nor the desire to open the door and yet she had to tell someone, talk to someone. While she hadn't been able to confide in anyone for a long, long time, she knew that it was long over due that she should talk to her mom about her life. With that thought, she took a deep breath, which made her stomach muscles ache and then reluctantly exited the bathroom. Her legs were wobbly and she felt slightly lightheaded but she managed to walk steadily into her mother's room and sit upon the bed as if everything was normal. As she adjusted her eyes to the dark room she saw Binta reclining in the side chair staring out of the window. Kinni tried not to look at the bright blotch on Binta's face illuminated by the daylight. It had become harder and hairier since the last time she saw it, still transforming itself from a sore to a scab. Kinni's impulse was to say something about it but she didn't want a repeat performance of her mom refusing to believe that anything was wrong.

"You feel like cooking something for tonight?" Binta asked wearily.

"Sure. Chicken? Beef?" Kinni asked trying not to move too much for fear that she might have to run back to the toilet.

"Sure," Binta said blanched.

"What?" Kinni queried.

Binta stared at something for a long while before recognizing that Kinni was still there.

"…kay," Kinni mumbled responding to her mom's lack of a response.

Then Kinni sat uncomfortably wondering why Binta appeared to be sleep-walking through the day. She seemed like a porcelain doll, all lashes and mouth posed in an 'awe.' Binta was not herself lately and Kinni couldn't seem to penetrate the thin but powerful veneer that covered any explanation. Kinni doubted that Binta would ever tell her all that was actually going on with her.

"Was that all you wanted to talk to me about?" Kinni hesitantly asked, "It sounded like something else."

"What?" Binta moaned as if she were swatting a fly.

Kinni just wanted to run tail out of there at that point. It was clear that Binta was otherwise occupied, in her own head and resolute about staying there unaccompanied. Plus, Kinni had to get over to Tse's and really have a little chat. Yet she patiently waited a little while longer for her mom to wake from her daydreaming. As she did she thought about the idea of Tse being the father of her baby realizing that the thought wasn't entirely unpleasant. His little studio apartment could have a little bassinet in the corner off by the window. She thought once again about buying drapes. She'd suggest that he purchase a real dresser and that they'd all have a drawer, hers, his and the baby's. Sure it would be tough at first but other women had done it and survived just fine. She decided that it might even be a welcome change in her life this baby, this new born, her child. She had to admit that she liked the sound of it, 'her child.' She smiled and could immediately feel Binta glancing over at her.

Now they both looked lost, entertaining their own thoughts, totally in their own worlds.

She glided so quickly pass Barnes & Noble's that she didn't even see Khadyjah's trying to flag her down to say something to her. Kinni hadn't bothered to follow up on the job position once she and Tse started working together. In fact, she hadn't thought about or gone into the book store at all. She hadn't thought about books or reading or any of the things that she and Khadyjah used to discuss during her long visits. She was now on a, albeit shaky, mission. Her future was revealing itself or unraveling itself right before her. That was all she could think about interspersed with thoughts of her mom. Allah, help her, she was about to be her mom. She was no longer nauseous but noticed her once flat belly protruding outward in a small bloat. That and the lack of her period were the only indications so far. She figured that she was probably an entire month with child. 'What if it's a boy?' she thought. 'What if it's a girl?' she marveled. Either way, she'd love it. Either way she wouldn't raise it the way she or her mother was raised. She'd make sure that they knew they were Americans with all the freedoms and privileges that birthright afforded and allowed them. She would never sell her child into forced marriages or any other servitude customs that Gambia held. Suddenly, she stopped short in the middle of the street. A Malibu skidded within an inch of her leg as it slammed to a halt.

"Hey, what you gonna' do?" an irate seventy-something gentleman yelled out at her.

Kinni scurried across the street and didn't look back. She was thinking about Tse and his heritage, his traditions and his homeland ghosts. 'What kind of superstitions did his people have?' she pondered. Between the two of them, their kid might end up even more messed up than they were. Suddenly with that realization, she was having second thoughts about telling Tse at all. Now with this absurdly grave fear of her unborn child's future came a magnified type of loneliness that threatened to topple her over. Once again she reminded herself that she needed her own place, her own business and definitely her own money. That way she could raise her child any which way she wanted. She wouldn't have to be dependant on Tse, her father or mother or anybody else. She could cook whatever foods her child desired, not just a bunch of throw backs from Gambian culture. The child wouldn't be subjected to her father raping her either, or disowning her because she wasn't born of the right wife. There would only be one mother and one father who would love him or her shamelessly, recklessly even.

She looked up to her dismay and discovered that she was already on Tse's block. She always walked fast when she had things on her mind. His apartment building loomed only two doors down. Her steps became labored. She wanted to turn around and several times did only to remember that she had no place to go. So, she pressed on towards his front door and rang his doorbell. No answer. She loved the fact that the decision was made for her. She wouldn't have to tell him at least not today. She was halfway down the steps before she heard the intercom buzzing her in. She raced hesitantly back to catch the door. It was heavy in her hands as were her thoughts. The elevator smelled of urine and had her wholly doubled over by the time she reached his floor. Each step forward made her want to retreat. Though, she was not the type of person to run away from a challenge, sniveling and crying at every hardship and she wasn't about to do so now. She would walk in and simply tell him with her head held high. He would either accept the news well or he wouldn't. Her hand was poised to knock when his door flew open before she hit it with her fist. First thing she saw was a woman's back facing her. Then she felt the woman's foot pressing down upon her shoe.

"My ride's here," giggle, giggle said the woman.

"Ouch!" Kinni snapped at her, "Watch where you're going."

"Oh," the stranger said turning to see Kinni's angry face, "Sor-ry," she said a little too territorial for Kinni's taste.

'Who's she?' seemed to be the general sentiment on both of their minds as they each turned to Tse who was standing by the sofa with a cup of something in his hand. Kinni's eyes scanned his body to see a knotted up towel draped around his waist. It was the only garment he had on. She stood frozen for several seconds before any sound escaped her lips.

"What the f-'s going on here?" she bellowed breaking the pregnant silence.

Her voice caught Tse in mid sip and he jerked and spilled what looked like coffee down his bare chest. The woman who now stood a fair distance from Kinni flipped her head from Tse to Kinni in rapid succession as if she didn't know who to scream at first. Her wide mouth was stretched wider still and her face appeared to be on fire, it was so flushed.

"Tse!" Kinni and the stranger called simultaneously.

Tse gulped down his drink and lowered his head. Kinni wasn't sure but he looked as if he had a little smirk upon his all too calm face.

"Who the f- is this?" Kinni yelled again and this time stepped into the apartment, getting right up into Tse's face.

"Kinni…Kinni…come on now," Tse tried.

"What the hell is this? Who do you think I am that I'm gonna' put up with this shit?" Kinni yelled some more.

As she did Tse moved her slowly and painstakingly backward

and toward the open doorway. He knew that he had to separate the two women quickly before they came to blows or worst hit him.

"I don't know who she thinks she is but this is my man and you can just get the hell out of here before I cut you," the stranger said to Tse and to Kinni as a matter of pure fact.

Kinni could hear the Puerto Rican accent in her voice now, though she looked to be the typical around the way girl, Black American.

"I don't need this drama! I will hurt somebody to-day!" she continued.

Tse kept ushering Kinni to the door gently but firmly.

"Who's gonna' hurt who today? I know you're not talking to me, bea-itch!" Kinni went all out around Tse swinging at the woman.

The girl ran toward Kinni circling her arms windmill style with her fingernails protruding out to scratch her. Instead of getting at Kinni, her nails dug into Tse's arm. He flinched and instinctively shoved the girl back. She went sailing down against the end table. She quickly dusted herself off and got up swirling her arms around again. One or two of the flails managed to strike Kinni on her side but Kinni recoiled her arm and punched the girl dead center in the face. Kinni put her weight into it too and the power of the blow knocked a tooth or something out of the girl's mouth. The girl hollered so loudly that neighbors began to appear at their doors searching the hallway for the origin of this commotion.

"Ah no! Ah hell no! No body hits on me!" she promised retaliation in her wails and went rummaging for something deep within her over stuffed purse.

Tse quickly ran over to the girl and grabbed the bag away from her.

"Hey. Hey, Tanya. No. No. No, girl. Woo…woo now. Listen…lis-ten…" Tse spoke softly to her, again too softly for Kinni's taste.

"I'll cut this little hussy in half! You don't know me. You do not know me. You better watch your back. You better be glad he's here. I'll cut you, you hear me!" Tanya went on and on.

"Nobody's gonna's cut nobody," Tse said to everyone including his nosey neighbors.

Then he sat Tanya down on the end table and ran to the kitchen for paper towels. He forced the whole roll into her hands and then went quickly over to Kinni who still had her fist poised and ready for another go around.

"Kinni," Tse said with his voice almost in admiration of her, "Kinni, bab.., I mean, Kinni, listen. Can we…can we talk later?" he gently asked.

To which Kinni responded bluntly, "Hell no!"

"Baby, pleeeeeeasssssse," he whispered.

"I hear how you talkin' to ha'. Tse, who the f- is she?" Tanya asked in angry tears.

Kinni felt like crying too but refused to give either of them that pleasure. Her temper with so high that her heartbeat was slamming against her ribs.

"…I….I…" was all Tse said on the subject looking guilty as sin.

It was obvious to all present exactly what was going on but Tanya demanded verbal confirmation.

"I better have all my teeth in my mouth, you wit-ch!" she said in several different directions as if there was an audience there.

Kinni caught Tse cracking a smile as he escorted Tanya into the bathroom, no doubt to check herself out in the mirror. He was obviously pleased to have two women fighting over him. Tanya leaned upon him and whimpered like a puppy. She was suddenly a femme fatale. Meanwhile Kinni looked like a prize fighting champ after a knockout. She was beaming with pride herself. She was pumped with adrenaline but had no idea what to do next and just stood in the doorway shifting her weight from one leg onto the other. She had the urge to pee again too and knew that that was a totally inappropriate response to the current circumstances. Sure, she'd been lied to before, mistreated and even deceived but this was a new one, something she hadn't seen before – romantic relationship betrayal. In truth, it was betrayal and at the same time it wasn't. She and Tse weren't exactly a couple, legitimately speaking. For all she knew, she was the other woman. She remained in the entrance of his apartment stoic and wondering what comes next while the other apartment dwellers sauntered back into their abodes. There wasn't anything else to see. All was quiet save Tanya's breathing loudly and sucking in air through her mouth. Kinni could hear Tanya whispering something to Tse and him "huh huhing" her to death. Whatever promise he was making with her, Kinni didn't know. However, she did know that she wasn't just going to stand there all day and wait for them to kiss and make up or whatever they were doing. Besides, she had some rights in this situation. After all, she was the mother of his baby. Then she thought that maybe just maybe she wasn't the only one with one of his kids. She got ill at that thought. She was tired of being the sucker. She wasn't going to take this crap from anyone. She was ready to knock them both out if that became absolutely necessary.

Then Tanya came flying out of the bathroom, bag in hand, eyes red from crying, hair everywhere, disheveled. Kinni regarded her with disdain and disgust but moved out of her way nonetheless when she came rushing pass. It did cross her mind to trip her but that would have just been over kill. She could see that Tanya had something very recognizable on her face too, fear. Kinni could read that emotion so well on just about anyone's face but especially on another woman having seen it so many times herself in her own reflection.

"This ain't over," Tanya shouted at Kinni.

"Girl, please," said Kinni sucking teeth and looking straight at Tanya as if she were a bug to be crushed.

"I'm not leaving because he said I should. I'm leaving 'cause I got somewhere else to be," Tanya declared.

"Whatever, girl. I'm not your social director," Kinni said as an aside.

Kinni's apathy made Tanya's blood boil. She stood staring at Kinni thinking that had she more time, she'd cut her to bits then go on about her business.

"Tanya, go on and do what you got to do, 'kay," Tse told her leaning into the hallway shooing her to the elevator.

Tanya left but not before giving Kinni the wickedest look she could muster. Kinni wasn't worried. Besides, Tanya would have to stand in line behind her father and Mandinka husband. By comparison, Tanya was like a tadpole surrounded by sharks.

Kinni stood immobile for a long while just staring through the narrow of her eyes at Tse. He didn't move either. It was as if he were trapped within her penetrating gaze, bewitched. What could he do? What could he say? What could possibly fix this? How could he smooth this over? Would he want to? He was caught red handed so to speak. Kinni was so caught off guard and disgusted that she refused to even ask the typical questions, 'Who was that?' 'Are you in love with her?' 'Are you going to choose me over her?' 'What she got that I don't got?' Kinni wasn't going to go out like that, down that road of insecurities coupled with self-doubt. She didn't really care, or did she? At least she didn't want to. She'd deny it if she could but she did feel hurt like he had taken a knife and cut her wide open.

"Look, Kinni…you know what I'm saying… we…you and me… you know what I'm saying, Kinni," Tse's lips moved but he wasn't saying nothing.

Though, somehow, Kinni was getting the gist of it.

"What?" Kinni grunted.

"You know, we, you and me…" shrugged Tse.

"Yeah?" Kinni shrugged for him to continue the thought.

"Well, you know what I'm saying, we're not like, 'clusive or nothing," he finally concluded.

"No, we're not "clusive," right?" she breathed and held in the air for a few minutes before expelling it.

'Men,' she thought. 'Cowards,' she thought. They remained on opposite ends of the small apartment like two lions stalking each other in the same cage. Each trapped in their own hopes and dreams about their future together. Kinni would have, she realized, preferred something a bit more exclusive. While Tse, obviously did not. He made his position crystal clear. The evident of which was Puerto Rican slasher, Tanya. No, Kinni wasn't going to bombard the man with a bunch of foolish questions. Why bother. 'So, Tse, you want both of us now, right?' 'Is she better in bed, is that it?' 'Who sucks you off better her of me?' 'Does she let you stick it anywhere you like, is that it?' 'I bet its because she likes to swallow, right?' No, Kinni refused to dignify this entire little episode by giving him an anxiety show. He didn't deserve that. He deserved to have his head blown off but she wouldn't do that to him either. Tse looked like he didn't know what to do with himself. Kinni was literally cursing him with her face in the attitude of sheer revulsion.

"What?" he asked her hesitantly.

"What the f- do you mean, 'what'?" she threw back at him.

He tilted and fanned his head from side to side unable to find a voice for what he was thinking. Kinni realized that he wasn't ever a big talker. That was another trait that Devon possessed and Tse lacked.

"What you got to say?" Kinni placed her hands on her hips and stomped down her foot against his floor.

She waited for a moment but not patiently.

"Look, Kinni, I'm not tryin' hurt you or nothing. I have these feelings you know. I just get lost sometimes in these feelings, you know?" Tse admitted.

"Feelings," Kinni stated looking at him as he were a one million piece puzzle.

"You know, it's not like I go out looking for nothing like that. It's just there, you know and before you know it, you know, Tany…" he said.

"Don't. Don't say her name to me like you're making an introduction. And I don't need to know about your little problem of dragging girls home with you because you just can't help yourself," she said sing-songy like he was a little baby.

"Hey, you don't have to go there," he suggested feeling the pinch of her condescending tone.

"Go where? Did you or did you not pick her up off the street…too?" Kinni crossed her arms over her chest and waited.

She wanted him to squirm.

"Like I said, we're not 'clusive, right?" he chanted like an anthem.

"No, Tse, we're not ex-clu-sive, like that makes everything alright," she told him with a smirk.

"Well, it's true, right? Right?" he asked determinately.

"Look, Tse, what we had, we have right now with a child, okay," she simply said.

"A what?" he questioned.

"You heard me," she yelled.

"A baby?" he asked.

To which, she just glared at him, turned on her heels and walked out, pushing air through teeth in an exasperated sigh. The door slam practically hit him as he ran after her.

"Kinni! Kinni, wait! Kinni!" he yelled trying to catch the elevator doors before they closed on him too.

He sliced his arm between them narrowly capturing the electric eye. Kinni didn't even acknowledge his presence.

"Kinni, come on. Let's talk about this. A baby?" he asked.

Kinni looked up at the ceiling and wondered what in the world had she seen in him in the first place.

"Yes," she uttered, 'Can't you hear straight?'

She was reticent to continue any further dialog with him.

"Well, what we gone do?" he asked.

"What in the hell do you mean by that?" Kinni asked thinking the worst.

"I mean, just that," he said.

"Look, it's my baby. I don't need anything from you. You can go the hell on with whatshername and leave me and mine alone, okay?" Kinni told him sternly.

"Why you gonna' be like that? Why you got to get all like that about it?" he asked.

Kinni pushed the first floor button of the elevator and it jerked trying to obey that command. Tse resisted for a few moments but then released his grip on the doors and road down to the first floor with her.

"Listen, Kinni. I'm just a little shocked, you know. I'm not trying to make any decision right now about nothing. I'm just…you just…surprised me is all, damn," he said.

"Well, I'm surprised too what with you wrapping your thing

up the way you do…" she told him, "…but it is what it is. What we going to do about it now?"

"I don't know. I don't know! I don't know," he said three different times in three different ways.

Then they both stared at the floor indicator, fourth floor, third floor, second floor, first.

Chapter Thirty-Three

Kinni practically ran home. She was definitely escaping. If she could, she would have escaped her entire life. She didn't want to think about anyone or anything, not about Tse or Tanya or her father, the dumb fight she just had over the equally dumb man, or the baby, the baby, Harlem nothing. She couldn't help but feel utterly drained. That little excuse for a man, Tse, had just made everything she had recently hoped for seem dull and stupid. 'We're not like 'clusive right,' Kinni thought. He couldn't even pronounce the word. Didn't that make the whole thought invalid? What he did made the entire relationship invalid. Once again, she had been duped by a man, actually not a man but by a mere boy this time. Were they all just incapable of telling the truth? Did they wake up and decide one day that what they desired in life was more important than anybody else's feelings? Were they all just a bunch of self-involved jerks? He wasn't even trying and he still managed to pull a fast one on her. She tried telling herself that she wasn't really interested in him in the first place but somehow, somewhere inside, she did believe that there was hope. That elusive kind of hope, that of having a real honest to goodness happy life which in turn propelled her forward and nagged at her heart. She just thought that even with all of his and her flaws that they could have still made it work. She was foolish. She may have leapt too quickly into this dream and now before it even began, it ended. Deep down she knew that she couldn't even blame Tanya although she really wanted to. She wished she could have knocked all of her teeth out. Just the thought of doing so made her smile, of slamming Tanya to the ground and then going to work on sorry behind Tse; him standing there grinning as brightly as the sun like he was the nucleus of their argument. Tse, as some kind of war prize, in a battle of the fittest, where Kinni and Tanya were supposed to kill each other over him and for his amusement. He didn't even have sense enough to know that women could fight that passionately over a shoe sale, and not even a very expensive shoe sale. He was just there really, nothing more than a hood ornament on a car, a symbol. He was just the object of their fantasies. He wasn't even a good replica for either of them, a rather piss poor example of what they desired. He was like a mirage. Kinni saw him as possibly a future husband, a real father to her baby. Tanya saw him as a loyal boyfriend who would never hurt her, never cheat on her, never place her anywhere in his life except at the top of his priority list. 'We were both wrong,' Kinni thought, 'Both foolish.' Men were incapable of making a simple dream come true? All of the ones she knew at least. All save one and he was dead and long gone.

She turned the corner onto her block at last and immediately saw a truck near her house. On top of it was a red flashing light. She wasn't sure whose house it was parked in front of. She couldn't completely make it out, but it looked like her father was standing at the foot of the steps and carrying Bina in his arms or at least that's what he seemed to be holding. She thought, 'What now?' Kinni slowed down wondering just what God awful thing her no good father had done this time. Men. As she drew closer, she saw Deebal and Jumu standing by the front doorway, straddling the saddle. They had such worried expressions on their faces. Kinni could see that, even though she was still at least ten doors down. Her little sister, Sara, was behind Matar crouched down. Kinni could hear her before she could see her.

She was crying. Kinni paused, stopped right there two doors from her house. It had suddenly occurred to her that everyone was accounted for except, except her mother. She broke into a run towards the house.

"Mom!" she screamed.

At that point the siren began to wail. Its shrill screeched and bellowed through the block echoing loudly off the buildings. Kinni slowly turned towards it and peered through the windowed doors on the back as it was pealing away from the curb. She saw a man, a paramedic sitting down next to a cot. Beside him was Binta. Somehow Kinni knew that it was her before she recognized her limp body, legs daggling off and to the side. Another paramedic was pumping away with both of his hands down upon her chest. Kinni scanned her eyes over to Matar. She was searching him for answers. He looked utterly helpless, an usual expression for him. He was in shock.

"No!" Kinni yelled and went running after the ambulance again.

She made good time but couldn't catch it before it zoomed down around the corner and down Malcolm X Boulevard.

"Wait! No! Stop! Stop, damn-it. Stop!" she yelled futilely.

Kinni caught a quick glance at one of the paramedics who was shaking his head at her basically saying that they couldn't stop for her. She was too late. All Kinni could do was stand in the middle of the street watching it disappear. Eventually car horns startled her out of her trance and she quickly moved back onto the sidewalk. Reluctantly she turned back around and headed back toward her house. She could still hear Sara crying an unconscious kind of sob with a load of stops and starts and sniffling. Her brothers, Deebal and Jumu, were still gathered at the top of the steps frozen. And there was her father, holding Bina in his arms, he too as stiff and rigid as Kinni's heart felt.

"Take her," he barked at Kinni.

Kinni didn't move. She refused to. 'How dare he,' she thought. She imagined that he probably did something else to her mother and that this time she'd take months to recover. She had to get her mother away from this horrible excuse of a man. She had to. She simply refused to help him do anything. 'Why don't you be a man for once and take care of your own child for a change,' she thought. She half wanted to see how he would cope without Binta taking up the slack for all of his shortcomings.

"Please take her. Please…" he requested this time surprisingly nicely.

Kinni felt a little more inclined with the please besides she didn't want him to drop her. She hoisted Baby Bina from him and into her arms.

"…I have to go and bury my wife…" he said underneath his breath as if it were an after thought.

"What?" Kinni asked loudly, waking the baby and everyone else on the block.

At that Matar turned and sadly faced Kinni. He just managed to catch her and the baby before Kinni's knees buckled and she slid down onto the stoop. She rested there, clutching the wailing baby within her arms and Matar supporting her back so she wouldn't slam her head against the cement. Sara's sobs grew more intense causing Deebal and Jumu to join in. They whimpered and shook and gripped onto the doorframe as if it were a crutch. The whole family sat for several minutes, each in their own private hell of collective grief weeping for poor Binta but none more than Kinni.

Chapter Thirty-Four

That entire next week during Binta's burial will be forever etched in Kinni's memory as the single most painful era of her life. She was a walking and talking statue and nothing and no one could chip away at the slab of stone that she had become. She absolutely hated every minute of her existence, the relatives carrying huge trays of food to the house, patting her back and lowering their heads in pity. The cards that began with 'deepest sympathy' or 'thinking of you' or the flowers that died a day after they arrived sitting in their tombs of still water welting over the side of their vases. Everything was a distressing reminder of what she had just loss. Not one soul came close to discerning how a loved one couldn't be replaced by mere trinkets. This concept cannot be readily understood by those who have never experienced such emptiness. This feeling was only reserved for those who have been left behind while their very reason for existing has crossed over, gone to the great by and by, or was taken up to Heaven never to be seen or heard from again. Binta's lovely spirit lingered still. It was practically embedded in the walls of the house, every crevice smelled of her freshly washed skin and her aura hovered in the now stale atmosphere that filled each room. Binta was the one in the flesh who loved Kinni unconditionally, the one who forgave and forgot and smoothed over all ills. Who would be there to do that now? She was irreplaceable. There was no amount of words, or tokens or hugs or kisses that would be able to fill that peculiar void that managed to suck all the air right out of Kinni's lungs. She was now just an empty shell, like saw dust on the floor to be discarded. So wounded was she that she could barely concentrate on anything else besides the gapping hole in her heart. She hadn't the faintest clue that she could be this miserable and having the life that she had led, the death of her mother lowered her cessation for life into a realm of the unknown, the undead. She, herself resembled a corpse. The gray body of the only person who really and truly loved her was lowered into the earth. Kinni hated the way the funeral home director, Mr. Raymond Wilkes, had bragged about making Binta look like she was still among the living. Why? So that everyone could still believe that she existed? It was sheer cruelty to sit and watch as they sunk that wooden box beneath the ground, thinking the whole while, 'Why are they burying my mother alive?' So disturbing to witness this ritual with its speeches about a better place on the other side, that Kinni looked past the smiling redirect spouting mosque leader, Honorable Mohamed Isaac, bragging about a life after death, to the other tomb stones at the grave site. 'Allah is as dead as my mother,' Kinni thought, 'Deader, even, because he allows the innocent to perish.'

Kinni couldn't help but to think of Binta's life. It was as if she were taking a tour of it in her mind, a moving picture, images, impressions and speculations. To her, Binta's life had been a life of pure misery. First she had her womanhood stolen away from her before she was even able to fully realize it as a gift. Cut out, as if someone had sliced her tongue from her mouth. They might as well have done just that because from that day forward she didn't have a say in anything. Her entire childhood was diminished, truncated and shrunken by the dictates of selfish men who lusted to control the whole world yet settled on their vulnerable, insignificant families. Binta's father didn't offer her in marriage to Matar, he sold her out as if she were a common slave to shoulder and bear all of Matar and his hopes and dreams. Binta, merely cheerleading Matar throughout his life with her hands raised and her skirt swinging and swaying in the breeze, forever chanting his name and applauding his so-called accomplishments. Meanwhile, there wasn't anything left of her. Her essence had been ripped to shreds, her soul had been twisted up and squished into the equivalent of a toe nail which contained someone else's foot placed firmly upon her neck and their core purpose for her own life. She was to marry and raise children – period. For no other purpose was she made. For no other thought was she ever given. For no other use, save for his. Man. 'To hell with this life,' Kinni thought, 'To hell with it!' It was not what she wanted for either one of them and definitely not for her baby.

Matar was so knocked out that he didn't even hear Kinni as she tip-toed in and opened and closed his bottom bureau drawer, the very same one that Claudia had rummaged through looking for hidden treasure. Kinni found what she sought too. It was right there on top of his nice, clean, folded shirts - fully loaded. 'He didn't even bother to hide it. What if Deebal or Jumu found it?' Kinni wondered. She lifted it up and began examining it. It was heavier than she had imagined it would be. It didn't seem so the way he continually brandished it in her face. The weightiness of it brought a smile to her face. She would aim. She would not miss. This weapon was assured to rip the flesh from the bone at a fair distance. She didn't intend to be that far away. She'd be tight and up close and personal. She had done this once before leaning to one side and scared out of her wits. It would be undoubtedly easier this time. She'd simply hold the thing steady and pull back and down on the trigger. That much she knew she could do. She wasn't troubled about it at all. She wasn't even worried about the hereafter. 'Who cares?' she thought. If she could resurrect her mom from that cold earth she'd ask her if she even cared. 'She'd probably say, "Blow his damn head off!"' Kinni thought. She grinned just thinking about it. Matar may not have actually been the one to give Binta the aneurysm but he was the cause of that effect as sure as rain follows cumulus humilus clouds. Just as Binta may not actually be the one to finally send him to hell, but it will be done in her honor. Kinni smiled. She may not have been able to take her to Mecca and to bow down for the five Salah prayers especially the maghrib towards the setting sun but she would allow her to rest in peace. Kinni would have her revenge for all of the hateful things he had done to her, the rape, the imprisonment, the never-ending torture. She gripped the gun steadily and gently placed the barrel just a half an inch above his skull.

"Kin-ni!"

Kinni jumped.

"Did I scare you?" Sara asked, lids still closed.

Kinni hid the weapon, turned back and looked at snoring Matar who had rolled over on his side.

"I'm hun-gry," Sara said rubbing sleep from her eyes.

Kinni could hear rumbling coming from the back of the house. Suddenly, both Deebal and Jumu appeared in front of Matar's door.

"Somebody say food?" Jumu joked.

Deebal quickly looked down to see what Kinni had hidden in her hand. He frowned. Kinni tucked the gun underneath her arm pit and rushed to the door. Then she grabbed hold of Sara and walked her into the kitchen. Deebal kept eyeing her and then peeked over at his sleeping father. Matar's chest rose in inhalation and sank back down three or four times before Deebal comfortably followed Kinni.

"What do we have in here?" Kinni said immediately swinging

open the refrigerator door and sticking her head inside.

"Hope you found what you were looking for," Deebal stated and slumped in a chair.

She and he both knew that he wasn't talking about the food. His face was fixated on the way her arm clutched her side.

"It's not what you think," she told him recognizing that she had to say something.

"Well, then what is it?" Sara innocently asked.

Kinni brought out one of the many trays of food that had been left for them by well wishers.

"Looks like pasta. Lasagna, to be exact. Who wants lasagna?" Kinni asked, sniffing it then popping the entire glass dish into the oven and switching it on to three hundred degrees.

"I do," Jumu said yawning from the doorway.

Kinni realized that not one of them had eaten much since Binta died. They all looked as if they were shriveling up, skinny and colorless. They had each suffered from it differently but had arrived at the same place, scared about the future and tired.

"You think I don't understand, but I do," Deebal told Kinni plainly, secretly.

"Is it ready yet?" Sara inquired.

To which, Kinni and Jumu just smiled at her. Then Kinni looked at Deebal. She hadn't realized it before but he was a man now, three years younger than she but nonetheless, a man. As far she was concerned he was the man of the house. Matar was just an empty chair at the table. She imagined for the first time that maybe, just maybe he did understand. He wasn't too young to have seen and heard what was going on in their house. Although he and Jumu were Matar's favorites, surely he could see that she and Sara weren't. Baby Bina didn't count. Everyone loves a baby. Deebal studied Kinni as she leaned against the counter and held her focus on the floor.

"One death in the family is, is enough," Deebal told Kinni solemnly.

To which, Kinni raised her head and stared at him, through him. She hadn't thought about how killing Matar would have affected them, his children, his boys especially, his heirs. As much as she truly hated Matar, she just couldn't in good conscience do that to them. Could she? They were her family. She wanted what was best for them.

"By the way, I moved out of your room," Deebal informed her.

As she looked into Deebal's sympathetic eyes, eyes that were literally pleading with her to cease the mission she was on of doing harm to his father, she couldn't help but honor his request.

Chapter Thirty-Five

"...forgiving sets you above..."

Everything in her life seemed to change once she had her baby girl. She named her Binta in honor of her mother. Even Matar approved. He was a broken man by then, after Binta's death, and actually marveled at the child of her namesake. Kinni didn't know what to make of it, him playing with her baby, coo cooing and holding her gently on his knee. She decidedly didn't trust this new Matar not one bit but alas with a new born there were a great many things that were quite out of her hands. She peered over at Matar from time to time sensing that he had simply given up on life or rather on the life that he once so diligently sought. When he wasn't working, he was tired and just slept for hours on end all cooped up in his room even in the middle of the day. Kinni furtively did enjoy that latest development. It was as if he wasn't there at all. Growing older had mellowed him and smoothed the once angry, controlling nature that drove everyone and everything far from him. In truth, her mother was in a lot of ways his only real connection to the old world he came from. Without her, he seemed disoriented, alone and off-balance. Kinni never thought she'd see the day when he didn't walk around the house roaring like a lion. Though without his wife, Binta, who would be impressed by his prowess? Despite his constant confessions of not loving her, she was a central part of who he was. Like a reflection in a glass, when he looked at her he saw in her eyes the man he thought himself to be, successful, strong, a Gambian king who made good in America. Currently there was a shift in that certainty, because with Binta's death that image died and no one else in the family could or would support it. He was simply the man who paid the bills, widowed father and not much else. To Kinni's amazement, she unofficially became the mistress of the house. She marveled at the notion that even that new fact didn't seem to disturb Matar. He was more than pleased with whatever she cooked, cleaned or didn't clean. He was content with it all, resolute in fact. Sometimes he was just there, like a flat tire, quietly occupying space. It was he who took Kinni to the hospital when it was time and waited patiently the thirteen hours in the waiting room while she delivered, which was one of many firsts for him. He refused to do it for his own children, but was apparently there for his grands. Kinni wouldn't have believed it if she hadn't seen it with her own two eyes. Was it possible that he had learned something about life after all?

"Are you comfortable?" he turned and asked Kinni as she sat in the back seat of the taxi snuggling with the baby.

He had brought her the car seat that Binta used for Bina. Kinni didn't rightly know how to answer him.

"Huh...huh..." she stuttered glaring at Matar in shock.

She wondered if he was genuinely concerned about her comfort or was he just putting on an act for the cab driver.

"Yeah. Yeah. Fine," she mumbled staring down her nose at him.

Once they entered the house, Kinni discovered a brand new crib in her room. Kinni was speechless. Deebal, Jumu and Sara fanned their arms out displaying it together with all the other baby gifts and gadgets, presents all from Matar, who actually went out by himself and bought them, Kinni was told. Also, to her utter amazement, were two crisp one hundred dollar bills placed neatly on the nightstand. 'Okay,' she thought, 'What the hell's going on?'

"What's this for?" Kinni shouted at him, stomping out into the hallway, waving the bills in front of his face.

She just couldn't get over how presumptuous and arrogant he was in assuming that she would now be his new wife, which was completely and utterly and profusely and ridiculously out of the question. If that was what he had in mind, she would definitely finish the job she started that night in his room. She still possessed the weapon and knew how to use it. She stood there fuming expecting a knock out, drag out fight. However, Matar simply shrugged and walked into the kitchen to get a beer.

"Thought you'd need some spending money, that's all," he said and kept on walking away from her.

He didn't even raise his voice. It took a long time before Kinni could fully close her mouth. She was, to say the least, shocked and kept staring at his back and the money for several additional seconds. At best, she was apprehensive. At worst, she was confused. Deebal raised an eyebrow at her and just smiled.

"I told him," Deebal whispered.

"You told him what?" Kinni asked him in a huff.

Deebal pulled her back into her room. The baby was sleeping in her new crib. They both could hear Bina calling for Matar sweetly, "Papa! Papa!" she called.

"You told him what, exactly?" Kinni asked completely perplexed.

"I told him about the other night," Deebal said silently.

"What about the other night?" she asked curiously.

"About...you know...about...the o-ther...night..." Deebal pointed to Matar's room and Kinni's face went white.

"What?" Kinni shouted.

"I told him to treat you nicely from now on..." Deebal smiled, "...or else."

Then he walked out of her room, leaving Kinni to chew on his powerful words. Had Deebal, Matar's son, a man, managed to do the impossible? Had he changed the entire genetic make-up of her father? She didn't know what to think. Days later she would still be downright astounded as Rehema Twyman, a house keeper came to live with them. Her bed was Kinni's old floor pallet in what used to be Bina's room. From that day forward, Kinni didn't have to lift a finger in her house. Rehema was all too eager to please and simply loved taking care of the baby and little Bina. Plus, besides the two hundred dollars that was now given to Kinni weekly, she also received money for food and clothes for all the children in the house save Deebal, who got his own allowance. Against her own will, Kinni forced herself to simply accept the money her father gave and even opened a savings account for her baby, Binta. Though she was still uneasy about this new found kindness of his and sincerely believed that one day it would vanish as mysteriously as it began, she recognized that his money was neutral. Things had certainly changed. Kinni even found herself smiling about her life at times, especially those spent with Devon when he used to call her queen. She was finally beginning to understand exactly what he meant by that term.

Then Rehema came into Kinni's room one day and placed a stack of papers on her bed.

"What's this?" Kinni asked her.

"I dun't 'no but it have your name onit. They was in the hamper," she told Kinni and continued on with her chores.

Kinni looked over at the pile. It was roughly thirty envelopes taped round with her name in magic marker written across. Right off she could tell that it was Binta's handwriting. Her heart stopped. 'What on earth…' she thought. She leapt atop the bed and tore open the package leaving bits and pieces of it scattered in every direction. Once the tape was unraveled, Kinni could clearly see that it was a stack of letters and not at all for her but rather addressed to Matar. Some were sent from New York, others from Mexico, Aruba, even one of two from Gambia. Kinni burst out laughing and immediately rushed over to close and lock her door, for the sender was none other than wayward Claudia, and she had the nerve to use her married name, Claudia Bragia. Kinni ripped one open and began to read.

> *Dear Matar,*
>
> *Baby, why haven't I heard from you? I hope that you are fine. I am fine also. It is warm here in San Juan and I wish you were here. Do come. I'm at the Playa San Juan now.*
>
> *Love, Claudia*

'Playa San Juan, the nerve,' thought Kinni. She shuffled the letters into date order and realized that the one she just read was one of the earlier ones. The later ones weren't as friendly.

> *Dear Matar,*
>
> *You must still be angry with me because I have not heard from you. Why have I not heard from you? Please, please write to me soon. I'm back in the Gambia. Mother was not really pleased to see me back. She's worried that I will grow old alone.*
>
> *Write. Please write.*
>
> *Love, Claudia*

'So...' Kinni thought, '...Matar hasn't seen these.' It would be a long while before she would stop laughing about that fact. Then she recalled how Binta had always made it seem as if she hadn't an inkling of what was going on between Claudia and Matar. Meanwhile, she had orchestrated this little pay back of sorts. 'Serves them right,' Kinni thought. Then she spent the remainder of the afternoon reading the little notes from Claudia. It didn't take long. Claudia's letters were no more than two to three lines each. The gist of which was that she apparently, stole Kinni's money then left town wealthy only to then catch a conscience and have second thoughts about splitting. She flat out refused to come back home and requested that he, Matar, join her for some adventurous travels. If she had returned, he probably would have killed her. Being Gambian, she most definitely knew that as the God's honest truth. Matar wouldn't let her live with that kind of shame brought upon his family. It seemed that she had also gone through the money faster than she'd anticipated and had to run back home to her mother. 'That must have been some kind of homecoming,' Kinni thought, then, 'Serves her right for stealing my money…mines and Devon's.' She didn't want to dwell on the past but Claudia's letters had led her right back to that time where everything she hoped for suddenly vanished into thin air. Kinni was still angry over it all too. Both Claudia and her father caused Devon's death, not directly but they may as well have pulled the trigger. The only thing besides her baby that stopped a sudden urge for vengeance was an acknowledgement that somehow justice had been served. It wasn't how Kinni would have envisioned it happening but neither Claudia nor Matar were still among the living. Claudia's thievery had severed her own American dreams forever and Matar loss two of the greatest love's of his life. Sure, both Claudia and Matar still breathed in air but there was nothing left for them to hope for. Life only gives two choices either it's filled with anticipation or regret. Matar and Claudia were most probably deeply ensconced in the latter. Matar, when he wasn't sleeping, would stare out of the window for hours. Maybe he foolishly believed that one day Claudia would return to him.

While Claudia was back in Gambia with her disappointed mother who'd sent her off on the wondrous journey to America in order to marry the man of her wildest dreams. There were no other hopes for Claudia save death. Each had to surrender to defeat. Kinni knew that feeling well and as she read Claudia's letters she couldn't help but feel some satisfaction.

Then she picked up her baby girl, Binta, and gently rocked her in her arms. The love she had for her was almost overwhelming. She brushed her hand across Binta's face and almost wanted to weep for the joy in feeling her soft, delicate skin. It didn't matter anymore about how she conceived her and with whom. Her angry thoughts toward Tse had subsided as she forgave him his tryst with Tanya. Kinni hadn't the strength or the energy to maintain hatred towards anyone while she was pregnant, least of all Tse. After all, he had given her a precious gift; a gift, that she now held in her arms thinking of the enormous plans that she pictured for her. Baby Binta would be and do all the things that Kinni only thought were possible. Kinni reflected on how she had been on a journey too, of how strong the Gambian traditions and her heritage had tried to make her into something and someone she just couldn't be. She realized that they were trying to choke the life out of her, trying to dictate to her who she was supposed to be and how far she could go. She had overcome that ancient curse, that old mystery. She was no longer among the living dead. Now, finally she was in control of her own destiny and she would never, ever allow another living soul to take that away from her. **The End**

About the Authors

THE WRITER: Beverly A. Burchett placed second in the Billie Holiday Theatre Poetry Contest and thusly her love of writing was spurred. She's a graduate of the famed High School of Performing Arts, and has acted in a number of national commercials as well as a few popular films, including "Fame." *The Girls from Heritage High*, *Open Doors*, and *Random Arts of Kindness, a journey*, are three other books to her credit and soon to be released. She's a published lyrist. She resides in Queens, New York.

THE INSPIRATION: Fatou K. Goumbala, of whom this story is about, grew up in Harlem, New York and now resides out of state.

www.ingramcontent.com/pod-product-compliance
Lightning Source LLC
Chambersburg PA
CBHW051747040426
42446CB00007B/258